'Most of us know Rowan Williams as one of our greatest theological minds, but he is also a talented poet and gifted teacher. Over the years, Rowan and I have talked literature and culture often, and this book reminds me of what I've received from those conversations: startling insights, warm humanity and a constant reminder that we are connected by love and beauty to the Divine.'
Greg Garrett, Professor of Literature and Culture, Baylor University, and Canon Theologian, American Cathedral in Paris

'Rowan Williams is one of our best readers of poetry. He is an "all-round" reader, attending to the full range of details, questions and possibilities in a poem, and arriving at a remarkable depth of thinking in response. The trans-national and "trans-religious" range of his ever-proliferating research matters too when he reads, illuminating much that we might miss in a poem's complex weave but in the same inimitably clear, direct, caring register that marks his theological writing. This collection goes one step further, given his desire to engage us all in the ultimate questions with which these poems struggle; we hear more of his own personal response, so that an intimate space opens up wherein we can indeed "search our hearts" in the company of not only these poets, but of Williams too, himself a poet. In my experience, spending time with Rowan Williams's writing changes your life, as does great poetry. This book offers both.'
Romana Huk, Associate Professor of English, University of Notre Dame

'These are not so much Rowan Williams's favourite poems as verses chosen for the way they shape an "appropriate grammar" for thinking about faith. Unusual and often surprising, they begin with the practical care of a cathedral verger's polishing and end with an equally embodied embrace of the material world by a female philosopher. Williams's meditations on the works are themselves things of beauty that refresh our understanding of old favourites such as Mackay Brown and Elizabeth Jennings, while introducing new voices from Jewish and Islamic as well as Christian imaginaries. Reading this book is going on a spiritual journey in which we are invited to leave behind our "twined scaffolding" of fixed meaning to enter language as if from the inside and discern the divine "pattern that informs" everything.'
Alison Grant Milbank, Professor of Theology and Literature, University of Nottingham

'Rowan Williams and poetry have a lot in common. Both prefer honest complexity to dishonest simplicity. Both want to draw your attention to the space around words, to sound, epiphany and emotional resonance, so that a more distilled understanding appears on the horizon. The two are brought together in this book, in which Williams's patient reflecting on poems from the past hundred years offers nothing less to us than an undeceiving of the world.'
Mark Oakley, Dean of St John's College, Cambridge

'This is a compendium of poems you could spend a lifetime absorbing. Rowan Williams has gathered a diverse array of poets that grapple with mystery, ultimacy and the terrifying beauty of being human. These are deep wells, and Williams is a gentle guide into the depths of riches.'
James K. A. Smith, editor-in-chief, *Image*

'Each poem in this collection is a door ajar, which Rowan Williams nudges open, inviting us in, where he carefully shows us around. He leaves us in a room of many windows, the light streaming in, our souls enriched, this book in our hand.'
Frances Ward, Poetry Editor, *Theology*

'A poet's choice. A thoughtful, eclectic, original selection of poems, their power enhanced by conjunction with one another. No serious lover of poetry will want to be without this book.'
A. N. Wilson, writer and broadcaster

Born in 1950, Rowan Williams was educated in Swansea (Wales) and Cambridge. He studied for his theology doctorate in Oxford, after which he taught theology in a seminary near Leeds. From 1977 until 1986 he was engaged in academic and parish work in Cambridge, before returning to Oxford as Lady Margaret Professor of Divinity. In 1990 he became a Fellow of the British Academy.

In 1992 Professor Williams became Bishop of Monmouth, and in 1999 he was elected as Archbishop of Wales. He became Archbishop of Canterbury in late 2002 with ten years' experience as a diocesan bishop and three as a primate in the Anglican Communion. As Archbishop, his main responsibilities were pastoral – whether leading his own diocese of Canterbury and the Church of England, or guiding the Anglican Communion worldwide. At the end of 2012, after ten years as Archbishop, he stepped down and moved to a new role as Master of Magdalene College, Cambridge. He retired in 2020 and is now living back in Wales.

Professor Williams is acknowledged internationally as an outstanding theological writer and teacher as well as an accomplished poet and translator. His interests include music, fiction and languages. His *Collected Poems* were published in 2021 by Carcanet.

ROWAN WILLIAMS

A Century of Poetry

100 poems for searching the heart

First published in Great Britain in 2022

Society for Promoting Christian Knowledge
36 Causton Street
London SW1P 4ST
www.spck.org.uk

British Library Cataloguing-in-Publication Data
A catalogue record for this book is available from the British Library

ISBN 978-0-281-08552-1
eBook ISBN 978-0-281-08554-5

3 5 7 9 10 8 6 4 2

Typeset by Fakenham Prepress Solutions, Fakenham, Norfolk NR21 8NL
First printed in Great Britain by Clays

eBook by Fakenham Prepress Solutions, Fakenham, Norfolk NR21 8NL

Produced on paper from sustainable sources

Contents

Contents

Acknowledgements

A good many people have played a part in this enterprise, directly and indirectly. I'm grateful to Philip Law of SPCK for the initial idea of a collection along these lines and for his constant patience and encouragement. Burl Horniachek and Don Martin were hugely helpful with suggestions about poets from the USA and Canada, and Dominic Leonard and Gwyneth Lewis also steered me towards some names I had overlooked. The late and much missed Valentina Polukhina introduced me over many years to several significant names in contemporary Russian writing. Hugo Azerad shared his enthusiasm for Yves Bonnefoy and prompted me to explore his work. And Dr Irene Lancaster provided really invaluable assistance in selecting writers from the twentieth-century Jewish world, in Hebrew, German and Yiddish, as well as generously checking and improving several of my attempts at translation. Although these and many others with whom I have discussed poetry over the years – among them Eleanor Nesbitt, Ian Florance, Malcolm Guite, Michael Schmidt, Subha Mukherji and Mary Ann Clark – have contributed a huge amount to my poetic literacy, I must of course take sole responsibility for the interpretations I suggest here. Warmest thanks to them all – and, as always, to my family.

Introduction

The title of this book refers primarily to the fact that all or very nearly all of the poems here were written within the last hundred years. (I have stretched this just a little with one or two poets – like Avraham Kook – who were active within the period but whose poems may have been written before 1922.) It is not a book about the One Hundred Best Religious Poems of the Past Century, or even a collection of personal favourites. I am not convinced of the usefulness of trying to catalogue 'best' poems. I hope all the pieces here are *good* poems in some obvious sense – honest, linguistically interesting, metaphorically rich and surprising – and I think some of them are great poems by any standards. But the principle of selection has been simply whether or not they open the door to some fresh, searching and challenging insights about the life of faith: do they present the language of religious belief, the images and connecting patterns in what people of faith say about their world, as something worth thinking *about*, worth thinking *with*, and capable of leaving the reader with an enhanced perception of their humanity and all that surrounds it?

This allows the inclusion of some pieces written by poets whose personal religious convictions may be opaque or agnostic, unorthodox or semi-detached, but who assume that the world of faith is at the very least a serious dimension of the human imagination, rather than a set of intellectually incoherent and morally obtuse fairy tales. The writers included here stand on a broad spectrum: there are traditionally orthodox Christians (T. S. Eliot, Les Murray, George

Mackay Brown), less orthodox (Quakers and others: Ursula Fanthorpe, Kate Foley, Dorothy Nimmo), agnostics (Stevie Smith), Muslims (Imtiaz Dharker, Naomi Shihab Nye), a variety of Jewish voices (from the traditionally observant like Rav Kook to the impossible-to-classify Paul Celan), a Buddhist (Maitreyabandhu) and a Native American (Joy Harjo). The criterion is the same: do they allow the language of faith to question them at a certain level of seriousness and to enlarge their perception and sympathy?

As I've said, this book is not meant as a collection of 'favourite' poems exactly. I have reluctantly left aside a fair number of poets of diverse background and conviction whom I love and admire, and some (or much) of whose work would undoubtedly fit in a collection like this – Yeats, Carol Ann Duffy, Seamus Heaney, Ted Hughes, John Deane, Basil Bunting, Carolyn Forche, to name just a few. But part of my aim has been to balance much anthologized writers (those just listed need no advertisement from me) with less familiar names; and I have also wanted to keep the reader's eye open to an international landscape. Once again, I have not made an effort to be systematically 'representative' in my choices about poetry in other languages, but have followed what leads I found, hoping that some readers will be encouraged to explore poets who deserve to be better known here.

Readers will undoubtedly want to ask, with varying degree of indignation, 'Why isn't there anything by X?' The omission of any writer is not at all a judgement on their quality; it depends largely on an assortment of rather random factors, chief among them being a purely personal response to specific poems, and the reflections that have grown out of that response. There are poems here about which I feel a bit ambivalent, even if they strike me as significant and have generated much thought; there are poems I have not included which I treasure, but which have not prompted quite the same searching. And this may explain why I have generally not looked to include poems that are – in one way or another – first and foremost devotional or celebratory; not because such writing is incapable of being poetically interesting, but because I have been listening for what I can only call a poetry that invites longer questioning and more sitting-with the tensions and teasings of language about the holy.

The arrangement of the poems included here is alphabetical: not ideal, perhaps, but a chronological scheme might imply that the collection was setting out to tell or at least suggest a story of development, which has not been my aim. The relatively arbitrary order of the alphabet may help readers to take each piece in its own right, though I have noted echoes and overlaps between poems and themes from time to time. I also decided early on not to include extracts from longer works, though I have sometimes reproduced individual pieces from sequences of linked but self-contained poems. The fact is that some of the most significant religiously inspired poetry of the last century is to be found in longer-form works – Eliot's *Four Quartets*, Auden's *For the Time Being* or *Horae Canonicae*, Vernon Watkins' *Ballad of the Mari Lwyd*, and so on – perhaps most notably the works of David Jones, whose omission from these pages leaves a very substantial gap, I realize. Something of the same challenge arises with the later work of Geoffrey Hill, which sits somewhere on the boundary between linked sequence and continuous poetic argument. But the point of this book is not to present a representative sample of 'religious poetry'; it is to select individual poems for close reading and reflection. The more extended works I have mentioned simply do not lend themselves to this and a note simply discussing an extract would not be a fair or even useful guide to the context in which that extract is set. The longer work requires a different approach; you could break it down into a series of meditations on successive sections, but a treatment of the entire work would push this collection out of proportion, and I have to be content with gesturing expansively towards these more expansive achievements.

Which brings us back to where we began. A 'century' is a hundred years; but the word has a few other meanings as well: a detachment of the Roman army, a score in cricket – and, less familiarly, a genre of spiritual writing, as most famously in Thomas Traherne's *Centuries of Meditation*. From the time of the early Byzantine Church onwards, Christians would compose 'centuries' of texts from particular authors, a hundred (usually brief) extracts from the works of a great theologian, thematically selected and arranged for contemplative reading and reflection. This book is something like that kind of 'century': although it is not drawn from one writer, it presents fairly brief texts and comment, in the hope that it may prompt the same kind of contemplative reading and rereading. Both texts and comments have in view the possibility of providing a shared space for believers and non-believers to explore together. Whether a particular poet is or is not a confessing believer, the works collected here are meant to encourage what ought to be a constructive curiosity about how religious language actually *works* – not as a crude fantasy but as a resourceful (and sometimes bewildering and alarming) way of putting human lives in context. And these poems may also help the reader grasp how the way religious language works intersects with the way poetry itself works as a means of real *knowing* and learning, in a mode not always grasped or valued in an impatient, two-dimensional culture.

Rowan Williams

Gillian Allnutt

Verger, Winter Afternoon, Galilee Chapel

Durham Cathedral, March 2004

Careful, here,

as polishing cloth across a floor,
police officer,
voyeur.

Air closes over the angel's departure.
Always, in the air. The river
in the floor

inhabits it, as light inhabits water
or the heart's interior
or here.

Gillian Allnutt's poems are typically extremely spare: enigmatic and sharp at the same time. Here we are taken into the chapel at the west end of Durham Cathedral where two of the great saints of the region (Allnutt's home territory), Bede and Cuthbert, are buried. It is a smallish space that gives an impression of airiness and openness (especially in contrast to the massive Romanesque arches of the cathedral's nave). The poem begins with very diverse images of what being 'careful' might mean: the care of the verger doing routine cleaning, the care of the policeman charged with keeping the peace and watching for signs of irregularity, the care of the voyeur, immobilized in eager viewing of what should be hidden. We are being enjoined to all those kinds of carefulness as we step into a holy place – the routine dusting-off of our souls, the care not to disturb the stillness of the place, the anticipation of catching a glimpse of some secret.

One of the experiences many people report in places with a reputation for holiness is of something just missed, activity just beyond the corner of the eye, a presence just departed, like the angel in the air here, which is always present and always departing; though 'Always, in the air' also articulates the sense of suspension in mid-air that the architecture generates. The windows of the Galilee Chapel look down almost perpendicularly to the River Wear; those who know the space will understand the imagery of 'the river in the floor' as well as the mid-air sensation. The poem evokes light reflected from water illuminating a space in which everywhere and nowhere is 'occupied' by the holy. 'Presence' turns out to be a complex affair: no angels to be literally seen, but an unambiguous affirmation of the indwelling of this space by light, in just the way light inhabits or indwells water, and this all-pervading intangible indwelling as a metaphor for the indwelling of light in the heart.

Allnutt skilfully upsets what might seem the obvious progression of ideas in the last lines: light inhabits water, light inhabits this space, light metaphorically inhabits the heart. But instead we have light in water, light in the heart and then – implicitly – *the same light that indwells the heart* (the light of grace or love) indwelling the physical space. We have to be carefully on the lookout not for a fleeting glimpse of some 'supernatural' visitant but for the recognition that 'presence' is (as in Eliot's famous phrase in the *Quartets*) 'grace/dissolved in place'. The holy presence is not one item to be noticed among others; it is something that inhabits or saturates the finite place in which we find ourselves. And this is a theologically weighted perception: if God is what God is said to be, then divine presence is never an object among others, and divine reality can only be truthfully imagined with an analogy like that of light in water, not displacing the medium in which it lives but irradiating it in every corner.

A poem about grace, then, and so about the appropriate grammar for thinking about God or opening up our imagination to God with 'care': the care of the floor-polisher, prosaically attentive, the care of the watchman entrusted with keeping the peace, the care of the avid spectator, not daring to take a breath. Stone, air, water are all fused in the economical imagery of the poem, so as to introduce us into and hold us in a consecrated space, in which we are enabled to see – however fleetingly – how God *is* in the world of time and space.

Yehuda Amichai

Jews in the Land of Israel

We forget where we came from. Our Jewish
names from the Exile give us away,
bring back the memory of flower and fruit,
  medieval cities,
metals, knights who turned to stone, roses,
spices whose scent drifted away, precious stones,
  lots of red,
handicrafts long gone from the world
(the hands are gone too).

Circumcision does it to us,
as in the Bible story of Shechem and the sons of
  Jacob,
so that we go on hurting all our lives.

What are we doing, coming back here with this
  pain?
Our longings were drained together with the
  swamps,
the desert blooms for us, and our children are
  beautiful.
Even the wrecks of ships that sank on the way
reached this shore,
even winds did. Not all the sails.

What are we doing
in this dark land with its
yellow shadows that pierce the eyes?
(Every now and then someone says, even after forty
or fifty years: 'The sun is killing me.')

What are we doing with these souls of mist, with
these names,
with our eyes of forests, with our beautiful
children,
with our quick blood?

Spilled blood is not the roots of trees
but it's the closest thing to roots
we have.

Yehuda Amichai emigrated from Germany to what was then the Palestine of the British Mandate in 1935, and his poetry (and other writing) turns back frequently to the experience of *aliyah*, return from exile, and all the complex emotions and perceptions that go with this for Jews moving to Israel. This poem explores the different kinds of memory that live on in the minds of exiles – more particularly European Jews – who have never known the first homeland to which they return. These immigrants carry names connecting them with Europe, and a history of the various European settings in which Jewish communities lived (and suffered: 'lots of red'), the vanished, enclosed worlds of spices and jewels and regular persecution; but these memories are not the deepest roots of identity. Being Jewish cannot depend on these. In Israel, 'We forget where we came from.'

What matters ultimately is the primal fact of being circumcised, being included in the history of God's covenant. But circumcision can be painful (Amichai alludes to the story in Genesis 34 of how Simeon and Levi, the sons of Jacob, are enabled to defeat and kill the inhabitants of Shechem because the men of the city have been persuaded to be circumcised and so are weakened), and, says Amichai, the pain does not ever go away.

So what the returning Jew brings to Israel is pain. The fruitfulness of the land (Amichai uses with deliberation the near-cliché of the 'desert blooming') and the beauty and health of the next generation cannot quite extinguish this; the actual history of the return is woven through with more pain, the wrecked ships, the vessels turned back (as happened, notoriously, in 1947, when British forces attacked the *Exodus 1947*, carrying Holocaust survivors to Palestine). And – prosaically enough – the unfamiliarity of the climate means that the returned exiles cannot feel at home in any obvious way. Amichai voices the inner debates and doubts that go with all this in the repeated 'What are we doing?' The exile still carries the alien name, the memory of European forests, the memory of 'souls of mist' – this last phrase suggesting the insecurity of the Jewish presence in Europe and the half-life allowed to Jews in Christian society. But now the same exile lives with 'beautiful children' and 'quick blood' – a dramatically different future and an extroverted and impassioned social climate in which no one has to show deference or crippling patience. The pain of what is remembered is also the pain of these inner tensions ('"The sun is killing me"' – a gently ironical version of the profoundly serious homelessness evoked).

Most societies think of their roots in terms of place and kinship. Jewish identity is bound up with the Land of Israel, but not by way of an unbroken history of political control: Israel is not the stable setting of common life across the centuries but the place which is always there to be longed for and rediscovered.

And for Amichai, the blood that unites and anchors the Jewish identity is not the blood of ethnic kinship alone but the blood shed – in circumcision, in persecution and murder. In contrast to the regular caricature of Jewish self-understanding as a purely ethnic affair, this is a picture of the Jewish community as united precisely in a divided and fragmented history, and in the common memory of bloodshed; circumcision functions as a sort of foretaste of the sheer physical fragility of Jewish life in exile. The exile returning to the Land is able to live with a new and unfamiliar sense of having agency or freedom in regard to the future. But Amichai seems to be saying also that the tension he maps out here is not to be forgotten, despite the poem's opening line. The gift of 'covenanted' existence that is the heart of Jewishness is from the very beginning also a wound, a gift that pierces self-sufficiency and mere optimism about the future. The poem prompts the reader to imagine, through the lens of a very specific Jewish experience, what it might mean to think of a human community united not by ethnic uniformity or triumphant historical continuity but by the acknowledgement of shared hurt, shared fragility; we are asked whether *this* is what it is that the human family has to learn from the divine covenant with the Jewish people.

Yehuda Amichai

The Real Hero

The real hero of The Binding of Isaac was the ram,
who didn't know about the collusion between the
others.
He was volunteered to die instead of Isaac.
I want to sing a memorial song about him –
about his curly wool and his human eyes,
about the horns that were so silent on his living head,
and how they made those horns into shofars when
he was slaughtered
to sound their battle cries
or to blare out their obscene joy.

I want to remember the last frame
like a photo in an elegant fashion magazine:
the young man tanned and pampered in his jazzy
suit
and beside him the angel, dressed for a formal
reception
in a long silk gown,
both of them looking with empty eyes
at two empty places,

and behind them, like a colored backdrop, the ram,
caught in the thicket before the slaughter,
the thicket his last friend.

The angel went home.
Isaac went home.
Abraham and God had gone long before.
But the real hero of The Binding of Isaac
is the ram.

This subversive, even transgressive, reading of the story of Abraham's obedience to the divine command to sacrifice his son (Genesis 22.1–19) was written against the background of the Israeli invasion of Lebanon in 1982. There was debate in Israel over this, and there were those who felt that the lives of young soldiers were being put at risk in a conflict that was not understood; a feeling that sacrifices were being imposed not chosen. Amichai – one of the most popular and acclaimed Israeli poets of his time – gives voice to this unease, and the poem's perspective broadens out on to the whole territory of 'sacralized' violence pursued at the cost of lives randomly drawn in to lethal conflict.

The ram caught in the thicket, slaughtered in place of Isaac, is ignorant of the 'collusion' or 'pact' (as it has also been translated) between 'the others'. The biblical story is set in the context of the covenant between God and Abraham, who are presumably the others in question: it is this agreement that has to be honoured and preserved – but the ram is not a party to it. The ram is 'volunteered' to die; the Hebrew is literally 'as it were [*kemo*], it volunteered itself' – as if the animal 'presented itself' in a free offer of involvement. To put it slightly differently, there is an inexorably *tragic* element in the story: Isaac – and so the future of God's people – is saved, but at the cost of an innocent life. What is more, the slaughtered ram provides not only the sacrifice but also the means by which the victory of the divine plan is celebrated: the blowing of the *shofar*, the ram's horn, is part of the ceremonial around the celebration of the New

Year in Jewish practice, and is also mandated on the Day of Atonement. It is mentioned many times in Hebrew Scripture in connection with the festivals of the Jewish year. Talmudic texts associate the blowing of the *shofar* with the events of Genesis 22, the *Aqeda*, or 'Binding', of Isaac: God hears the ram's horn blown and remembers how he delivered Isaac on Mount Moriah, providing the ram as a substitute victim.

Amichai underlines the irony in using the ram's horn, cut from its corpse, to glorify the kind of militarism that imposes sacrifice on those who have not accepted it, effectively making possible the killing of the innocent. The strength of his language – this glorification is 'obscene' or 'gross' – expresses a revulsion at the idea that the *shofar* can or should be used to celebrate military triumph. But Amichai is not satirizing or criticizing the traditional liturgical use of the ram's horn as such, but pointing to the coarseness of a perception that clothes violent *Realpolitik* as tragic necessity or voluntary and heroic martyrdom. And he poses the deeper question about the collateral suffering of the innocent in the course of the unfolding of the divine purpose. The reference to the ram's 'human' eyes tells us that the poem is about ongoing human suffering, the suffering of those who have no real choice about their involvement in the drama of violence. A Christian reader might think too of the 'Massacre of the Innocents' narrated in Matthew's Gospel, where once again an appalling fate is visited on the guiltless as a consequence of the outworking of a divine plan and the saving of a child of promise.

Abraham and God vanish from the scene, and we are left only with two figures, as if in a posed photograph – the angel who gives the command to kill the ram, and the ransomed Isaac, with the ram itself as a painted 'backdrop'; the collateral body-count is reduced to a bit of scenery. Why do Isaac and the angel look with 'empty eyes'? They are looking into empty spaces: the two places where the ram's horns once grew, perhaps; or the spaces vacated by God and Abraham, who have, we are told, left the scene. On either reading, the real story of the sacred covenant has vanished, and all that is left is the appropriation by violent power of the signs of God's providential action. The angel and Isaac pose with the slaughtered innocent and then go home.

It is a bitter, difficult poem. The ram is a true hero (and it is worth noting that the last line in the original is not quite the same as the first: in the first line, the ram 'was' the story's hero; in the last, it '*is*'): the sacrifice is not unreal or ineffectual. What is troubling and shocking is the double slippage of meaning by which the death of the innocent is trivialized, and the celebration of the sacrifice is secularized. Both these shifts of meaning have the effect of normalizing and absolving violence. Amichai is implying that an authentic covenantal faith looks to a God in whose eyes, in whose presence, violence is never to be normalized.

Mia Anderson

Prayer Is Scrubbing

Prayer is scrubbing a carrot with plastic bouclé
  bath-gloves on.
Prayer is another carrot, and another.
Prayer is opening the door to the mudroom and
  then the door
from there to the garden steps
and throwing the muddy water out into the leaky
  bucket.
Prayer works like the leaky bucket:
there's an 'is' and an 'ought' but the 'is' takes
  precedence.

Prayer is standing at the other garden door after
  midnight
and breathing in the dark and
seeing someone's white cat the White Cadger
  mid-stalk stand stock-
still in the middled night
and watch the watcher – and watch the watcher
  watch her,
another cadger cadging prayer bytes –
then stalk off into more dark, more garden, more
  bytes.

Prayer is dreaming that you asked if he had any
time today,
the last day, for a chat,
and he confesses with alacrity but chagrin that he
hasn't,
and you have asked because
you are pretty sure this is the last time you will be
on the same
continent, before the great divide.
And you are dreaming of Last Things. Prayer works
like that.

Prayer is that sudden intimation that just perhaps
you might
forgive the one you know best,
(who is that? you? him? the other?)
might find how to be able to let or might be
empowered
(as they tediously say) to let at last the last
nearly midnight shadow of whatever it is that
stands between
you and the shining carrot
shuffle off its muddy coil and let the soil cleanse it.

Prayer is soil.

Scrubbing removes what coats something, letting its actual contours or colour come through: hence the triumph of 'is' over 'ought', the importance of being in touch with what is rather than what we think should be. And so prayer, in this intricate poem (one which grows in subtlety and wit as it is read aloud) is seen here as what holds us to that realism; it encompasses the midnight moment of watching the neighbour's cat hunting (the repeated 'st' sounds perhaps allow us to imagine the almost inaudible heartbeat of the watcher or watchers). Then, more poignantly, we are shown how it also encompasses another kind of truth-telling that belongs with or in prayer, the way in which our dreaming lives show us what daylight hides.

The strange lucidity or luminosity of the white cat in the garden prepares us for this probe of the nocturnal consciousness; and what comes to light is the haunting knowledge of unfinished business in relationships, especially the closest relationships of all. The poem is overshadowed by the impending death of a partner; the dream tells the speaker of the shortness of time before 'Last Things' – the end of a life, the arrival of exposure to the truth in final judgement, the *imminence* of separation and of an inescapable reality of loss. What is not done *now* stays undone. Hence the swift turn to the 'sudden intimation' that you are postponing the most necessary task of all – forgiveness, including self-forgiveness. Notice the challenge as to who it is you actually 'know best': it is equally disconcerting to think that the person closest to you isn't necessarily the one you know best and to think that *you* are not necessarily the person you know best. And 'the other'? Any other? A specific other? An other you don't know you don't know?

The poem begins with images of muddy water thrown out of the kitchen after cleaning carrots fresh from the earth. How shall we allow the deceptive habits of our darkened daytime life to be worn away so that we see what is there to see? The difficulty of this is indicated in the halting syntax of the lines: 'how to be able to let or might be empowered/ (as they tediously say) to let at last the last/ nearly midnight shadow . . .' The 'shining' of the reality that confronts us must be allowed to break through the shadow of what we place between ourselves and it. And what 'cleanses' that shadow is – paradoxically – the soil itself, the fundamental reality on which and from which we grow. Prayer is ultimately that ground; derivatively, it is any and every practice that opens us up to that ground. The images at the beginning of the poem of opening the door and throwing muddy water away are in the background here; but the final turn of the poem takes us back to the imminence of death. The cleansing soil is the grave; prayer introduces us to the grave, we might say, the place where we can no longer hide from who we are. Finding our way to forgiveness is part of our movement towards the grave as an open door, a gateway ('the grave and gate of death' is the phrase in the Book of Common Prayer).

So prayer is the beginning of a kind of death and at the same moment our anchorage in the truth of life. We live to the extent that we can die to the world of shadow we constantly reinforce for ourselves. The practice of prayer scrubs away at the mud and wears away the plastic gloves as well. Our praying will be sporadic and 'leaky', like the bucket for the muddy liquid, but it is steadily punctuated by the gifts of darkness – by what is given in silence and obscurity that will wear away the deceptive daylight in which our unscrubbed souls live.

W. H. Auden

Friday's Child

In memory of Dietrich Bonhoeffer, martyred at Flossenburg, April 9th, 1945

He told us we were free to choose
But, children as we were, we thought –
'Paternal Love will only use
  Force in the last resort

On those too bumptious to repent' –
Accustomed to religious dread,
It never crossed our minds He meant
  Exactly what He said.

Perhaps He frowns, perhaps He grieves,
But it seems idle to discuss
If anger or compassion leaves
  The bigger bangs to us.

What reverence is rightly paid
To a Divinity so odd
He lets the Adam whom He made
  Perform the Acts of God?

It might be jolly if we felt
Awe at this Universal Man
(When kings were local, people knelt);
  Some try to, but who can?

The self-observed observing Mind
We meet when we observe at all
Is not alarming or unkind
   But utterly banal.

Though instruments at Its command
Make wish and counterwish come true,
It clearly cannot understand
   What It can clearly do.

Since the analogies are rot
Our senses based belief upon,
We have no means of learning what
   Is really going on.

And must put up with having learned
All proofs or disproofs that we tender
Of His existence are returned
   Unopened to the sender.

Now, did He really break the seal
And rise again? We dare not say;
But conscious unbelievers feel
   Quite sure of Judgment Day.

Meanwhile, a silence on the cross,
As dead as we shall ever be,
Speaks of some total gain or loss,
   And you and I are free

To guess from the insulted face
Just what Appearances He saves
By suffering in a public place
   A death reserved for slaves.

This is a particularly densely composed poem: it moves along rapidly and teasingly; its syntax is complicated and elusive, its imagery is subtle, and it presupposes rather a high level of familiarity with the ideas of the theologian Dietrich Bonhoeffer, who was executed in the concentration camp at Flossenbürg in 1945 for his complicity in a plot against Adolf Hitler. His letters from prison, first published in English in 1953 in a much abridged version, provoked a good deal of puzzled comment in the decades that followed. They were often read – superficially – as foreshadowing the theological radicalism of the 1960s, with its scepticism about traditional doctrinal formulations and (at the furthest extreme) its ambivalence about the very idea of an active and actual God.

In contrast, Auden's reading (the poem was probably written in or around 1958) is one of the most nuanced and insightful responses to Bonhoeffer, going to the theological heart of the German thinker's meditations; and it is arguably one of the most profound poems about faith written in the last century. Human freedom is not a kindly but provisional concession to us on the part of God (a concession that may be withdrawn 'in the last resort' if we prove stupid and intractable): God means what God says. We are given the freedom, without reserve or qualification, to 'Perform the Acts of God' – to act, think and speak as if God were not there (Bonhoeffer uses the Latin phrase, *etsi Deus non daretur*, paraphrasing – and somewhat reinterpreting – the words of the legal theorist Hugo Grotius about how certain duties would still be binding even if we did not presuppose the existence of God).

Yet the liberated, elevated human consciousness we might expect to see emerging is in fact 'banal', self-deluded, profoundly confused and ignorant. Bonhoeffer had written of how theology had to come to terms with 'Man [*sic*] come of age'; and some of his interpreters in the 1960s took this as the respectful recognition of a human moral maturity that no longer needed supernatural sanctions for good behaviour. Auden takes Bonhoeffer's admittedly ambiguous phrase less optimistically: we may have 'come of age' in the sense of discovering our liberty to act as if God were not there, but this does not mean that we have arrived at any kind of maturity. The human mind is no more impressive than it ever was. All we have learned is that we have no guarantee of God's existence and are left with a freedom that turns out to be not such good news after all, a freedom that leaves us alone with our triviality and muddle, our mixture of technological sophistication and imaginative poverty.

Conventional religious certainty has indeed vanished. Proofs of God's existence are 'returned/ Unopened to the sender'. And this image is skilfully turned around in the stanza that follows: has God 'broken the seal' – the seal fixed on the grave of Jesus according to the Gospel of Matthew, the seal on the 'letters' sent to God with proofs of his existence? We are not in a position to answer; but the idea of a God who will call us to account – not in any very sympathetic way – persists, even in the irreligious. As Auden notes early in the poem, we are 'Accustomed to religious dread'; we are haunted by the God we don't believe in, the God who does not really give us authentic liberty but still reserves the power to damn us.

The final two stanzas of the poem are an extraordinary key shift, a jolting change of focus and register. '*Meanwhile*': while we worry away at the memory of the God we don't accept and try to make what sense we can of our incongruous lives, abandoned as we are by any hope for authoritative vision, *something else* is happening. The 'silence on the cross', the unequivocally dead body of the redeemer, is either a wholly new vision of God or a final closing down of all hope. We are 'free/ To guess': Auden leaves the word 'free' hanging for a moment in the break between the stanzas, as if to remind us that the whole poem has been about freedom, about the complete seriousness of the gift of liberty that God gives humanity. The cross sets us free from the need for proof, we might say; but whether that means faith or its opposite is an open question for us.

The death of Christ is a matter of 'saving the Appearances': Auden, with more than usual allusiveness and elusiveness, picks up a phrase first used in ancient Greek thought, where it designated what would be needed in any theory claiming to account for the phenomena in front of us without making it necessary for us to ignore some aspect of those phenomena. If the cross is indeed the act of God, then seeing it as such is a recognition that the freedom of the world to be itself without God – the freedom that is in fact implied in God's very act of creation – must involve the possibility of God's presence in creation being totally, definitively unrecognizable, the presence of God as a dead body, the utter opposite of what we associate with God. God dies the death of a slave, a person without freedom; and in doing so both expresses the divine freedom (God is free to be present even in what is most unlike God – that is, slavery and death) and confirms once and for all the reality of our freedom – freedom to guess, certainly, but something more than this if we can indeed see God in the crucified: freedom to see more than our own embarrassing deceits and confusions, to see what the gift of life actually is.

W. H. Auden

Luther

With conscience cocked to listen for the thunder,
He saw the Devil busy in the wind,
Over the chiming steeples and then under
The doors of nuns and doctors who had sinned.

What apparatus could stave off disaster
Or cut the brambles of man's error down?
Flesh was a silent dog that bites its master,
World a still pond in which its children drown.

The fuse of Judgement spluttered in his head:
'Lord, smoke these honeyed insects from their hives.
All works. Great Men, Societies are bad.
The Just shall live by Faith . . .' he cried in dread.

And men and women of the world were glad,
Who'd never cared or trembled in their lives.

This sonnet is a marked contrast to Auden's Bonhoeffer poem, which we have just read (it was written about a decade earlier). Its argument is simple, its imagery spare; not one of Auden's major poems, but – like so many of his shorter pieces – embodying a single critical insight with an economical and detached formality. The insight, to put it simply, is that one person's radical and traumatic release from guilt and terror can be twisted into an alibi for complacency.

In the mediaeval landscape of the first quatrain, Auden evokes the mental anguish experienced by the young Luther, obsessively conscious of his sin and the sin of the whole institution he is part of; the young monk who insisted on going to confession more than once in a day because of his awareness of failure and corruption. It is as if sin is as unavoidable as the wind blowing through the gaps under the door and bringing to the 'nuns and doctors' (doctors of divinity, that is; Luther took great pride in his academic title) both the urge towards transgression and the paralysing guilt that follows. Luther sees human beings as trapped in these two compulsions, of transgression and guilt; there is no way to cut through the thorny hedge that surrounds us. We should be 'masters' of our bodily needs and passions, but the wordless drives of the flesh turn and wound us. Our sinfulness sinks us without trace in the 'still pond' of the world. It is worth noticing in passing how Auden makes the flesh and the world 'silent' and 'still' (just as the devil, to complete the traditional triad, is busy in the wordless passage of the wind) – the opposite of any sort of raging passion: the problem is not the noisiness of emotion, temptation, struggle, moral drama, but the inexorable silence of the mechanisms that drag us down so insistently and have no voice, no ideas, no way of being adequately talked about.

Luther's protest, then, is a kind of breaking of the silence. The mechanism must be named, the word of divine judgement must explode in the face of this deadly circling back into stillness. And what is said is, above all, that the structures we erect in order to tell ourselves that we are safer than we actually are have to be torn down – 'All works, Great Men, Societies'. The good news is that faith alone delivers, faith in a power infinitely beyond all our striving. Good news, but also the source of another kind of terror: it says to us that there is no way out of fear except by recognizing and embracing our absolute helplessness.

This explosive rejection of human achievement is, by the worst of ironies, good news of quite the wrong sort for 'men and women of the world' – those who have never been at odds with the compulsions of the world or the flesh. Luther's passionate exposure of the falsity of human myths of virtue and success becomes an excuse to forget about any hope for or aspiration to transformed human life – at worst, a plain cynicism about the possibilities of holiness or justice, at best a self-congratulatory acceptance of things as they are in society. Auden is surely thinking of the way in which Lutheran pietism in Germany had made generations of German Protestants uncritical supporters of existing political power – as in the notorious letter of support for Wilhelm II's military policy at the outbreak of the First World War, signed by all the leading Protestant theologians in the country; and, more shockingly, the passivity of so many German Christians in the face of the rise of Nazism. But it is also about the idle 'worldliness' of all who treat the grace of God as an excuse for human inaction ('God will forgive; that's his job', to quote the old French maxim). Bonhoeffer himself was to write scathingly of how the myth of what he called 'cheap grace' had corrupted the Christian mindset in this way; whereas, from Luther's own point of view, only the person who has been through the hell of self-doubt and self-loathing had the right to talk about grace.

And the repudiation of 'works' carried its own internal risks of corruption, not just the risk of misunderstanding from a spiritually lazy public. 'Righteousness by works' was associated with Judaism and the 'Old Law', and Luther's hostility to Jews reached a pitch of unprecedented and murderous hysteria in his later life. Auden would have been well aware of this, too. Perhaps one of the things the poem is saying is to do with the need to be sceptical even in our scepticism, especially when that scepticism is grounded in a traumatic personal history. We can see the hollowness of human aspiration and the nonsense of human self-deception; but the savage refusal of aspiration and deception can breed its own demons. Openness to grace need not entail creating new demons to hate and subdue.

Jay Bernard

Tympanum

Wood smoke of black Anglicans behind the body.
As he was in life, he is heavy. Pallbearers lock knees
against the weight and tilt the coffin over the lip.
The tips of my father's fingers guide me by the back
  of the head.
Blown cheek of the roof, ulcer and teal, gas pipe
  and cherub.
The radiator prays for warmth. As in life, my
  uncle's body
is raised like a newborn. People are gentle with
  him, speak slowly.
Black feathered congregation missed breakfast
  sharpening their shoes.
My cousin throws a low grin between the pews and
  we play
muffled *had*, skidding along the rows as though
  sitting still.
Until the singing, I had been thinking of that warm
  night
legs slung over either side of the church wall,
  ankles locked
with my lover drinking Stella, the song said I am
  here,
I don't have to worry, you can see your tears. Can I
  open my mouth

and say such things, can I let this song see me cry?
My cousin went up to the body, alone, and looked.
She turned to me. The answer, as it is in heaven:
something about a child with its hands over its
  face.

The Grenfell Tower fire of June 2016 was and is a focus for deep grief and anger, showing as it did the level of criminal indifference to the lives of so many regarded as marginal, even dispensable, in British society. For many people of Afro-Caribbean heritage, it woke recollections of the terrible loss of life in the New Cross fire of 1981, very probably the result of deliberate and racially motivated arson, never adequately investigated or explained; for a whole generation, a stark reminder of which lives do and don't matter in the UK today.

Jay Bernard's poetry connects these traumatic events of violence and loss in a sequence of diverse poetic responses, both nuanced and unvarnished, voicing the perspectives of the dead and the bereaved alike, and mapping a broad landscape of loss and powerlessness – 'Losing and losing and loss./ Never recouping the cost', as one of the closing pieces in the collection *Surge* puts it. But that poem itself firmly situates this activity of detailed, unsparing remembering and memorializing as the way in which we face loss, refuse to pretend it is anything but what it is, and keep that unrecovered cost in view for everyone. Many of the poems focus on specific individuals, unique moments and perspectives of trauma within the collective disasters of the two fires, while some are related to particular family or local bereavements. This poem is about a family funeral; but in its context it is shadowed by the larger shared tragedies Bernard addresses.

Thus the 'Wood smoke' of the opening image evokes not only the sombre clothes of the dutiful Anglicans gathered in the church but also the glimpses of violent and nightmarish death that we see elsewhere. The weight of the coffin tells us that death does not lessen the 'weight' – in another sense – of a human life; and despite the weight, the dead man is lifted by those who love him, 'As in life', lifted as gently and securely as we might lift a newborn baby. Dignity remains in death, and the gentleness and nurture we give to the newborn is also the dead man's right. 'People are gentle with him, speak slowly' – as we would with a small child. If our minds turn to other, harsher deaths, including the deaths of children, it is with both this imperative of gentleness and this sense of weight.

In spite of the vividly rendered physicality of the first section of the poem – the touch of the father's hand, the random visual details of the church and its shabby décor, the inadequate radiators – the speaker is still a bit detached, casting an ironic glance at the plumage and the shinily polished shoes of the congregation, reliving childhood games. And then the well of emotion is opened by the singing: the relaxed summer night that has been recalled is all at once gathered into something else as the song announces its presence, there and here (is the June night of the Grenfell fire in the background here?). Who is the 'I' who speaks in the song? We might have expected '*You* don't have to worry, *I* can see your tears.' But what is happening is that what speaks in the song speaks from beyond anxiety and allows the speaker to pay attention to what is being felt and risk articulating it. 'Can I let this song see me cry?'

And the deep and economically evoked feeling of the closing lines brings together the silent appeal for solidarity in grief with an oblique picture of what it might be for human grief to be recognized in a more 'absolute' way. 'As it is in heaven' is, of course, the conclusion to the prayer, 'Thy will be done in earth.' The concluding image is an 'answer' to the speaker's question about whether to give full voice to the scale of the grief that is felt: if there is a divine will to be done 'as in heaven', it must be 'something about' what recognizes and speaks for the desperate, inarticulate terror or grief of the child hiding its eyes – overcome with weeping, or shutting its eyes against what can't be borne.

The 'tympanum' of the title is the name commonly given to the usually semicircular panel over the west door of many mediaeval churches depicting Christ in majesty or the Last Judgement; and it is also the technical term for the eardrum. What the poem must do, it seems, is to appeal for judgement, to deliver an apocalyptic cry against a culture in which some people's deaths are held to be meaningless. But that begins when we allow the eardrum to be struck by the song that breaks down our resistance, that tells us something of what lies beyond anxiety, shame, evasion or embarrassment. If human lives and deaths *mean* for us what these moments uncover, then we owe them something more than evasive silence.

John Betjeman

Norfolk

How did the Devil come? When first attack?
  These Norfolk lanes recall lost innocence,
The years fall off and find me walking back
  Dragging a stick along the wooden fence
Down this same path, where, forty years ago,
My father strolled behind me, calm and slow.

I used to fill my hand with sorrel seeds
  And shower him with them from the tops of
  stiles,
I used to butt my head into his tweeds
  To make him hurry down those languorous
  miles
Of ash and alder-shaded lanes, till here
Our moorings and the masthead would appear.

There after supper lit by lantern light
  Warm in the cabin I could lie secure
And hear against the polished sides at night
  The lap lap lapping of the weedy Bure,
A whispering and watery Norfolk sound
Telling of all the moonlit reeds around.

How did the Devil come? When first attack?
  The church is just the same, though now I know

Fowler of Louth restored it. Time, bring back
  The rapturous ignorance of long ago,
The peace, before the dreadful daylight starts,
Of unkept promises and broken hearts.

Anyone who has written seriously about Betjeman has recognized how fatally easy it is to underrate him. The flippancy, the self-conscious skilfulness of his playing with the clichés of Victorian versification or the hidden passions of suburbia, even the displays of religiosity, all of them draw attention away from the sceptical, sometimes anarchic intelligence underlying so many of the poems. He can channel with great imaginative sympathy the voices of people who have deep-rooted faith, and he can also express a naked fear, shame and guilt impervious to the reassurances of belief. One of his best-loved poems, 'Christmas' (yes, I did think about including this in the present book), pivots on the question, 'Is it true?' and the well-known last verse begins, 'And is it true? For if it is . . .' The affectionate picture he paints of the ordinary sentimentalities of Christmas is abruptly framed by this larger challenge. *If* it is true, what it claims is indeed, of course, beyond comparison more beautiful and life-giving than any human cosiness. But the poem itself doesn't answer its own question. The triumphant last lines ('God was man in Palestine,/ And lives today in bread and wine') are still prefaced by that 'if', even though most readers may have forgotten it.

A lot of Betjeman's poetry celebrates – with varying levels of irony – suburban cosiness and childhood memory, children's parties, holidays, and – less happily – schooldays. 'Norfolk' (printed in the same collection as 'Christmas') sandwiches such a celebration between the stark repetition of the question, 'How did the Devil come?' How is it that the harmless comfort and confidence a child enjoys with its parents can be invaded by something alien that leads to betrayal and disappointment? We grow and we learn: Betjeman, with a touch of self-mockery, notes that he now knows that 'Fowler of Louth restored' the local church of his early Norfolk holidays. But that kind of knowledge is only a sliver of what we actually learn as we grow older. We learn that we can break promises – and (implicitly) that promises *to us* are also broken, the promises that seemed to be encoded in childhood security, with the water lapping at the sides of a well-caulked boat.

We look back at the memory of safety and realize that we were never safe. The world was never actually insulated from the corrosive possibility of 'attack'. William Golding's 1959 novel *Free Fall* is in some ways an extended probing of Betjeman's question, looking back over a life that has its share of betrayal and disappointment in the vain attempt to track down the exact moment at which 'the Devil' arrives and the freedom to be good is lost; wherever we look, it seems, is either too early or too late – though Golding hints that the crucial points are perhaps when we make a *decision* to believe that we are not free, and when (in consequence?) we make the further decision that the material of the world around us, especially other persons, are first and foremost there *for us*, not in themselves. And even then we can't trace exactly what makes such a decision inevitable.

So we are always looking back at a life in which something is already lost, whatever the point at which we pause the video. We may have been experiencing 'rapturous ignorance' or 'peace', but we have (like the young Betjeman) been 'gathering seeds' – surely not a casual choice of words on the poet's part – without realizing it. The security of human love is appallingly fragile, and Betjeman in his wonderful verse autobiography, *Summoned by Bells*, recognizes just how far back guilt goes in his memory, and how inseparable it is from his love for his parents. The 'lamp-oil light' of the Christmas poem, echoed here by the 'lantern light' on the holiday boat, is an unreliable illumination. We were always coming to know things beyond our choice and comfort. That is what it is to grow as a human being.

In that connection, there is no way back to the innocent trivialities. We are not redeemed by the reassuring and very temporary generosities of Christmas – the John Lewis Christmas ad vision, we might say. The poignancy of the Christmas poem is that these heart-warming moments are debris floating on a very dark ocean. Perhaps they are a distant glimpse of what genuinely might be; or perhaps they are moments that only intensify the darkness, encouraging the cruel illusion that darkness is not ultimately inevitable. To believe the former, to believe that something other than guilt and disillusion and betrayal might be real, means believing that, just as it is possible to be attacked or invaded by something destructive that is more than our own self, it is also possible to be open to something that is *not* destructive, to be open to grace in the widest imaginable sense, to a daylight that is not dreadful. 'And is it true? For if it is . . .'

Chaim Bialik

Alone

All of them the wind lifted, all of them
The light swept on their way, a new song
Reviving their morning. But as for me,
A fragile bird, I am left deserted
Under the Shekhinah's wing

In solitude. Left here in solitude, and the
  Shekhinah,
Its right wing shattered, quivers above my head.
My heart knows hers, my heart knows the terrors
She bears, her fears for her son,
Her one and only.

Exiled from the mountain heights, and only
This secret corner making space for her –
The *beth ha-midrash*, where she takes refuge, where
She and I are alone with one another, no-one but me
To share the suffering.

I long for the window, the light, like one robbed of
  her children,
And the place under her wing is a prison to me.
She nestles her head against my shoulder,
And a tear drips down and falls
On my completed page.

She clings to me wordlessly, weeping over me,
Her broken wing like a shelter stretched above:
'They are all gone, the wind has carried them away,
All of them flown the nest, and I
Am left bereaved, alone.'

Like listening to some immemorial dirge's dying
  fall.
Like listening to a pleading prayer. Like harsh
And fearful cries. In all that silent weeping,
That scalding tearfall, this is what I hear
By the hearing of the ear.

Like other Jewish pieces in this collection, Bialik's poem makes use of the great theological image of the Shekhinah, the personalization of the divine presence in creation, distanced from heaven in this world of suffering and defeat. The central metaphor in the poem is the exiled Shekhinah, with its broken wing, hiding in the *beth ha-midrash*, the study-house or synagogue, a mother-bird still protecting the one among her offspring who has not yet left the nest – the speaker, whose loneliness mirrors her own. A full commentary would need to track the varied echoes of biblical phrases, very evident in the Hebrew – the restoration of 'joy in the morning' promised in Psalm 30, the many references to hiding under the shadow of God's wing and the understated allusion to the 'shelter' or 'tabernacle', *sukkah*, of the Feast of Booths (see also the poems by Rav Kook in this collection, pp. 167 and 171), the lament of the mother whose children have been taken away or killed (Jeremiah 31.15), the archaic formulation of the 'hearing of the ear' (as in Job 42, for example). It would also need to note the echoes of Kabbalistic language and practice – the 'only son', *yechidah*, as the term for the highest state of union with the divine (suggesting that the 'solitude' of the poem alludes to the contemplative practice of Lurianic Kabbalah), and the 'shattered' wing of the Shekhinah, calling to mind the primordial 'shattering of the vessels', which scatters the divine presence abroad in the created universe.

But the protecting heavenly presence is overwhelming, stifling; the speaker, muffled in the darkness under the divine wing, yearns for light as urgently as the Shekhinah yearns for her children (once again, there is a Kabbalistic echo in the idea that God is glimpsed only through a window). The poem is probing a Jewish identity in which the only place left for the divine is the study-house, and the only language for Jewish faith is one of lament for loss and disruption. Bialik (who wrote elsewhere of the frustration of confinement in the study-house when the outside world is green and bright) implies that this, with all its deep pathos and gravity, is a prison; he was one of those who returned to the Land early in the twentieth century, already scarred and shocked by the violent anti-Semitism of 'Christian' Europe; and the very fact that he chose to write his poetry in Hebrew (rather than what was then the more obvious medium of Yiddish), well before the full-scale modern revival of the language, was itself a sign of rebellion against the confinement of Hebrew to the study-house. Writing in Hebrew, you could say, was his own attempt to bring the divine out of the *beth ha-midrash*, to reconnect the words of revelation with a complex modernity.

Yet for all this, the mother-bird clings on, and the pathos of loss and dispersal still marks the speaker's writing: tears have fallen on the page. As in Sutzkever's poem about raiding the printing presses (see p. 305), there is a challenge as to whether the sacred alphabet can be re-forged as a defence against the distinctive barbarity of the contemporary world, whether the poignant integrity of a community faithful to its Scriptures and its memory of suffering can give birth to something new. Bialik's poem does not try to give an answer to this, except in the bare fact of its being written in Hebrew. But there is a sense here that the speaker's fidelity to and unity with the wounded Shekhinah, his understanding of her loneliness and grief, is significant. He has not 'flown the nest' of the tradition, and his ability to hear what the Shekhinah's silent weeping is saying is what animates the poem as an exploration of two interlocking solitudes. To be able to decode and share the weight of wordless grief that shapes Jewish identity, and not to turn away from what the *beth ha-midrash* represents, is what enables a renewed capacity to make the historic language work again. The mother-bird is desperate to protect this, her last remaining child, and that terror has to be recognized and taken seriously: something must be remembered and spoken of and transmitted to the next generation, the history of faithfulness and loss must not be forgotten. Articulating that remembrance in the world beyond the European ghetto or *shtetl* may be a lonely task, but it is a task fitting for the Hebrew poet: the written ('completed') page will still display the marks of tears even as the language looks to another kind of future. The phrasing in the last verse, the biblical idiom of the 'hearing of the ear', may well point to that best-known instance of the usage at the end of the book of Job: after his sufferings, his anguished protests of integrity, his silencing in the presence of the divine self-revealing, Job says that until now he has 'heard of [God] by the hearing of the ear', but now sees God directly and repents; and a new world follows.

Ruth Bidgood

The Pause

‘A wonderful Great and unknown Creature’,
wrote Traherne, waking his readers
to some idea of the strangeness
of a divine Lover.
                    Is there a sense
on this tawny silent moor with its drift of rain
glittering in stormy sun, its rainbow flung
from hill to cloud and back to autumnal earth,
of that being’s elusive presence?

Nothing I see matches the map. Getting lost
here seems inevitable and good.
Till the rainbow fades, till patterns
of time and direction grow clear again,
in a stormlit pause the Creature roams the moor
and breathes with the breath of the bright rain.

For many readers, Thomas Traherne’s work, celebrating a material world suffused with God’s beauty and welcome, still frames the way that the English–Welsh border is experienced. Three and a half centuries after Traherne, Bidgood, whose home is on this border, here picks up in a poem that is part of a short sequence on the region and its vistas (indoors and out of doors) a phrase from the seventeenth-century writer, a phrase of exemplary simplicity: ‘A wonderful Great and unknown

Creature'. The 'strangeness' of divine love is what the phrase evokes, we are told: encounter with, or the hint of encounter with, God is like discerning the traces of some as yet undiscovered animal in the wild, with just enough in those traces to let us know how beautiful it would be.

That strangeness is what comes to the fore in this particular landscape, the silent moorland under a glittering shower, with a rainbow overhead. There is no way of locating on a map where it is that the speaker is standing, and this is appropriate to the moment of 'discerning the traces'. The rain and the light together obscure the ordinary landmarks (those who know the landscape in question will know what she means). There is a pause when we do not know where we are: we are strangers to our immediate physical setting, strangers also to *who* we are. We have no identity, no reference grid, to put between ourselves and the brightness of the rain. We are surrounded and (literally and metaphorically) soaked through by the unknown greatness.

God is in the pause, in the 'breath' of the rain across this uncharted landscape. Breath – the same word as 'spirit' in the biblical languages – sustains life, and so the moment of alienation from self and place and time, which could be terrifying, becomes a glimpse of grace. It is a 'stormlit' moment, born out of the tumult of unsettled weather: we are being reminded that this is not the predictable fruit of quiet meditation but a gift arriving in the heart of the turmoil, not quite the 'eye of the storm' but almost the reverse, a perspective that is somehow in and around the storm. The clear markers of time and place are suspended in this storm-scape of water and light, and the imagery is not that of a hidden centre into which we are invited but a vast openness in which 'the Creature roams', a God 'at large', breathing freely.

Bidgood will be perfectly well aware of the irony of calling the divine presence 'the Creature': God, of course, is creator not creature. Theology 101. But the point is twofold. First there is the surface sense of the metaphor, that of the unknown animal whose presence we faintly sense (by sound or smell, perhaps); the reality and specificity of God's nearness is underlined by this very physical imagery. But then there is the hint that we who genuinely are 'creatures' have become new and strange in this moment. *We* are the ones who roam in this great moorland space, breathing differently. The pause in which the divine becomes fleetingly perceptible is a time-out-of-time when we grasp that who and what we are is bound up with this disorientation in our usual habits of compass-setting.

The contemplative writers of the Rhineland in the fourteenth and fifteenth centuries – Eckhart, Tauler, Suso – would compare the contemplative experience with being in an unmapped wilderness, no pathways to be seen. Ruth Bidgood builds on this, and gives it a strong and unexpected turn, so that the mystery of the divine lover comes to be inseparably woven in with the mystery of the strange, newly uncovered selves we see in the inseparable moisture, light and rapid shadow of the landscape.

Yves Bonnefoy

Noli me tangere

In the blue sky, the flake hesitates once more,
the last flake of a heavy snowfall.

And it's as though she were coming into the
  garden,
she, who must surely have dreamt how it might be,

This gaze, this simple God, with no remembrance
of the grave, no thought but bliss,
no future
but dissolving in the blueness of the world.

'No,' he would say to her, 'don't touch me.'
But even saying no would be a ray of light.

Yves Bonnefoy wrote a memorably beautiful sequence of poems about snow – the different sorts of transformation in landscape and objects that a snowfall produces. But this brief piece is distinctive, evoking as it does the story of Mary Magdalene coming to the garden where Jesus' tomb is located, finding it empty and then encountering the risen Jesus; not at first recognizing him, then realizing who it is as her name is spoken. Bonnefoy sketches this allusion very lightly, his language employing a series of conditional verbs, as if to underline the tentative nature of the perception he explores.

The heavy fall is over, and a few last flakes are dropping as the sky clears into blue. The last flake is melting as it falls; it cannot be taken hold of. But just for that reason it is exceptional and precious. It carries nothing of past or future; it exists in a present moment so fleeting that there is really no way of capturing it at all. The only words that in any way express what is happening are 'Don't touch!' Don't try to seize this because there is nothing to be held on to and you will destroy not so much the melting physical object but the actual lightning glance of perception, the moment of receiving that fugitive knowledge of – what? Being part of something, being held in something, not being alone, not being a random bundle of mechanisms?

The snowflake's refusal to be grasped is at one and the same time its ability to be a means of grace. It somehow embodies a 'gaze', it opens up to us the awareness of just being looked at, a wholly 'simple' moment in which I know that the source and totality of existence is focused on me – but without in any way promising some outcome, solving some problem, even healing specific wounds. So the 'No' that the snowflake utters is *illumination* for us: there is nothing but the recognition of being recognized, the simplicity of being seen and acknowledged, yet without any of our routine wants or fears or hopes being met in any straightforward way. I am recognized; yet my turbulent and confused ego is sidelined.

The flake melts; Bonnefoy teasingly turns the picture upside down by speaking of the 'blueness' not of the sky but of the world. In one sense the snowflake is dissolving into the sky it's falling from, but it is also melting into another 'infinity', the depth of our world, the world of our thinking and sensing. The ray of light released by the 'No' dissolves into what we are, it becomes us. It disappears *into us*: which doesn't mean that it's swallowed into the processes of our busy mind and imagination. It means that we are made able to live in the presence of the vanishing, virtually invisible 'simple God', the whatever-it-is that tells us we are seen, and so liberates us from the frenzied effort to *make* ourselves seen, to make ourselves real, the effort that in fact deafens us to the 'Yes' hidden in the snowflake's 'No'.

It is an almost Buddhist perspective on the familiar resurrection story. The moment when Mary knows she is known, when her name is spoken, is the moment when she has also to learn that what she has seen and what has been given to her cannot be made into a possession. The risen presence of Christ has to 'disappear into us', as we move beyond a simple picture of my self and Christ's self, so to speak, connecting in external ways. To have the reality of grace within us is to know that we are not sealed-off lumps of selfhood, but are always open to receiving life and illumination. The 'gaze' in which we stand does not falter. When the snowflake has melted, we are different. We are freed from the craving to grasp and possess.

And it is not an easy or obvious lesson to learn. We need to be out in the snow quite a lot. Or to read more poems about snow.

Euros Bowen

Lazarus

No; there is not a thing he can remember
of how it felt inside the tomb,
or anything belonging
to that dead season,
only the noticing, as he woke up.
of memory whited out,
the memory of the unboundedness
of the last moment of dark sickness.

Breathing is pleasure, breathing the goodness
of wind at the cave's mouth,
listening to his tongue's surprise
as it comes to itself again
eating bread at the table.

He knows that what he died of
was familiarity, the same old things
day after day.

But now there is more than sound
in the noises around him, feelings
feel more, taste tastes more, smelling
is more than smelling. He cannot
hold back the smile, standing
at the back door, watching the boundlessness
of the almond tree whiting out the yard.

Like R. S. Thomas, Euros Bowen spent his working life as a parish priest of the Anglican Church in Wales; but his poetic voice is as different as could be, an incantatory, slow-paced brooding over symbols, with a powerfully sensuous – but also at times curiously abstract – atmosphere. 'Lazarus' is a tantalizing poem about the frontier between life and death, between what can and can't be said, between the very particular and physical details of human life and the blinding light of whatever it is that we meet beyond death or beyond words.

Lazarus, coming back from the dead, has nothing to tell us. Bowen echoes, consciously or not, the encounter in Per Lagerkvist's 1950 novel, *Barabbas*, between Lazarus and the confused and angry Barabbas, whose life has been saved (like all our lives, Lagerkvist hints) by a stranger he has never met. He wants to know something about this stranger and seeks out Lazarus – whose presence is opaque and disquieting, and who can only say that he has been into nothingness and returned. So too in Bowen's poem. Nothing *happens* in the tomb, there is nothing to narrate. All Lazarus can think of is the way in which, as he died, memory was buried in a 'whiteness' of oblivion, a sense of limitlessness that overtakes his 'night of sickness', *nos ei glefyd* in the original Welsh. And when he returns to an awareness of the physical world, it is with sharply enhanced senses: in retrospect, he sees that he was already dying, long before his actual death, in the flatness and sameness of his perceptions. *Actual* death has given him back his capacity to see, hear and taste. There is more, not less, to sense in the world as life is given back. And in a skilful and unexpected metaphorical twist, Bowen connects the return of speech with the return of the tongue's other use in savouring the texture of food. The tongue 'comes to itself', 'comes home', in eating bread – implicitly, eating with others at a shared table, so that the Christian Eucharist is not far away. Words and bread come together on the tongue; the Word made flesh is made bread at the table of the Eucharist. In another poem ('The Word'), Bowen presents the physical action of sharing the Eucharist as what prevents the living Word becoming no more than an 'ideology of Christ'.

Lazarus stands at the cave mouth, at the 'frontier' of his burial place, and he stands at the door of his house, on the edge between two worlds; and it is at this edge that he senses the fullness of reality most acutely – and most *physically*. The grace of dying and returning is presented here not as a matter of transition to another and more 'spiritual' realm, but as going deeper into the life of the body itself. There is a well-known Buddhist adage that, before enlightenment, mountains are just mountains, rivers are just rivers, trees just trees; when meditation begins, mountains cease to be mountains, rivers cease to be rivers and trees cease to be trees, but when enlightenment arrives, mountains are mountains again, rivers are rivers and trees trees. No clue again as to whether there is any deliberate echo, but the point is clear.

And the imagery of a shower of white blossom smothering the backyard or garden has a distinct flavour of the Zen imagination. Bowen carefully links this new and joyful vision with the whiting out of the moment on the margin of death, as if the perception of abundant and purposeless beauty were a sort of dying. Poetry and faith here exist at the cave mouth, on the edge, inviting us to some kind of 'dying' to stale and routine perceptions of the material world; they do not promise that on the far side of this there will be lots to talk about, an exciting story of risk and deliverance; they simply begin by pointing to the blinding shower of blossoming light that makes it possible to see and sense everything again as if for the first time. This is what ideology keeps trying to eradicate, and what faith keeps returning to us.

George Mackay Brown

Epiphany Poem

The red king
Came to a great water. He said,
Here the journey ends.
No keel or skipper on this shore.

The yellow king
Halted under a hill. He said,
Turn the camels round.
Beyond, ice summits only.

The black king
Knocked on a city gate. He said,
All roads stop here.
These are gravestones, no inn.

The three kings
Met under a dry star.
There, at midnight,
The star began its singing.

The three kings
Suffered salt, snow, skulls.
They suffered the silence
Before the first word.

George Mackay Brown's poetic voice is typically one that takes the reader into a world of pre-modern image and music, with a directness and physicality in its symbols and a simplicity of diction and syntax. To call it 'archaic' would be misleading; it is not nostalgic, and it has no trace of pastiche in word or tone. It is not polemical about modernity (though his prose can be that at times), it merely directs our imagination to themes and rhythms that do not alter when the furnishings of a culture change.

The colours associated here with the three kings of the Epiphany legends are at one level arbitrary, part of the vividly material environment that the poet conjures. If there is any allusion to the traditional association of the kings with Europe, Asia and Africa, as in so much mediaeval and Renaissance art, it is at most subliminal: the diverse aborted journeys of these three magi do not derive their significance from geography, let alone race. They are to do with the points at which the human quest is halted by the apparent blockage of the way ahead. The kings 'Suffered salt, snow, skulls': the unexpected alliteration (skilfully understated, with the marked variation of the other, non-alliterating, consonants in the words) brings together these very diverse blockages. And all are then gathered up into the 'silence' that is common to what the magi suffer.

The star above them when they meet is at first 'dry': it does not immediately yield its secret. But the kings are travelling because it has already broken the silence of their worlds. Each has said that the end has been reached, and said no more. In a way that calls to mind St John of the Cross writing about the 'Dark Night' in which the spirit is eventually transformed, it is at midnight that things begin to change, when it cannot get any darker; or, with other contemplative writers like Eckhart in mind, we might think of the silence that is the condition for the divine Word to be born in us. The imagery is of grace appearing when we have come to the end of the resources we know, understand, and in some degree control. Coming to the point of ultimate frustration with the human search for meaning or search for God is what frees us, under the dry, cold and distant presence of the star, to hear what we had not imagined. If the three journeys are to be very loosely read as voyages of discovery, the mapping and following of trade routes, and hopes for urban civilization, the termination of all of them in a despair about going further is bound up with the necessity of letting go of our fantasies of ever-expanding dominance over our environment. The trackless ocean, the uninhabitable regions of freezing cold, and the sheer fact of death (the city's 'gravestones', with 'no inn', no place to stay) must be our teachers.

The parallels with Eliot's 'Journey of the Magi' – in thought if not in style – are not difficult to see. Eliot's magus has nothing directly to say about what was found at the end of the journey except that it was 'satisfactory'; and the aftermath of the moment of vision or presence is bewilderingly inarticulate. But there has been a passage between worlds, an unmistakeable transition that could be called equally birth or death. For George Mackay Brown, though, the perspective is even larger: what the kings 'suffer' is what is there before the 'first word', before God's 'Let there be light' is uttered over the formless waste that is all there is at the very dawn of creation. What the Epiphany discovery is has something to do with the Nativity or Incarnation as the start of a new creation. It is a passage between worlds, but ultimately a passage between chaos – the chaos of human achievement and power – and the new condition of openness in which God can be heard, and so life can be sustained.

John Burt

Sonnets for Mary of Nazareth III

Because he was so plain a god, so calm,
Riding at her heart like any child,
A stirring and attentive passenger
Wakeful in her wordless rush of breath,
She would have been amused, not terrified.
What did he have in mind? she thought at nights
While patient Joseph snored and shepherds woke.
It came to her at last: he didn't know;
He himself would catch it up from her.
What could he want, except to want like her?
To know what weakness is, and casualty,
How being done to teaches her to be,
How losing love enables her to learn
To make of fear her honor and of death her gift.

This is the third in a short series of sonnets, the first two of which explore the ways in which we make gods in our own image, projecting on to them our anger and our restlessness. The gods of Homer, with a rather detached curiosity, observe the 'secret in them [human beings] they don't know', the elusive interiority that haunts human life and seems to disappear when we turn to look at it directly. Homer's Achilles tries 'to kill his way to fame', seeking to be divinized by sheer force and excess. But in Homer's epic, Achilles only 'matters' when he is brought up short by Priam's grief for his slaughtered son; his aspiration for a divinity seized by extravagant violence is less important than the humanity he briefly comes to share in the fleeting compassion he shows to Priam, when he for a moment understands why and how he matters as a *human*.

So we have had two poems about the divine as the image of our pathologies and the product of our failure to know ourselves. The God incarnate in Mary's womb is 'plain' and 'calm', not a repository for our furious resentment, not a home for wish-fulfilling fantasy, not a myth of the triumph of raging excess. Mary is not 'terrified' by being the body that bears this God, because he is simply alive at the centre of who or what she is, picking up the cues her body gives him – 'stirring and attentive'. Mary's revelation is that this is a God who does not come into the human world with an *agenda*: she has to teach God what his human calling is.

'What could he want, except to want like her?' It is a particularly strong statement of what theologians have often tentatively stated: Mary has to teach Jesus how to be human, as any mother teaches a child. And if this humanity is uniquely the vehicle of the eternal Word of God, Mary has to teach her child how to be *that* unique human. Jesus must learn to be God incarnate from his mother; that is, he must learn how to make his life gift not campaign; to do what has to be done by 'being done to', by loving and attentive receptivity that will embody the eternal loving receptivity of the Son to the Father in the Trinity; by making loss and catastrophe and death a means of growth. Mary's familiarity with receptivity and the transformation of risk or vulnerability becomes the specific concretely human means of Jesus growing into a humanity that is the agent of universal renewal, the door opening into a new humanity and a new creation.

The God who is made flesh within the fleshly womb of Mary is the opposite of a wish-fulfilling idol. This God does not have to fight and defeat; this God is a stranger to the rage and denial that mythology projects on to an all-powerful visitant from somewhere else in the universe. This God is not a limited and tormented consciousness defending itself against others, but a genuinely transcendent – different – reality. But just because of this, God needs to be 'shown' how to be human, since he is not (like the pagan gods) a massively inflated version of the human ego to start with. Jesus must learn how to be the embodiment of an absence of angry ego, how to offer his very identity as unreserved gift, how to act liberatingly and transfiguringly through what looks like passivity and defeat. And there is nowhere else to learn it except from his mother.

Devotion to Mary has taken extravagant forms in Christian history, and some of those forms have had the effect of removing Mary a fair way from the ordinary fragilities of human experience. Burt wants us to think of her as being free within those very fragilities to induct her son into a form of human living that will be completely transparent to the shattering *difference* of God, the God who is not the projection of human rage or resentment. The poet's picture of Mary is in its way more startlingly ambitious than any amount of extravagant devotion to the Queen of Heaven. It is the picture of a human being liberated by grace to the degree that she can teach her son to be divine in a human way.

Charles Causley

I Am the Great Sun

From a Normandy crucifix of 1632

I am the great sun, but you do not see me,
  I am your husband, but you turn away.
I am the captive, but you do not free me,
  I am the captain but you will not obey.
I am the truth, but you will not believe me,
  I am the city where you will not stay.
I am your wife, your child, but you will leave me,
  I am that God to whom you will not pray.
I am your counsel, but you will not hear me,
  I am your lover whom you will betray.
I am the victor, but you do not cheer me,
  I am the holy dove whom you will slay.
I am your life, but if you will not name me,
  Seal up your soul with tears, and never blame me.

In the traditional Catholic liturgy for Good Friday, a series of texts is sung called the 'Reproaches', *Improperia*. They are inspired by a passage in Micah 6, beginning 'O my people, what have I done to you? In what have I wearied you? Answer me!' God confronts God's people with the record of divine guidance and gift, and asks why their response should be so reluctant or hostile. The fully developed liturgical text carries the uncomfortable shadow of anti-Semitism that haunts so much of the devotional language of Good Friday in Christian practice; it is true that nearly all Christian preaching today would say that the focus of this and comparable elements in the liturgy is meant to be primarily *Christian* betrayal and unfaithfulness. All the same, the dramatic premise remains: God is complaining against the people that God himself has brought out of Egypt.

Causley's version of the Reproaches begins from another place simply by addressing any and every human passer-by. The crucifixion of Jesus is not a remote historic miscarriage of justice, nor even an occasion for conventional moral or religious self-accusation. It is the sign of a global refusal of life. The reality that in fact illuminates everything is ignored; and the poem continues with a relentless enumeration of the ways in which we both refuse love and refuse to see that we are refusing. We will not set free what it is that we imprison by our wilful ignorance – that is, the self we might become, but are afraid to be. We will not 'obey'; we will not let a reality outside us shape us according to its own unchanging nature, and so are left in a perpetually distorted and distorting relation with a truth that will not bend to our convenience. We will not 'stay', we will not commit to city, spouse or child; we slip away from the hard permanence of our human task, our calling to be with and for one another, whether in family or society.

The voice from the crucifix demands a recognition that we shall *live* only when we have turned again to look into the face of all we have rejected, ignored and hurt: our hope is with our victims. It is a deeply convicting thought for Good Friday simply because, for two millennia, the self-proclaimed followers of the crucified have created more and more victims in his name, not least the Jewish people whose imaginative role in the Christian liturgy is to provide a prototype for betrayal. For anyone accustomed to using the Reproaches in worship, the challenge is inescapable, the challenge of recognizing the hideous irony by which the event that summons us to look at our victims so as to find our hope becomes, in the Christian imagination, an occasion for the creation of a new category of victims.

'If you will not name me': the voice from the crucifix cries out against a corrupt silence that will not face the nature of human perversity. And the concluding phrase, 'never blame me', is a stark declaration of our responsibility to open our eyes and mouths, to see the 'Great Sun' and to name our sickness. So far from the cross of Christ being only a lifting of our guilt, it is *first* a summons to acknowledge it. Looking at the tortured and rejected embodiment of hope or truth or love, we must learn to say, 'This is what we do; this is the engine that moves human interaction, this process of refusing who we might be and so of refusing one another.'

The force of the poem, its air of almost impersonal, timeless austerity, has much to do with the way in which it repeatedly brings us to the edge of intense emotional recognition, but refuses to exploit or elaborate that emotion. Only in the last line does something like passion flare up, both in the metaphor of sealing up the soul with tears (evoking the sealing of Christ's body in the tomb at the end of the Good Friday narrative) and in the uncompromising, unmerciful concluding words. The mercy we seek on Good Friday is not an indulgent pardon for our misdeeds but an abiding reality – light, commitment ('your husband', another echo of the imagery of the Hebrew prophets), stability and common life ('the city'), the unchanging possibility of peace ('the holy dove'). It is a reality that we not only ignore but also actively fight against and seek to destroy. Good Friday cannot bring us to life until we acknowledge the ways in which we are deeply at war with life. Turn to the victim of your violence, and find there the face of the God you have refused to see. Have mercy on the self you have imprisoned and you will find the mercy of God.

Charles Causley

Eden Rock

They are waiting for me somewhere beyond Eden
  Rock:
My father, twenty-five, in the same suit
Of Genuine Irish Tweed, his terrier Jack
Still two years old and trembling at his feet.

My mother, twenty-three, in a sprigged dress
Drawn at the waist, ribbon in her straw hat,
Has spread the stiff white cloth over the grass.
Her hair, the colour of wheat, takes on the light.

She pours tea from a Thermos, the milk straight
From an old H.P. Sauce bottle, a screw
Of paper for a cork: slowly sets out
The same three plates, the tin cups painted blue.

They beckon to me from the other bank.
I hear them call, 'See where the stream-path is!
Crossing is not as hard as you might think.'

I had not thought that it would be like this.

We dream of people we have loved who have died, often in settings or landscapes that evoke a sense of repair or completion. In this simple and overwhelming piece, Causley steps without preface into such a dream landscape – both vague ('somewhere beyond Eden Rock') and highly particular (the details of the parents' clothes and of the picnic meal, so lovingly redolent of the early twentieth century). 'Eden Rock' is not the name of any local landmark that anyone has identified, and may be just the kind of name overhead in dreams that is felt to have deep significance in the dream context; and of course it alludes to the garden where our 'first parents' lived (and lived in brief harmony with the animal world; we should not ignore the youthful dog accompanying the father).

The familiar and everyday persons and activities are suffused with a visual intensity that is anything but everyday (the mother's hair 'takes on the light'). The three plates, like the three suns, set a number of associational chains running. At the most mundane level, the plates are for the three members of the family, about to be reunited; but somewhere in the background may be the three angelic visitors to Abraham in Genesis 18. The light of the three suns calls to mind the phenomenon of 'parhelia', optical illusions that give the impression of three suns in the sky (as happened before the battle of Mortimer's Cross during the Wars of the Roses, for example); but it also seems to hint at the vision of interwoven circles of light at the end of Dante's *Paradiso*. The domestic scene of the picnic's preparation is clothed in what is literally an aura of radiance, as the speaker is invited to join his parents, who assure him that crossing the little stream between them is not difficult. The closing line, separated by a gap from the rest of the poem, has a monosyllabic density worthy of George Herbert: 'I had not thought that it would be like this.' The 'it' is the prospect of death but also the sense of a numinous homecoming within and beyond death, a homecoming as utterly uncomplicated as a child on a day's outing rejoining its parents after wandering away. The abstruse vocabulary of 'negative theology' is reduced to these bare syllables of wonder. This is what we could never have expected; not because it is so remote from us but because it is (to borrow a phrase from St Augustine) closer to us than we are to ourselves.

Causley is not writing a poem 'about' immortality or heaven or anything like that; he is creating a lucid dream in words, the substance of which is to do with the hope of overcoming loss and understanding death. Like any account of 'enlightenment', it refuses to elaborate or explain: it involves an irresistible awareness of light and presence within the ordinary, and attempts no further theorizing. The deep subtexts – of the love and trust between parents and child, the trauma of losing a parent at an early age (Causley's father died when the poet was seven), the fear of death and the hope of recognition and welcome in, around and beyond death – are all left implicit. In contrast to much of Causley's work, with its heavy and confident balladic beat and strong rhymes, the rhyme scheme here is regular but tantalizing (consonantal groups chiming but vowels varying), and the metrical pattern in each line loose and subdued. 'Somewhere beyond Eden Rock' is a location that can best be mapped by these indeterminacies and half-rhymes of the form; and yet *what is seen* is in no way vague, even under the dazzling light of the whitened sky.

What makes this – I believe – one of the most compelling 'religious' poems of the last century is this combination of absolute clarity and profound reticence in the account of what is seen. If there is a 'poetics' of faith, this is it. The words are shot through – shaken, we might almost say – by the subtexts, yet they hold their own; they 'take the light', like the mother's hair. What the poetry can and must do is just to bear witness, to acknowledge: we did not know that it would be like this.

Paul Celan

Count Up the Almonds

Count up the almonds,
count what was bitter, what kept you wakeful,
count me in with them all.

I sought out your eye as it opened, when no-one
  was watching.
Spun out that hidden thread
along which the dew of what you were thinking
slipped down into pitchers
protected by maxims that never reached anyone's
  heart.

There, whole for the first time, you walked into the
  name that is yours,
stepped into yourself, sure-footed,
and in the bell-frame of your silence, the hammers
  swung free,
and what was being listened for came out to meet
  you,
and what was dead put an arm around you,
and together you walked on through the evening.

Make me bitter, then.
Count me in among the almonds.

On the surface, not apparently a poem about faith or religious identity; but the key to this deeply elusive and complex poem is the chain of association carried by 'almonds'. In Hebrew, the almond is *sheqed*; in the first chapter of Jeremiah (1.11–12), the prophet turns it into a sort of revelatory pun on *shoqed*, 'the one who watches' – more specifically, God who 'watches over his word to perform it'. It also shares the consonants of *qadosh*, 'holy'; and almond blossom features in the decoration of the menorah in the Tabernacle (Exodus 25.33) and Aaron's staff produces almond blossom (Numbers 17.8). It is both bitter and sweet: in the last chapter of Ecclesiastes (12.5), the blossoming of the almond is one of the signs of fear and mortality that attends old age, as if a portent of the bitterness of loss to come; but the almond eye is one of the conventional marks of Levantine beauty, just as the almond can serve as a signifier of delight and sweet savour. In a later poem, 'Mandorla', Celan links the human eye and the almond: the almond contains the 'nothingness' within which dwells 'the King'. The almond and the watchful or wakeful eye are again paired: looking at the almond, the poet is also looking into the transcendent emptiness within itself that mirrors the sacred nothingness it confronts, the hidden King. But Celan can also write (in another poem, 'Remembrance') of the 'almond eye of the dead' – evoking the dead as watching the living, the dead as witnesses.

All this builds up a background for reading this challenging piece. The poem is addressed to Celan's mother, murdered in an internment camp. The first presenting image is a domestic one, counting almonds as if in a kitchen, a mother baking cakes with almonds; but it immediately shifts focus to a bitterness that 'kept you wakeful' – a reference to the *shoqed* echo that Jeremiah sets up.

Who is the 'you' of the poem? It is primarily the poet's mother, who is 'wakeful' – watching for God's faithfulness to be realized as promised by the God who is 'watching over his word'? But she will find no merciful conclusion to this wakefulness. The bitterness will not fade. And the poet demands to be reckoned with those, like his mother, condemned to such wakefulness; he demands to be counted among his people, reckoned as a Jew. Commentators on the poem have noted that the repeated use of the verb *zahlen* conjures up the roll-call (*Zählappel*) of the prison camp.

The speaker/poet is waiting (watching) to catch the moment when someone's (his mother's, anyone's) eye opens before anybody else has seen or can see it: the moment when something like the clarity of dew at dawn comes to light, a sense of unique identity that almost at once slips down into concealment – into a vocabulary of conventional wisdom ('maxims'), a set of storage jars, that doesn't resonate with the depths of anyone else's life. In that moment of waking, before the stale words have taken over, the bell sounds that gives voice to the most central identity of all, and calls for the dead to embrace and welcome. The poem rises out of that silence, giving the dead mother her true name, her true presence, among all those counted off for destruction in the camps (those reduced to numbers, not names). What is 'listened for' becomes fully present: it may be God or simply the numinous presence of the slaughtered people of God. All that has died embraces the speaker's mother, and they walk in the evening – as God walks in the garden of Eden in the cool of the evening, perhaps; as if the embrace of the dead somehow restored a world still unbroken by deception, disobedience and exile.

But the 'you' is also the poet addressing himself. It is he who experiences the sleepless bitterness, he who has to find a truthful identity for himself that can be embraced by the dead – a kind of absolution for his survivor's guilt. The final walking in the evening would have the same possible significance, with the poet embraced by his mother, by his people, perhaps by God. On either reading, though, it is clear that the poet's goal is to be among those who are 'counted' – counted off for slaughter, counted among the chosen; counted for bitterness and for sweetness, summoned to stay awake and (in both senses of the word) to witness – to see and to testify. The almonds being reckoned up are images of the Jewish people themselves witnesses to the possibility of truth or of God. The poem's ending voices this longing for solidarity; but it also – for those who remember the Hebrew – suggests a prayer to be kept awake, to be kept aware of the ineradicable bitterness. Poetry coming out of the nightmare of the camps must be a poetry of *wakefulness*, almost a poetry that has to 'stand in' for a God whose fidelity to his word of promise is so deeply and terribly invisible. This is a poem about the profoundest contradiction in the experience of a people defined by divine promise or covenant; a poem about how the names of the lost can be truthfully remembered.

Paul Celan

Your Beyondness

Your
beyondness tonight.
I spelled you back again with words, and there you
  are,
and everything is true, and everything is
a waiting for the truth.

The beansprouts are climbing up outside
our window: be aware of
who is growing tall alongside you, of who
is watching you.

God, so we read, is both
a single part and another, scattered:
it is in the death
of all who are cut down
that he grows into himself.

That's where
the looking leads us,
it's with this other half
our business lies.

Another poem about loss or absence: the poet's words are there to summon again what has been lost, and the cumulative force of these words allows something to grow alongside us, the lost presence in some degree restored as something that observes us. We have seen already how Celan can deploy the picture of the survivor who stands under the gaze of the murdered fellow Jew. The poetry intensifies this gaze or, rather, our awareness of this gaze.

The focus of the poem shifts slightly, with an allusion to Jewish esoteric thought – to the idea that the glory of the divine presence, the Shekhinah, is split apart in the act of creation, and dispersed in fragments throughout the finite world; the calling of the saint is to reunite the 'presence above' and the 'presence below'. Here, that 'presence below', the Shekhinah fractured and scattered throughout the world, is linked with the dead, whose fate testifies to the brokenness of the world we know: in the remembrance of the slaughtered, God 'grows into himself'. This seems to mean that the presence growing alongside us ('in front of the window') is God gathering back into himself the scattered sparks of his life that are the lives of those who have been killed. For God to be fully God is for God to act in and through those hideously aborted lives; for those lives to be made alive again, not in a comfortable or consoling happy ending, but as a living presence calling us to judgement.

And this is where the poet's business lies. If we are not to settle for the famous dictum that poetry is impossible after the Shoah – and Celan clearly does not – what can poetry do without talking a kind of unspeakably painful nonsense? It can 'raise' the dead as witnesses. Its business is with the 'half' of God that is the Shekhinah in humiliation, in filthy rags, broken and dispersed, bound to the terrible fate that overtakes God's people. And yet, in speaking or writing about this, the poet is looking towards the unimaginable end where God has 'grown into himself', and the 'above' and 'below' are together again.

Celan's response to the Shoah is therefore many-faceted; this poem and the other one we have just been considering point to a variety of ways in which speech about the uniquely dreadful can still be possible. And at the centre is the conviction that the poet/speaker has to be exposed to being 'seen' by the hosts of the murdered: the poet's voice has to articulate the sense of being under their eye, under their judgement. At the same time, the speaker affirms the longing to be included with them, takes the step of risky solidarity: he does not want a separate fate, a security they cannot share. And ultimately, looking into the eye of the dead is inseparable from looking into the emptiness that is God, 'the King'; looking at or into a God who is 'no thing', no object *for* us, yet always moving *alongside* us, or in some sense *in* us as we struggle to find words that will not allow us to stop looking into the 'almond eye of the dead'. What poetry does here is not to console or explain; it seeks to hold our eye steady. And that steady gaze, directed to the eye of the dead, looks also towards God; but it is a vision of God that brings no simple absolution or hope, only the possibility of some sort of truth. The poem is, as the opening lines state, a 'waiting for the truth', waiting for the words that conjure the absent ones to create a present moment where 'above ' and 'below', present and absent, are held and seen together.

Jack Clemo

Cactus in Clayscape

To know the God Who answers by fire,
To pray for rain and flee from Jezebel:
The cactus throbbed at voice and footfall
Of these prophetic urges. They seemed to stir
Deep in its stem, but were always outside,
Merely echoed in its prick of desire,
In the dry shaken leaf of a sentinel
Scorned like the sighing juniper.

The cactus prayed for death
Because the elect were too few for the battle,
And the priests of the evolving light,
The pruned approach, the sleek interpretation,
Ran glib and gloating over the holy mount.
They brought no fire and no rain
From the transcendent heaven, and Jezebel
  embraced them
With expert harlotry, craft of proud science
And decadent religion at the false fount.
The cactus bristled in searchlight glare;
The hills turned white around it, and the air
Filled with the odour of an open sickness –
A growth, through man's discoveries,
Of godlike claims that breed disease.

Seer of judgment and grace,
The cactus would stab to save the primal mountain
For the true fire, the pure rain, the embrace
Of the holy Queen, conceived without stain,
Who halts the advance of man and nature
With a humbling flash in which they are emptied,
Re-fertilized and born again.

Anyone familiar with Jack Clemo's poetry (and prose) will agree that the cactus is a very apt metaphor for this stubborn and resolutely un-ingratiating writer. His traumatic personal experience as someone who lost both sight and hearing at a young age combine with his uncompromising Calvinist Christianity to produce a formidable, unfashionable poetic voice. But he is never just a reactionary contrarian. He will unhesitatingly pass critical (even patronizing) judgement on great Christian figures of the recent and remote past, from John of the Cross to Dietrich Bonhoeffer, as well as on secular oracles like D. H. Lawrence. Yet the originality and clarity of his images of grace as a kind of industrial ravaging of a corrupt and decaying nature – like the great wounds in the earth that dug out the bleak clay pits of his native region in Cornwall – have their own integrity, even beauty. And his obstinate refusal to adopt a conventional modern evangelical negativity about sexuality is a persistent theme in his work, both before and after his marriage. He looks forward to the plain physical fulfilment of a Christian marriage, both exclusive and unreservedly passionate; when this longing is granted, he celebrates it without prudery or reserve.

This gives an extra edginess to the present poem. There is an inescapably sexual resonance to the image of the cactus, throbbing, pushing, stabbing, the prickly flesh searching for a place to enter – but initially to enter so as to wound or repel the treacherous world around. The poet is Elijah, confronting the idolatrous queen Jezebel and her deceitful priests who know nothing of the true God: the poem takes aim at the unredeemed sensuality of a pagan world, in thrall to a myth of scientific emancipation, but also at a religiousness that has accepted this slavery and, through 'sleek interpretation', accommodates itself to falsity. As so often in Clemo's work, the baldness of the polemic ('decadent religion at the false fount') introduces a jarringly prosaic and abstract element into the poem and is a drag on its verbal energy. But the energy surges back. The immense frustration of being a lonely witness to forgotten truths in a desert landscape (and here the hills turning white, evoking the clay pits again, serve unusually as an image of desolation not of the wreckage created by the violence of God's grace) leads to a wish for death as a release from the bitter stand-off of the conflict – a much intensified version of Eliot's magi being 'glad of another death'. The assault both born of and embodied in sexual frustration, the displaced masculine violence, is troubling to the speaker because it does not come from far enough inside. It discharges only an 'urge'.

So the poet meanwhile prepares to 'stab' so as to save; to preserve somehow, in the very aggression and arrogance of the verse, the possibility of fire and rain on the mountain, the forces (divine, not natural) that will change everything. The unexpected introduction by this uncompromisingly Protestant poet of the figure of 'the holy Queen, conceived without stain', the mirror image of the destructive Jezebel, produces a dense and conflicted web of images at the poem's end. The fire and rain are the signs of that divine violence celebrated so often in Clemo's early poems. But here it is assimilated to the 'embrace' of the Virgin, to Mary's assent to God's will at the annunciation; and this act of female assent, making possible the incarnate life of God with us in Christ, becomes a masculine force of fertilization, both emptying the engorged pride of human ambition and 'feminizing' the space thus left by sowing the seed of new birth.

Thus the poem begins with but moves on from a restless, unconsummated sexual tension, partly discharged in the would-be 'prophetic' assault on godlessness and pseudo-progress but itself not yet fully realized, fully impregnated. The revolutionary receptivity of Mary is what changes the whole economy of frustrated desire, invading an exhausted humanity so as to bring it to rebirth. It is difficult to say whether Clemo was entirely conscious of the deep and fruitful confusion of sexual imagery implied here; but the effect is in fact to challenge the male-centred narrative of protest and aggression that seems to be taken for granted when the poem begins. Grace, in other words, may be violent, but it does violence to the violence of our instinctive categories of force, division and opposition.

Adam Czerniawski

Self-judgement

shaped from babylonian clay in the image
of man I ruled ruthlessly through the ages
until the revolt and betrayal crucified under
  pontius pilate
I died but rose again educated in athens
I survived the days of oppression and scorn lately
  I've been crumbling
rusting they still see me now here now there
on an altar and in dreams

                                        but some
proclaim me long dead others a fiction from the
  very
start they falsified the testimony bribed the gawkers
someone is still proving my existence I'm tired
I'd like to leave now the snow outside the windows
  forms a geometry
of white the real shroud is more perfect shaped
on the sixth day succulent leaves dewy in the
  morning
people speak of me think of me so I still exist

Like so many other modern Polish poets, Czerniawski has a vigorous and tangled relationship with the Catholic culture he inherits. This poem is a kind of divine curriculum vitae, a record of how the image of God – specifically the God of Hebrew and Christian Scripture – has changed, adapted, faded and survived. From the ancient Mesopotamian projections of human power on to the heavens, through the revolution of the crucifixion in which that power is overthrown, through the refinements of philosophical theology that seek to make of this a coherent metaphysic, and so to the dissolution of faith in our contemporary culture, the process is reviewed: and today, all that remains is the fleeting glimpse 'on an altar and in dreams'. It is a telling phrase: what abides is sacrament and buried symbolic intuition, altar and dream, the world of sign rather than argument. There are those who still work at 'proving my existence'; but the divine voice shrugs this off, weary of debate and defence.

'The snow outside the windows forms a geometry/ of white.' There is an implicit contrast between what the poem's opening line describes – the image 'shaped' in the beginnings of the biblical text by our own imagining of ourselves – and the white 'shroud' cast over the world by the snow which is 'more perfect shaped'. The shroud may suggest death, yet the geometry of the snow which falls from heaven is precisely what is not and cannot be projected from earth and, as such, it is akin to the dew on the plants growing on earth the morning of the sixth day of creation – that is, just before the creation of Adam. God is about to 'leave': but the shadowy double sense of 'leave' is pointed up in the echo of this word in the dew-covered leaves of the vegetation in Eden – as if God is also about to 'come into leaf', to show signs of life. Somehow the distance opening up between the speaking voice and the self-centred dramas of humankind renews the awareness of what the divine really is as well as distancing us from it.

'People speak of me think of me so I still exist': but the poem implies that *how* we speak and think continues to change. The eclipse of the human-centred drama in which God serves our passions and anxieties is not an eclipse of God (R. S. Thomas's vision has something of this in its acceptance of the passing away of expected and familiar styles of prayer and of theology). In the awareness of the 'more perfect' structure of the world's order and of the world's self-renewal (the dew on the plants), there may be something discovered – or unveiling itself? – that can be spoken and thought; there may be a witness to the continuing reality of what older words and ideas have been feeling for.

Does the language of God come alive more fully today when the apparent simplicities of narrative and personal description fade away? It is an uncomfortable thought for the Jewish/Christian/Muslim world, yet one that has haunted that world's own reflection, in the various kinds of warning issued by contemplatives and philosophers against freezing and solidifying the words we use about God's dealings with us. After the crucifixion, with its implicit emptying out of images of ruthless power, God's 'rising again' into a philosophical language ('educated in athens') may in fact be an evasion of what is really going on – the steady stripping away from the divine as it exists in our minds of that original 'shaping', in which our own human self-image plays so great a role.

We can (must) believe in divine persistence, divine fidelity; but we must also believe in the process of what has sometimes been called 'divine iconoclasm', God breaking the images in which the divine has been carried and venerated through the centuries. In Christian terms, we have to take seriously what the revolution of the cross means; it is not a final confirmation of the myths we create about a God in our own image, but a final dissolution of them – or, better perhaps, a final declaration that all such images are on the way to something more expansive, maybe even to the 'love beyond desire' that Eliot writes about in the *Quartets*.

Hilary Davies

Penance

Not known in what sort of afternoon
The knowledge fell like a knife.
And yet it must have been that time of day
Most aptly suited to standing at the window
Or listening to desultory voices on the courtyard
  floor.
Into that wasted moment the roar starts up
As whisper, the physiognomy
Of one known long ago, and loved once.

And then the face begins to multiply:
Not thousands sinned against, but more
The myriad of ways in which it gained house room
Was even fêted, finally growing as everyday
As tables, dangerous as acid in a flower jar.

What is this reeky charring of the so familiar?
We cry deliverance as the gimlet closes on the nail
Of what we are, our mind crackling with
What's done, and done by us, never will be undone,
The realisation that the manège is real, ugly and
  eternal.
Father and mother are wraiths against this.
Friends useless. Lovers the writing on the wall.

So when her mind began to blaze
And blaze with understanding,
She bought the oils and lavished all the jar
Upon the manifestation of penance.
This is the beginning of it: not the singling out
Of feet, nor head, nor individuals,
But the return of floreat
Into the no man's desert of the heart.

One of a sequence of poems on the seven sacraments of the Catholic Church, this uses the story in St Luke's Gospel (chapter 7) of the 'sinful woman' who anoints Christ's feet and head with oil, imagining the moment of deciding on this both extravagant and humiliating act. The afternoon is somehow the appropriate time, a sort of restless in-between period of the day, when memory surges up, only a whisper to begin with but swelling steadily – the memory 'Of one known long ago, and loved once.'

This memory may be the sinner's memory of a self before sin; the primordial offence is against oneself, and all later sin is a hall of mirrors, reproducing that basic denial. And the shock is not in the numbers sinned against but in the normalizing of sin, welcomed, ignored, corrosive of what is around it ('acid in a flower jar'). We come to sense sin as fastened on to our very identity, driven in to who we are as if a screw were gripping the nail. What's done remains forever done and forever defines us. We have trained ourselves to 'perform' like this as surely as a horse in an equitation compound being urged round and round the track (the meaning of the rather exotic term, *manège*). Nothing in the past or present offers release; lovers are a threat not a promise, 'the writing on the wall', because the self that once was capable of being loved is now buried or absent.

But this moment of understanding is itself the moment of change, even before the oil is poured out over the feet of Christ and even before the mind identifies the particular individuals from whom forgiveness must be sought. Davies tacitly picks up her earlier image of the acid in the flower jar, noting the 'return of floreat' in the moment of self-recognition, as though the unexpected recollection of 'the physiognomy/ Of one known long ago, and loved once' has stirred into life the possibility of change. The blaze of self-loathing is also a blaze of light and hope. Not that this alone can bring about the change, but the penitent needs first to learn how to turn around in the hope of re-creation. 'This is the beginning of it.'

'The no man's desert of the heart' seems to allude to Auden's famous line in his elegy for Yeats: 'In the deserts of the heart,/ Let the healing fountains start.' In that context, Auden is commending the poet for probing to 'the bottom of the night', the depths of human despair and alienation: only at this point does something begin to spring up that is restorative, a word of praise even in the prison of the human condition. Davies's poem enacts just this sequence. The recognition that sin is indeed screwed in to the substance of our identity is the turning point, the bottom of the night.

So the irony is that as long as we deny that sin has become fully grafted in our selfhood, we are not able to be free from it. When we know that we are indeed slaves, when we know – even distantly – the self we have lost, we recognize what freedom must mean; and without this, freedom will remain elusive to us. Penance – the bare act of getting up and going to seek forgiveness – is the uncovering of the loved self we have forgotten that we are. Penitence is not a kind of amputation of the wounded and wounding past but first and foremost the vision of the self as loved; the sacrament holds up the mirror for us to see that self again with clarity.

Imtiaz Dharker

Prayer

The place is full of worshippers.
You can tell by the sandals
piled outside, the owners' prints
worn into leather, rubber, plastic,
a picture clearer than their faces
put together, with some originality,
brows and eyes, the slant
of cheek to chin.

What prayer are they whispering?
Each one has left a mark,
the perfect pattern of a need,
sole and heel and toe
in dark, curved patches,
heels worn down,
thongs ragged, mended many times.

So many shuffling hopes,
pounded into print,
as clear as the pages of holy books,
illuminated with the glint
of gold around the lettering.

What are they whispering?
Outside, in the sun,

such a quiet crowd
of shoes, thrown together
like a thousand prayers
washing against the walls of God.

The worn sandal as 'the perfect pattern of a need' is the central image of the poem. Each of the sandals left at the door of the mosque has a unique set of indentations, a unique history of being pushed into *this* distinct shape by the unavoidable daily pressure of keeping moving. The prayers being recited inside the building share with the shoes of the faithful the unique shape given them by the weight of an experience that is different for each person. The prayer, like the sandal, may express more plainly than the face what is distinctive in each life.

Dharker, whose background is partly Pakistani, partly Scots, gives us an austerely compelling picture of what prayer actually is: it is something as inescapable as walking, something that has to do not with anxious petitioning or ecstatic thanksgiving but with the sheer hope of moving, or perhaps growing, into a future. She plays with the double sense of 'print' – the literal imprint of foot on sole and sole on ground, and the print of 'holy books', which (in contrast to the print of the foot) are likely to be gilded and decorated. The footwear, imprinted with the individuality of each wearer, records (as books cannot) the long processes in each separate story of wear and tear, damage and mending; like prayer, they manifest the cost and the abrasion of human living, something, it seems, beyond words (compare Naomi Shihab Nye's 'The Words Under the Words', p. 227). The piled sandals are quiet and their connection with one another is random, 'thrown together'. Again, we are invited to think of the faithful at prayer united simply by the fact of their need, something deeper than conscious belief or other kinds of local affinity.

The conclusion is skilfully ambiguous, depending on whether we read 'the walls of God' as 'the walls within which God belongs' or 'the walls that are God's own inaccessible being'. The footwear is heaped against the mosque's wall, and the evoking of prayer washing against the walls could suggest a tide pressing from outside against something firmly closed. Is prayer bound to be an unsuccessful attempt to breach the wall that is the impenetrable mystery of God, something that never reaches beyond that boundary? Or should we think of the tide of prayer going on *inside* the building, washing against the inner walls of the space where God is to be encountered?

On top of this, there is also a more unsettling subtext. The speaker is *outside*: so the likelihood is that the speaker is female, walled out from the collective activity of Muslim men at prayer inside the mosque, wondering, 'What are they whispering?' What male longing for God is really like remains hidden. Dharker has written forcefully about the challenges faced by women in this culture, and the poem quietly hints at the possible perception that the 'walls of God' are barriers against women. God may be inaccessible but is perhaps more inaccessible to some than to others. Yet the poem seems to look to prayer as something that dissolves purely human division. From one point of view, prayer is the throwing together of countless human hopes and terrors and raw need in front of a stark unknownness; from another perspective, the 'washing' of the prayers is their ceaseless, rhythmical contact with the fabric of a space where they are received or recognized; possibly, too, washing away the distorted images of God or self that are brought into prayer, even the washing away of barriers of distinction.

If we begin to think about prayer with Dharker's image of the 'pattern of a need', questions about which of these is 'correct', questions about the rationale of praying or the results of praying or who has a 'right' to be there praying, become pointless. The foot must go on touching the ground; the worn sandals simply belong with what we just *do* as human beings. Dharker likes to describe herself as a 'Muslim Calvinist', a not too serious acknowledgement of the strain of fatalism that might be detected in a poem like this. But the final verse, with its emphasis on quietness and the gentle 'washing' rather than any language of battering or contest, might point to something that speaks more directly to the 'shuffling hopes' encoded in the pile of worn footwear.

Imtiaz Dharker

Living Space

There are just not enough
straight lines. That
is the problem.
Nothing is flat
or parallel. Beams
balance crookedly on supports
thrust off the vertical.
Nails clutch at open seams.
The whole structure leans dangerously
towards the miraculous.

Into this rough frame,
someone has squeezed
a living space

and even dared to place
these eggs in a wire basket,
fragile curves of white
hung out over the dark edge
of a slanted universe,
gathering the light
into themselves,
as if they were
the bright, thin walls of faith.

In its original printed context, the poem accompanies the photograph of a structure from a shanty town in India, a fragile construction of poles and boards of rattan or corrugated iron propped against one another, with, in the middle of the chaos, a basket of eggs suspended. 'Not enough/ straight lines': we may be meant to recall the old axiom that 'God writes straight with crooked lines', or the philosopher Kant's image of 'the crooked timber of humanity'. But, in any event, the poem affirms that living space can be created in the middle of, and in the medium of, this absence of straight lines. That we can indeed live in what seems to make no sense, in the absence of 'straight lines' is near-miraculous.

Looking at a structure like this inclines us 'dangerously/ towards the miraculous', throws us off our rationalist/reductivist balance and suggests that more is possible within the disorderly world we inhabit than we could have believed. The eggs become a symbol of this 'unbalanced' possibility. The 'fragile curves of white' illuminate the darkness of a universe that is 'slanted' – out of true, as we sometimes say. They concentrate light; they can serve as a metaphor for faith by their clarity and their frailty alike.

So the poem sketches two related insights about the human world. The structures we live in are not safe – the moral and imaginative structures we build, the versions of ourselves and our societies that we construct, the levels of understanding we become accustomed to. The lines do not run where we would wish them to and the sense we make of them is insecure and badly connected. And in such a world, we continue to look for and to treasure what concentrates light, even when it is 'thin'. The thinness of faith can be both the frailty of it, the lack of solid evidence or predictive power or whatever – or the transparency of it. Dharker may be implying that anything which draws and transmits light in this way is *bound* to be 'thin' – in the sense in which people have come to speak of holy places as 'thin', letting through something that is genuinely other.

Is this a very minimal version of faith? Only if faith is thought of as something that ought to have a clear position among the things of this world rather than being 'the conviction of things not seen' (Hebrews 11.1). If we look to faith to provide the straight lines that can be guaranteed to prop up the chaotic edifice of our lives, we are in danger of reducing it to something that will simply fit our existing aspirations for security. A conviction of what is not seen is a freedom to inhabit the rickety structure of thought, desire, fear, imagining, hope that we live in with an awareness that the world's surface sometimes thins out to allow something to come through that is not part of the structures of our minds and passions. The light comes through; it does not replace the stuff of the world but makes it translucent.

It is a living *space*: there is room enough to live. And it is a *living* space; where we live is itself alive – not empty, not simply dark. Learning to live in this is indeed leaning into the miraculous, whatever the risk to what we think is orderly and safe.

Isabel Dixon

One of the First Times After

One of the first times after: church,
and Easter Sunday. Good Friday
we had skipped: too soon, and too severe
a day. The days of our desertion,

no resurrection yet. If it were thus,
already, brethren, he would be
the one to hold the chalice to my lips:
long now since he had the strength for this.

Christmas last he struggled into vestments,
held the bread-filled paten up; the cup,
its taste of silver and sweet wine,
not quite enough to bind us,

fractious family, his slow diminishment
our own unhealing wound. He couldn't say
the blessing till he'd gone to pee:
we waited with our silent fears and prayers.

We far-flung sisters had just one more chance,
communion at his bed. Surrendered now,
a calm and grateful ring of chairs,
a loving colleague with the book,

my father's lines now his. Too weak
for words, propped up, he took it in –
a deeper feeding than the drip
we let him veto, swabbing out his mouth,

and letting, breath by breath, the spirit go.
Here, in the pew, a stoic threesome,
we bear the sermon and the intercession
made for us, bereaved; but leave – no, flee –

during the last verse of the closing
hymn. My mother, capable of facing
up to anything but sympathy,
and we too glad of the escape:

the congregation's sincere looks,
this mutilated Eucharist,
the wrong priest's hearty clasp.

This is one of a substantial sequence of twenty-six poems about the death of Isobel Dixon's father, an Anglican priest, poems that are a precise and deeply moving record of the indignities of a slow dying in hospital and of the stages of bereavement. Here, Dixon brings into focus the way in which the consolation of Easter or the hope of resurrection can feel forced and premature for anyone still managing the newness of a loss. For a priest's family, accustomed to hearing and receiving the sacramental words and gifts from this particular person, the loss is especially acute in the context of the liturgy. Widow and children have avoided church on Good Friday ('too soon, and too severe'), but the Mass of Easter Day is no better; they have to endure a seasonal sermon (implicitly not a good one or one they can connect with) and put up with being prayed for and sympathized with. The service is overshadowed by memories of the father's last opportunity to celebrate the sacrament and of his last Communion – the 'deeper feeding' that nourishes a more durable life than the one supported by the surgical drip, and somehow releases the family to let the dying man go, 'breath by breath'.

Why is the Easter Eucharist 'mutilated', in the harsh language of the concluding lines? At the most obvious level, the mutilation is simply the absence of the dead father and the presence of 'the wrong priest'. We have been shown at the father's deathbed what the sacrament can be – the nourishment of soul that allows a letting-go, a breathing-out. But this Easter service feels to the bereaved like something definitively less than the reality they have experienced. The sympathy and sincerity of the congregation do not make real contact with the sense of loss; the words are empty, for all their good will. It is still 'too soon, and too severe'. A true celebration of the resurrection would be the restoration of the dead man as celebrant, holding the chalice for his daughter to drink from.

A straightforward poem about one aspect of bereavement, the portrait of a pastoral situation that many clergy would recognize easily, perhaps ruefully; but there are wider themes in the background. The Eucharist is the sign of the fragile possibility of family reconciliation, not quite realized at the father's last celebration at Christmas, offered again at the deathbed and, it seems, effective in that setting. There is a letting-go not only of the dying man's breath but also of whatever it is that has caused rupture and hurt: it is not clear in the poem what exactly is 'Surrendered now', but it must surely include all this. So the Mass is quintessentially a moment of *release* – release into the inevitable death of the body but also release into a 'death' for tension and hostility. But this Easter celebration fails somehow to speak of or indeed celebrate that kind of release, for whatever reason, and so has to be escaped from.

Is this, then, in part about how resurrection can be honestly hoped for only when we have begun to know what death can be, both the rawness of loss and the letting-go of the spirit? But this is a poem about a very concrete experience, and it is a mistake to make it too general, too theological in the unhelpful sense. Readers will have understood what needs understanding if they look at and listen to more candidly the ways in which even the most sincere and generous consolation or sympathy can 'mutilate' what is needed. Living through loss takes time, and demands more and more levels of letting-go. So we must trust the slow process of a 'feeding' that has to carry us through 'The days of our desertion', neither frozen in despair nor hurrying to consolation; we must learn not to speak too soon.

Emmanuel Egbunu

Farewell

This wilderness falls on my way
and though a wanderer like
Jacob of old
here I cannot stay.

I remember John the Baptist
who chose for his home
the wilderness;

I remember too
the wild sweetness
that I have tasted here
in these seasons
and the temptation
to linger.

But tents are not homes:
here I am a stranger
and the memories of
the sweetness here tasted
shall be my victual
the rest of the way.

So with bare fingers
I wave my farewell:

I shall wear a golden ring
when I get home.

The wilderness 'falls'. At first, the desert we experience is emphatically not what we have chosen; it becomes visible as we journey, an inescapable prospect. It is a consequence of the imperative to keep moving. Standing still is not an option, and so when the journey leads forwards into dry places, there is no possibility of stopping or turning back.

This deceptively simple poem, by a Nigerian Anglican bishop who has written movingly both about the scourge of the HIV pandemic and AIDS and about the wounds of civil war and inter-tribal or interreligious violence in Africa, begins with an acknowledgement that where we find ourselves is not our home. We may be, like the biblical patriarchs, destined to be wanderers, living in tents (there is an echo here of the language of the eleventh chapter of the Letter to the Hebrews), but the point of the journey is precisely that it *is* a journey, towards what is still unknown. In another poem, Egbunu neatly turns on its head the cliché about 'old familiar things', to speak of our 'old alien world' with its grip on our 'old alien affections', and the same point is just below the surface here. Our journey of faith is a task that requires us to continue letting go of what seems familiar or natural but is in fact not what we are made for as humans. At the same time we also have to learn – paradoxical as it may sound – not to cling to the restlessness of the journey itself, as if journeying were all that there was to be looked for.

John the Baptist chooses the wilderness for his 'home'; the desert's wildness has its own seductions and 'sweetness'. The temptation is to treat this as the end of the story: we let go of our comforts and set our faces to the journeying. But the wanderings of the patriarchs and the witness of John the

Baptist are stages on the way to something more, and the sweetnesses of the desert are food for our travelling, not provisions for a home.

To put it a bit differently, the patriarchs and John the Baptist are with us on the journey but the life they lead is not the journey's goal: 'tents are not homes'. We may accustom ourselves to the privations of the desert, and we may even relish its strange rewards. There is a satisfaction in the consciousness of brave endurance through pressure and struggle; there is a certain drama about the desert experience as it is sometimes presented that can mislead us into thinking that endurance is all we can hope for. But this is more a Stoic than a Christian perspective. We are not promised an endless journey but a homecoming.

In the evocative closing lines, what is it that the 'bare fingers' are waving goodbye to? Presumably it is the wilderness. We are stripped bare even of our privation; we have to let go even of the desert when it threatens to become another theatre for our self-orientated agendas. There is a Buddhist saying that even if you bring nothing to the act of meditation, you must 'lay down' even that nothing – that is, the *idea* of nothingness or selflessness. You must simply be there to receive. And Egbunu's final couplet points us to the end of the parable of the prodigal son, where the returning son is given a new robe and ring as a mark of dignity. But rings are also symbols of marriage. The reader might hear an echo of George Herbert's poem, 'Hope', with its poignant conclusion: the speaker here accuses hope of 'loitering', not delivering or perhaps committing as expected. 'I did expect a ring', he protests. But the ring arrives (so Herbert implies) only when hope ceases to be hope, when the longed-for reality has actually arrived, and we have arrived where we belong, where we are no longer strangers. Egbunu's poem gives us a skilful balance between the needful acceptance of the desert and its sufferings and the equally needful intensity of a trust that this is not all. There is a home to which we are called, a union like that which the ring sacramentally signifies – the union of God and God's people, Christ and Christ's Church, the created person and the divine love that sustains and transfigures.

T. S. Eliot

Journey of the Magi

'A cold coming we had of it,
Just the worst time of the year
For a journey, and such a long journey:
The ways deep and the weather sharp,
The very dead of winter.'
And the camels galled, sore-footed, refractory,
Lying down in the melting snow,
There were times we regretted
The summer palaces on slopes, the terraces,
And the silken girls bringing sherbet.
Then the camel men cursing and grumbling
And running away, and wanting their liquor and
women,
And the night-fires going out, and the lack of
shelters,
And the cities hostile and the towns unfriendly
And the villages dirty and charging high prices:
A hard time we had of it.
At the end we preferred to travel all night,
Sleeping in snatches,
With the voices singing in our ears, saying
That this was all folly.

Then at dawn we came down to a temperate valley,
Wet, below the snow line, smelling of vegetation,
With a running stream and a water-mill beating the darkness,
And three trees on the low sky.
And an old white horse galloped away in the meadow.
Then we came to a tavern with vine-leaves over the lintel,
Six hands at an open door dicing for pieces of silver,
And feet kicking the empty wine-skins.
But there was no information, and so we continued
And arrived at evening, not a moment too soon
Finding the place; it was (you may say) satisfactory.

All this was a long time ago, I remember,
And I would do it again, but set down
This set down
This: were we led all that way for
Birth or Death? There was a Birth, certainly,
We had evidence and no doubt. I had seen birth and death,
But had thought they were different; this Birth was
Hard and bitter agony for us, like Death, our death.
We returned to our places, these Kingdoms,
But no longer at ease here, in the old dispensation,
With an alien people clutching their gods.
I should be glad of another death.

This is a poem almost too familiar from the anthologies; but it deserves repeated reading, partly because it captures a moment in the experience of faith that is not always noticed or understood – though Christian Wiman's poem in this collection has some things in common. Eliot begins with a paraphrase of lines from a seventeenth-century sermon, with all the conscious musicality of rhythm and pace that characterizes the preaching of that era, and then shifts imperceptibly into a different register. A sort of greyness takes over both the language and the visual world evoked; lots of 'and's; a barely subdued resentment, a serial grumbling (we can hear the complaining colloquial note of 'and another thing . . .') at the trivial and not-so-trivial worries of 'such a long journey'; what sounds like a climax or resolution ('Then at last . . .') ends in disappointment. And then, the most low-key epiphany imaginable: 'it was (you may say) satisfactory.'

It looks forward to the way Eliot later, in the *Four Quartets*, insists that the journey towards home, God, illumination, reconciliation, arrives at a place where your expectations *have* to be set aside. 'What you thought you came for/ Is only a shell, a husk of meaning' ('Little Gidding', ll. 31–2). Epiphany is not simply the blazing fulfilment of all you ever longed for; it is at least as much the subdued, chastened recognition of how much baggage has to be shed, how much self-comforting drama and glamour need to be brought up against a truth that is raw, plain, absolutely demanding, absolutely non-negotiable. It does not console or tick off the answers to all your questions. It sends you back to a life among others who have no idea of what has been seen and shared. But 'There was a Birth, certainly'; the world has changed.

Like the other 'Ariel Poems' of 1936 published with it, this is a poem of exhaustion: these are compositions in which the speakers collapse into a drained quietness. But it is a quietness that comes in the wake of recognition. Something has happened, something has been restored or rediscovered or uncovered, even if the process of uncovering has brought us to the edge of what we can cope with. Eliot had made his peace with the Christian faith, but there is no sense here of triumphant proclamation or evangelistic fervour. The Eliot of the 1930s was still living with a depth of personal unhappiness bound up with the catastrophic failure of his marriage; his public persona was more than ever marked by a sort of nervous pomposity (which could lead him into the foolish and indefensible dogmatism of some of his critical and social commentary, including the notorious anti-Semitism of the 1933 lecture series *After Strange Gods*, a text he never allowed to be republished). The image in this poem of a solitary figure surrounded by an unchanged 'old dispensation', friends and colleagues who had become 'alien' in their thoughtless fidelity to idols, is vividly evocative of Eliot's state of mind.

Not many poems – or prose writings for that matter – speak out of this moment. Yes, change has almost imperceptibly happened, a change that is more radical than words can convey. It is birth and death – not the adoption of a few new ideas, but an immersion into a new world, a new set of horizons. And for now, it *feels* like a state of loss and helplessness. Not quite the mystical 'dark night' of intensifying pain as images and feelings are steadily stripped away; just a grey, chilly and overcast dawn, with not much sense of what the day will bring except the struggle to carry on, with no one around who knows what you're talking about. The journey to 'the place' where things turn on their axis is labour and struggle and the world afterwards is labour and struggle.

But 'I would do it again'. For a few lines, the tone changes, with the repeated staccato 'Set down this', the blunt monosyllables of 'Were we led all that way for/ Birth or death?', the sudden nakedness of 'Hard and bitter agony for us'. The words flare briefly; then return to the subdued grumbling of the earlier lines. Death is to be longed for; but is it 'another death' in the sense of 'another kind of death', the familiar kind of death that doesn't pitch you back into an unwelcoming world where you have to rekindle a deeply unlikely hope hour by hour? Or is it 'another transition that is both death and birth', like the moment that has been grasped at Bethlehem? Good poems leave questions like that open, as this one does.

Rhina Espaillat

Martha Considers the Lilies

Dancing above the field, they play the field,
unmindful of dark stems whose one desire
anchors them to the earth. Roots' work concealed
by summer green, they levitate, on fire
with nothing but the sun, as if to say,
'We need not spin the glory that we wear
unearned; it spins – it sings – itself.' And they
rebuke us in the prison of our care.
But they are not the field; the field is hard
and angular with stones, and yields no bloom
unless desire burrows past earth's guard
while each seed labors to prepare a room.
Labor's the truth that makes us more than free:
dancing above the field is fantasy.

This sonnet's title brings together two biblical passages: Jesus' injunction to 'consider the lilies of the field, how they grow' in the Sermon on the Mount (Matthew 6.28), part of a series of warnings about anxiety over material security; and the story of Martha protesting about her sister Mary failing to help with domestic tasks and preferring to sit and listen to Jesus (Luke 10). With a wit very typical of her poetry, Espaillat's Martha sees the lilies of the field 'playing the field' – flaunting themselves, avoiding commitment, implicitly denying the necessity of being rooted in the 'one desire' that in fact animates everything that they are. The lilies can briefly sustain the fiction that they exist simply in and through the sunlight around them, in 'unearned' splendour.

But it is a fiction. Those who live in that moment of gratuitous joy and radiant glory, and have no awareness of the single, deep anchorage that gives them life, have not understood that the field they grow in is full of challenges to growth – the 'angular . . . stones'; the root of desire has to work its way down into the soil through dense layers of resistance, 'earth's guard'. The field is not the same as the fleetingly beautiful blooms on its surface, and every seed must struggle 'to prepare a room'. Once again, the biblical echoes are clear, especially the narrative of the disciples going to find the room, 'furnished and ready' for the Last Supper (Mark14.15). There is no beauty without *labour* at some level, the labour of desire reaching down into hard and difficult depths. With another rather shocking twist of verbal wit, the speaker evokes the *Arbeit macht frei* motto over the gates of Auschwitz: 'work makes free'. But the labour that the poem's voice appeals to is something that 'makes us *more* than free'. The seed's labour to give birth to the 'room', the space, that it must make in order for growth to happen is the source not of some illusory freedom above and beyond commitment but of life itself, desire fully anchored in the depths of the soil and nourished from there. To live from this depth is indeed more than freedom as we normally think of it.

So this seems to be a poem about the risks of fantasy in the life of imagination or spirit; about the seductions of idealizing gratuity, spontaneity, instinct or immediacy and ignoring the dark downward push of the single root that makes space for ongoing life. Yet the Martha of the poem speaks of 'the prison of our care', a phrase that prepares us for the threatening undertones of the *Arbeit macht frei* allusion. The poem, in other words, can't be read as a simple endorsement of ‘Martha’s’ world. The unearned, self-generating glory that clothes the flowers is not a fiction, even if it is a fiction that the flowers have no roots. ‘It spins – it sings – itself’ is surely a fair enough account of grace.

A sonnet is, of course, a good place to stage a tension in our thinking. Here, the celebratory tone that emerges in the octet mutates at its end into a faintly resentful comment about the ‘rebuke’ that Martha senses: so far, the moral and imaginative weight seems to lie with the order of gratuitous beauty and contemplative delight. The sestet then reverses this effectively and economically. Yet the ‘prison’ image haunts the final couplet. There is a freedom Martha does not fully know, just as there is a deep anchorage and a summons to repetitive and strenuous labour that Mary does not know. Sun in the first part of the poem, earth in the second: but the seed in the earth doesn’t grow by its own effort, even though the growth is effortful, but because of what warms and moistens it. It is fantasy to think that flowers live literally ‘above the field’, but it is also the world above, the light of the sun, the ‘prevenience’, the ‘in-advance-ness’, of grace that makes the field fruitful. Martha’s voice matters; but not alone, or else we may be on our way back to prison.

Rhina Espaillat

Falling

Whatever is, harbors its own unease.
The spring aches, and the taut line sags to ground.
Green leaves pull skyward, blind roots hunger
  down
To dark necessities.

Even stirs restless and explodes to odd;
Odd strains for symmetry, limps home to even.
In the light-spangled solitude of heaven
God reels away from God.

And in the heart, born single as a kiss,
Broods the sad other – learner, yearner, dier –
That knows, uncomforted, its one desire
Was not for this.

Tension is built into things. Not tension in the sense of anxious or fearful anticipation, the tension of exam nerves or incipient panic attacks, but the tension of what is strung between two distant points, both anchored, both solid. This poem, earlier than the one we've just been reading, seems to fill in the background: leaves grow into the light, roots burrow into the dark. Rhina Espaillat's own identity as a fully bilingual writer, originally from the Dominican Republic, carries another kind of tension; it casts some light on why the concept recurs so frequently and suggestively in her work. There is a fine poem of hers, 'Bilingual/Bilingue', exploring the imbalances between two languages in the experience of a child growing up bilingual – the father's efforts to enforce a strict separation of languages, and the gradual realization by the child that her command of both languages and her willingness to let them speak to and 'in' one another was giving her a key to unlock what her father did not know. Growing into this dual belonging, 'still the heart was one'; but the experience of the two vehicles of perception coexisting opens new doors.

Whatever we say always reaches out to, asks for, what it is not saying. The poem's terse conclusion refuses a comforting synthesis: the single heart's single desire is for what it is not. The heart exists in time, and so it desires, learns and dies; it becomes strange to itself as it moves in time, as it grows. And the pattern is already laid up in heaven, so to speak: 'God reels away from God', even in the 'solitude' of heaven. How are we to read this? Some of Espaillat's other work highlights the tensions we encounter in trying to think about or imagine God, the seemingly irreconcilable contradictions of love and judgement. And the idea of the distance between God and God may have something to do also with the doctrine of the incarnation, God as human, God as mortal and suffering human, crying out to a God who has 'abandoned' him (Mark 15.34), God becoming a stranger to God.

The poem's title is 'Falling': something to do with the 'fall' from timelessness to time? The imagery is mostly of processes of movement and growth, as if growth could not be imagined without division of some sort – or at least without that moment of becoming-a-stranger-to-yourself that is built into growing. The image of God that we see resists any reduction to a static concept, even if we believe in the timelessness of God. We can have literally no image or idea about timelessness; to be outside time is to be outside language. And so we can only tell stories about the timeless God, stories the tensions and cross-currents of which could only be resolved in another order of vision or knowledge. Just so, we cannot tell a story of our own identity that is not a narrative of loss and discovery, something stretched out in time rather than space.

But the heart is '*born* single as a kiss'. At the root of the life of division and alienation and rediscovery, the life of irreducible tension, there is not only a unity but also a unity of difference (you can't kiss your own lips) or of love. The very idea that a kiss is a metaphor for *singleness* should give us pause (it is another very typical bit of Espaillat verbal teasing). The tensions we live through are not going to be resolved by reduction into sameness or even by some philosophical reconciliation in a higher sphere. Our restlessness, our oscillation between the solid poles of difference that hold our lives suspended, is not something to be cured by denying one or the other element. There is a single desire in us as in the cosmos and the divine will within which we live, but it is a desire not for some single outside goal that will satisfy its needs. The heart is orientated, in its poised and stretched duality, towards the state of non-duality, neither absorption nor opposition. If 'falling' is the recognition of the inescapable tension in our speech and action and imagining, 'rising' would be to recover the awareness of the 'kiss' of finite and infinite out of which we are born as subjects and speakers, so that the contradictions encountered on our journey become precisely those things that move us forwards into something more than the collision of differences.

U. A. Fanthorpe

Half-past Two

Once upon a schooltime
He did Something Very Wrong
(I forget what it was).

And She said he'd done
Something Very Wrong, and must
Stay in the school-room till half-past two.

(Being cross, she'd forgotten
She hadn't taught him Time.
He was too scared at being wicked to remind her.)

He knew a lot of time: he knew
Gettinguptime, timeyouwereofftime,
Timetogohomenowtime, TVtime,

Timeformykisstime (that was Grantime).
All the important times he knew,
But not half-past two.

He knew the clockface, the little eyes
And two long legs for walking.
But he couldn't click its language,

So he waited, beyond onceupona,
Out of reach of all the timefors,
And knew he'd escaped for ever

Into the smell of old chrysanthemums on Her desk,
Into the silent noise his hangnail made,
Into the air outside the window, into ever.

And then, My goodness, she said,
Scuttling in, I forgot all about you.
Run along or you'll be late.

So she slotted him back into schooltime,
And he got home in time for teatime,
Nexttime, notimeforthatnowtime,

But he never forgot how once by not knowing time,
He escaped into the clockless land for ever,
Where time hides tick-less waiting to be born.

A bit like Dorothy Nimmo (p. 219), Ursula Fanthorpe writes with imaginative compassion about childhood experience and language – and also shares with her a dry and deflating wit. This poem sets two schemes of timekeeping side by side: the time marked by the clock and the time marked by the actual rhythms of a shared life; it gently mocks, in those solemnly capitalized words, the blinkered earnestness of the teacher's world and her combination of godlike power with plain ignorance about the child's frame of reference. But its point is to reintroduce us to the uncovenanted moments that children in particular know about, falling between these two kinds of measurement, when the intensity of the immediate and specific suspends any awareness of time passing. The framing of the poem is – ironically – the sort of generic vagueness about time represented by the beginning of fairy tales ('Once upon a schooltime . . .'); the detailed location of the event has vanished, as has the detail of the offence for which the hapless primary school pupil is being kept in detention. And he is unable to explain to the teacher what he doesn't understand: how could he tell her that the gap is between her timekeeping and his when he does not share her relationships and patterns of living?

So the child is left in a time that is measurable neither by the clock (which he cannot read) nor by the ordinary rituals of life – even of love ('timeformykisstime') – 'important' as they all are. He is delivered from 'timefors': there is nothing to punctuate awareness. There is only the journey *into* what is immediately present – the flowers, the hangnail, the empty air outside. The mechanical 'legs' walking around the clock cannot help on this journey. It is the journey 'into ever' – a wonderful phrase for this consciousness of unmeasured time. The little boy is not having some sort of mystical experience of being lifted out of his body and the temporal world itself; he is admitted into the interiority of the moment in all its concreteness, into a sensing of the world that is not 'for' anything.

'Timefor' will reassert itself, and no doubt clock time will be learned in due course. But the 'clockless land' that has been encountered will not be forgotten, even though the date and occasion may be impossible to remember (the poem's end unobtrusively picks up the forgetting mentioned at the start). We might stretch a point and say that what the poem presents is *enlightenment*, the kind of perception that connects us with what is 'unborn', allowing us to sit in the middle of a changing world and be aware of the undivided stream of becoming, interior and exterior, of which we are inseparably a part. We break up time into units: the mechanism of the clock does this with more obvious artificiality than the times that we internalize as mapping out our days, but even the latter fractures what needs to be held together. Those with experience of meditation know that the removal of the signposts of passing time – whether clocks or patterns of action – can prompt something of this entry 'into ever'. The child in the poem is accidentally brought into the place that the meditator hopes to invite or be invited into. In the 'tickless' silence, time as we know it – events, narration, conscious shaping of what 'happens' – is still in the womb. Perception without happening, without awareness of purpose or function, is what is encountered in the moment where the only thing that is to be done is to look, to be aware not of where things are going but of where and what they are now.

Fanthorpe offers here a version of what Eliot's *Quartets* explore at length – the 'pattern of timeless moments' that constitutes history: not a process of mechanical progression interrupted by unconnected moments of ecstasy but a growth towards a kind of seeing and receiving of the world 'burning in every moment'. Of course time passes, of course time leads towards death; and of course things happen and purposive action (the realm of 'timefors') is required. But if the eye has been opened, like the child's in the poem, to 'ever', at least we may be delivered from the futile resentment of time lost, the futile anxiety about time to be filled. We have touched time as grace.

Caleb Femi

At a House Party, 'Ultralight Beam' Came on & It Started a Church Service

& in the corner, two spiders
watched us entranced
by the words of a little girl
pouring through the speakers
like anointing oil

One spider said to the other, *This is how*
they exalt so be careful; they'll not notice
treading on you: & the other spider said, *Yes*
we are watching our devils
pray away their devils.

The bass made your eyes heavy
like that time with the mandem
in a Vauxhall ringer, hotboxing –
searching for a name
the streets would know you by.

Things with names deserve deliverance.
That's why you don't name the spiders
you find scuttering across your kitchen floor:
otherwise, your house becomes a sanctuary.

The name given to you by your father
is not your right name. It is your occupation
in this world – determines how many friends
you will have, how many of your CVs will be
discarded
without a glance, how much Justice you will be
afforded,
how many lovers will think twice
before they introduce you
to their families; how much money you will make,
ever.

Did you know that God takes down the names
of everyone who pays their tithe,
everyone who says His name in vain?
– That there is a book in which the names are kept
of all who will see Paradise.

Caleb Femi's poems are a beautiful, harshly impassioned window into South London as experienced especially by young black people; they deal with the reality of naked racial injustice, the sheer daily risk of living in the supercharged environment of streets accustomed to violence of all kinds, the lure of gang culture, the intensity of friendship and the traumas of loss or betrayal, the corrosive knowledge that society is not on your side and that you have to build what communities you can to assure yourself of your dignity. Much more besides; but also the background presence, the electronic hum, of a religious language that can neither be ignored nor owned without irony.

'Things with names deserve deliverance.' The nameless spiders expect to be crushed by the 'exalted' emotions of the dancers responding to the famous Kanye West song, 'Ultralight Beam', a song that speaks of casting out devils: the song may be about hope and mercy and new beginnings, with the 'anointing oil' of a child's statement of faith setting the tone, but the spiders know that their namelessness leaves them unprotected. Their 'devils' have to be released to push back at the devils of destructiveness unwittingly set in motion by the passion and beauty of the song.

So it is a poem about the ambiguity of beauty and faith – healing, anointing, yet lifting people to a place where they stop noticing some things. Once you *do* notice and give a name – or, rather, *hear* a name, not impose one from outside – the unique substantive presence of something or someone other is there for you in a new way. But even names are ambiguous. What is your 'right name'? The father's name, the family name that is alien in the ears of a dominant racial majority, becomes an 'occupation' – not an assurance of belonging but the very opposite, a life sentence of trying unsuccessfully to explain or justify, to earn your place. You are, at the end of the day, in the same position as the spiders: and perhaps this makes sense of how 'devils' may be released to resist the ordered naming that the majority society uses so as to keep you confined.

How should we read the final section? God is the keeper of names, the names of those who discharge the duty of recognizing their creator, the names of those who exploit God's name for their own purposes, the names of those written in the Book of Life, destined for heaven. God's 'naming' is the opposite of the reductive labelling society inflicts; it acknowledges the deepest orientations of the heart. That is one reading. Or it could be that God's name-keeping is yet another register of success and failure, acceptability and unacceptability. It is not the poet's job to clear this up but to keep us reading and thinking. Is the name God records your 'right' name? Is it the name you find for yourself, the name 'the streets would know you by'? Is it something more elusive and unspoken?

No answers here, but we are nudged back to the earlier – very simple and powerful – image of the house that becomes a 'sanctuary' when things and people are rightly named; and to the insistence that 'Things with names deserve deliverance.'

The whole of this densely worked poem presents a challenge to the dominant culture: the naming that this culture uses and takes for granted, the use of names as part of a strategy to reduce, demean or frustrate because the 'father's name' is stereotyped as alien and threatening, is not the naming that creates sanctuary and opens the door to deliverance. How do we make or find a name that embodies our human presence as something that does not need to be justified or excused or explained? How does the dominant culture learn to listen for such names beyond and behind the stereotypes? And above all, is it true that there is an ultimate presence to which we are all present, an abiding sanctuary where our identity is held and affirmed? The lyrics of the Kanye West song affirm this with no irony or reservation; but Femi makes us work harder even to get to the question. Juxtaposing the child's expression of transcendent, anointing faith at the opening of 'Ultralight Beam' with the apprehensive spiders is both a teasing and a poignant move, quietly, unsparingly putting faith to the test, yet never losing sight of the possibility of sanctuary and recognition.

Kate Foley

Tikkun Olam: Mending the World

Season of jars and bottles when foetal plums
curl in on themselves, a bloodknot, rich on kitchen
  shelves,

when apples blaze like emperors,
when there are leaves on the line.

Though the cropped lion's ruff in fields
suggests a yield that never came,

because the Crack of Doom's so slow,
you can forget the scruffy bees

that rub their balding bodies
on scanty pollen while pigeons inch

on crippled feet.
You'd rather sweep out on a clean tsunami

with blackened fag-end flies, stained plastic,
disembowelled tvs

but now the virtual plastic of the Stock Exchange
in domino effect means Footsie's fall's

the only wave you'll get. Season of fruit
whose colours lend decay

romance, the world's wound stinks
like a bird in the chimney.

Mending is no hero's task. Think
instead, raw threads, cobbled patches,

tear-stained, blood-stained needle pricks
and where its rotten fabric parts

a patient, industrious makeover
of the heart.

The title is a Hebrew phrase, regularly used in Judaism for those activities that uphold, witness to and restore justice in the world; acts of 'righteousness' are not simply a matter of obedience to the will of God for individuals, they also contribute to restoring the torn or damaged fabric of the entire creation.

The poem is pervaded by strong physical images and contains a series of elusive verbal assonances and internal rhymes; there is an almost imperceptible effect of *interweaving*, which embodies the governing metaphor announced in the title. But it opens with a touch of elegiac autumnal pastoral, where decay is setting in after summer: her first line echoes Keats's 'Season of mists and mellow fruitfulness', and suggests one way of understanding the 'mending' that is the poem's theme by reminding us that autumn is also a season for preserving what would otherwise rot away. The 'foetal' plums are preserved in their jars as if awaiting an entry into new life. But the richness of autumn, the deep colour and golden light, is only part of the picture. Harvested fields, like a shorn lion's mane, the dying bees and diseased pigeons, speak of a world that has been left desolate, disappointed of its hopes. The promised End has not arrived, the fullness of harvest is somehow elsewhere, invisible.

So this period of conserving corruptible fruit against the backdrop of apples and falling leaves is one of doubtful and mixed feeling: there is an urge towards the dream of some catastrophic flood to clean away the debris of summer. The poem switches abruptly (a bit too abruptly, perhaps) to the decay and corruption of international finance. There won't be a cleansing flood: the only thing that will 'make waves', as we say, is the drop in the FTSE index (there is a nimble bit of wordplay around the 'fall' of the index as a correlate of the fallen leaves, the fallenness of the world evoked here and, of course, the American term 'fall' for the season). We cannot avoid the stench of corruption even when 'colours lend decay/ romance'. We must not let ourselves be deceived by the surface warmth and glow of the season; what is going on is slow death.

The temptation is to think that judgement and change, the Crack of Doom, the harvest home, the cleansing torrent, are realized by apocalyptic heroism. 'Mending the world' can sound like the task of a superhero. But what if it is like the painful and painstaking business of darning and re-darning ripped and decayed fabric? Tears and blood both fall on this work: the image evoked is of some Victorian seamstress whose fingers are rubbed raw and lacerated by the unending labour of mending, which is precisely not a once-and-for-all, near-magical restoration of the ruined fabric but a repeated and potentially heart-breaking task. Where things are torn and wrecked, as in the surreal and destructive world of global finance, we have to begin again and again the job of stitching together; and this can be grounded only in the healing of the heart. Foley uses the glib media term 'makeover' with conscious irony: the makeover, which promises so easy and gratifying a change, is in fact a 'patient and industrious' affair, undramatic and untiring. And the blood falling on the stitches recalls the vivid image at the poem's beginning – the preserved plum as a foetal cluster, a 'bloodknot'. Blood, the accepted cost of mending, forms a knot of connection, which is also a new possibility of life beyond decay. And the foetal imagery adds a subliminal hint that the masculine models (myths) of heroic decisiveness are less relevant to the world's conservation than the 'bloodknot' of connection in the womb and the labour of bringing to life.

A poem, then, about two kinds of illusion: the seductively consoling aura of a Keatsian autumn that conceals the miasma of decay; the temptation to look for instant and global change and for the dramatic flexing of the ego that will achieve it. It is not impossible to mend the world, but we must learn to diagnose its corruption truthfully and to respond – Foley's Quaker conviction is clear here – with the patient mending of our own torn and corrupted hearts.

Louise Glück

Vespers

Even as you appeared to Moses, because
I need you, you appear to me, not
often, however. I live essentially
in darkness. You are perhaps training me to be
responsive to the slightest brightening. Or, like the
poets,
are you stimulated by despair, does grief
move you to reveal your nature? This afternoon,
in the physical world to which you commonly
contribute your silence, I climbed
the small hill above the wild blueberries,
metaphysically
descending, as on all my walks: did I go deep
enough
for you to pity me, as you have sometimes pitied
others who suffer, favoring those
with theological gifts? As you anticipated,
I did not look up. So you came down to me:
at my feet, not the wax
leaves of the wild blueberry but your fiery self, a
whole
pasture of fire, and beyond, the red sun neither
falling nor rising –
I was not a child; I could take advantage of
illusions.

One of a number of poems under this title by the Nobel laureate of 2020, this is a meditation on God's visibility and invisibility. Although God responds to acute need – like God appearing in the burning bush to a Moses, who represents a whole community of suffering and slavery – invisibility is the 'default setting', the lack of a clear sense of God's presence. Is this God's way of prompting us to be more alert to the signs of presence? Or is there a magnetic attraction in the intensity of loss and grief, drawing God close to the site of suffering, just as the poet is drawn there? So the absence of God can be seen from two very different perspectives. It may be that the very depth of absence is a sort of vacuum that sucks into itself the divine presence, drawing in a God who cannot hold back from pouring the divine self into the dark emptiness of a fully devastated human selfhood – a model that some contemplative writers like Eckhart imply. Or it may be that we need the contrast between routine awareness of the world and the consciousness of God's presence in order to grasp how different the world looks when seen 'in God', as a dark background of cloud can accentuate the sharp sunlight on a tree trunk or hillside and mark out its contours more clearly.

So the poem talks about one of those moments of illumination, holding together these two approaches to divine absence. The speaker's self-questioning is what we encounter first, a potentially egotistical worry about whether they have suffered enough to be magnetically appealing to God; there is a wry hint that sufferers with the right intellectual qualifications may be first in the queue (the ones 'with theological gifts'). But this introspection, implying that God's presence is to be earned – so to speak – by seriousness or tragic extremity, is itself a way of delaying or diverting the vision; we are not looking up. So God meets us as we keep looking *down*. Consciously or not, this echoes something St Augustine wrote in his *Confessions*, about having his eyes drawn down from the heights of introspective contemplation to see 'the humble God at his feet'. In the context of Augustine's writing, it is a clearly Christian image: what is at the saint's feet is the dead and disfigured body of Jesus, which, as it rises from death, will lift us with it. Glück is not writing as a Christian (she is Jewish, and often makes use of themes from Jewish Scripture and tradition), and the epiphany that holds the eye at ground level is not so dramatically personal an incarnation. But it is no less comprehensively transfiguring, not a perception of one detail in the landscape but the grass reddened across the whole field of vision by a flaming sunset. Echoes of Moses and the burning bush again.

It seems then that the different perceptions we began with are in a way resolved. The real poverty, the damaging emptiness, that calls to God and draws God's fulfilling presence is precisely our sterile anxiety about whether or not our condition is serious enough to merit God's response; the divine answer is that the question is completely misconceived. God is always there at our feet, not at the summit of our imagining – including our imagining of our dramatic selves and their dramatic problems – and God's answer to our tangle of self-conscious, fretful probing is to open our eyes to the ground we stand on. The poem ends with a teasing twist: 'I could take advantage of illusions.' The child will mistake illusion for reality; the adult imagination recognizes that what is seen is a cypher for divine presence rather than a simple epiphany. But, being able to 'read' the experience as a sign in this way is to be able to receive it more fruitfully. What is laid open is a '*pasture* of fire' – not just the momentary flame of a burning bush but a space for feeding, for being nourished. If God's brief lightning flash, God's lifting of a veil, can free us from our preoccupation with whether we have 'deserved' to see God, we are set free to dwell *in* and *on* the world we inhabit, with a new patience and receptivity: the habits that make poetry possible.

Joy Harjo

Don't Bother the Earth Spirit

> Don't bother the earth spirit who lives here. She is working on a story. It is the oldest story in the world and it is delicate, changing. If she sees you watching she will invite you in for coffee, give you warm bread, and you will be obligated to stay and listen. But this is no ordinary story. You will have to endure earthquakes, lightning, the deaths of all those you love, the most blinding beauty. It's a story so compelling you may never want to leave; this is how she traps you. See that stone finger over there? That is the only one who ever escaped.

Harjo's poems combine an intense immersion in North American landscapes and her own Native American spiritual tradition with a strong contemporary feminist and political voice; they are formally very diverse, including pieces like this one which set aside the expected visual shape of a poem ('prose poem' is a singularly unhelpful way of describing such work).

Here we are taken into the numinous, welcoming and dangerous depths of what the 'earth spirit' is doing in a locality. Wherever we find ourselves, what is unfolding around us in our material environment is a story – a continuous, constantly self-adjusting memory. Immersing ourselves in that memory, letting ourselves become part of what will *be* remembered or narrated, is what we are invited into.

We must not 'bother' the spirit – that is, we must not interrupt and seek to take over the unfolding narrative as if it were simply *our* story. We have to learn how to be guests not colonizers or conquerors. Harjo's work often addresses the destructiveness of the colonizing mindset – and also celebrates the sacramental significance of hospitality. Another well-known poem of hers, 'Perhaps the World Ends Here', imagines the kitchen table as the site of all real human history, the place where human beings are shaped in their humanity. So too here, the spirit sets a kind of kitchen table for us; we are welcome if we do not try to take over.

But the story unfolding will not be the comforting one we might have imagined in such a setting. If the kitchen table with its coffee and warm bread is indeed the place where we learn who we are and might be, it is a place to encounter terror as well as (or terror *in*) beauty, and to come to terms with radical and devastating loss – a place where, in more traditional literary terms, *tragedy* is constructed, the attempt to speak truthfully about pain and horror without despair. It is a place that is hard to escape from once it has been discovered and inhabited. And trying to escape means you are turned to stone, it seems: run away from the earth spirit's story and you are left without heart, sensibility, mind, movement. The 'stone finger' points to the loss that is suffered if we try to tear ourselves away from what the spirit is doing.

It is a poem of monumental simplicity but one that opens perspectives in many directions. It is certainly about the poet's art (and, indeed, any kind of art), understood as grounded in the willingness to be absorbed into the rhythms of a world beyond the coming-and-going of human obsessions and ambitions. It is about how beauty and grief or anguish are inseparably the material of the spirit's work. It is implicitly about the violent disruption of the work of the spirit by colonial claims to possession, and about the cost of refusing to listen to the more-than-human story of the material world and the struggle to subdue and instrumentalize it. The 'earth spirit' is not exactly the 'God' of any organized religious system, but is unmistakeably an active and life-giving presence; it has something in common with the divine Wisdom, *Hokhmah* or *Sophia*, of Hebrew Scripture, developed in some Christian traditions as a way of conceiving the immanent harmonizing and transfiguring energy at work within creation (Thomas Merton was fascinated by this idea as he encountered it in some Russian Christian sources). Harjo speaks here for a range of indigenous religious practices and ideas that are not to be reduced to the conventional theological categories of the so-called 'world religions' and bring essential critical perspectives to bear on the language of those other more systematized and conceptually elaborate traditions; but this is not to say that these perspectives are completely alien to them. The point is that human agents or speakers are – if they choose to be – included in a narrative they have not scripted. This is alarming for the 'enlightened' ego, but also something that draws us with a sense of homecoming, despite the frustrating of our hopes for controlling the story. To adapt the conclusion to one of George Herbert's most famous poems, we must 'sit and eat' at the kitchen table. We must be ready to be fed, to be 'narrated' as part of a larger story, to be both welcomed and utterly transformed.

Kevin Hart

Facing the Pacific at Night

Driving east, in the darkness between two stars
Or between two thoughts, you reach the greatest
  ocean,
That cold expanse the rain can never net,

And driving east, you are a child again –
The web of names is brushed aside from things.
The ocean's name is quietly washed away

Revealing the thing itself, an energy,
An elemental life flashing in starlight.
No word can shrink it down to fit the mind,

It is already there, between two thoughts,
The darkness in which you travel and arrive,
The nameless one, the surname of all things.

The ocean slowly rocks from side to side,
A child itself, asleep in its bed of rocks,
No parent there to wake it from a dream,

To draw the ancient gods between the stars.
You stand upon the cliff, no longer cold,
And you are weightless, back before the thrust

And rush of birth when beards of blood are grown;
Or outside time, as though you had just died
To birth and death, no name to hide behind,

No name to splay the world or burn it whole.
The ocean quietly moves within your ear
And flashes in your eyes: the silent place

Outside the world we know is here and now,
Between two thoughts, a child that does not grow,
A silence undressing words, a nameless love.

Looking out over a dark expanse of featureless water brushes away the words we are used to deploying, the habits we take for granted of organizing and mapping the world. We are taken back to childhood – not the childhood of some innocent and bright sub-Wordsworthian vision of natural beauty, but the experience of the newborn or even pre-born infant, for whom the wordless rhythm of a liquid environment is all there is to know. The night-time moment of gazing into the anonymous pulsing energy of the ocean, never waking in its cradle between solid rock, is a moment that might equally be just before birth or just after death. It is a moment in which you have to leave behind a speech that hides the reality of a present moment in which travelling and arriving are indistinguishable. The 'web of names' is presumably not just the tapestry of verbal intricacy but also, surely, the spider's web of a neglected and stale inner landscape. And when all this is swept away, what is left to hear is simply the resonance between the movement of the sea outside and the movement 'within your ear', the pulse of blood; you are in 'the silent place'. The expanse that opens up 'Between two thoughts' is at first 'cold'; yet, as the poem advances, this apparent chill modulates into a nurturing and embracing quiet; and the eye's flash might suggest a touch of fire as well within this silence. And similarly, the sounds soften unobtrusively as the poem goes on, with a marked presence of liquid consonants and consonantal groups in the last two verses, so that the whole piece itself embodies the assimilation of the speaking subject and the ocean.

Eliot's *Quartets* – as so often – suggest an echo, perhaps a seed out of which some of this poem's imagery grows: the 'stillness/ Between two waves of the sea' at the end of 'Little Gidding' is not far from the evocation here of a moment 'between' worlds, where the passage of time pauses. But there is more going on: Hart points us to the violence, not only the futility, of language. 'No name to splay the world or burn it whole' suggests, in the unexpected 'splay', something like rape as well as a more neutral '*dis*play'; and 'burn it whole' is a literal rendering of the meaning of the Greek-derived 'holocaust'. The habits of speech are laden with the possibilities of outrage, forced penetration, final solutions. And correspondingly, the silencing of these compulsive dangers leaves nothing but love, just as, for a Buddhist, the extinguishing of the self's addictive longings is identical with the arising of compassion. There is literally nothing left to energize or activate violence, rejection, refusal.

And so the place from which the poem's speaker speaks and sees is both the transformed human sensibility that is free from time *and* the reality into which that sensibility looks – a 'nameless love' within, which is at one with, though not simply identical to, a nameless love beyond any speaker or subject. The ocean 'flashes in your eyes' – both a flash of perception *by* the observing eye, and a flash of light *from* the eye itself. This is a poem about union and enlightenment (Hart has said that the contemplative poetry of St John of the Cross helped to shape this piece), not as a simple denial of the world as such but as a freedom to be in a 'here and now' that is, paradoxically, 'Outside the world we know'. We have somehow to stop 'knowing' in certain ways; knowing in the mode of possession and conquest or assimilation. We have to know as the child within the liquid womb knows – to know in and by moving to the rhythms of what we swim in. The same thing is hinted at when we are told that the presence we encounter in this darkness is both 'nameless' and 'the surname of all things'. A surname: something that comes after a name that may be more individual and familiar, something that denotes kinship, relatedness? Is it that the dark sea is what ultimately connects all that we know, in a knowledge that is never going to work in the way our usual knowing does?

To 'know' what is present in this darkness, with all its overwhelming energy and all its uncompromising stillness, is to know the world we inhabit; and to know it like this, to know it from within the darkness of God, is to know what we cannot say, what we can only show in the renunciation of certain kinds of saying and acting, in the absence of violence and ambition in our speech.

Geoffrey Hill

The Orchards of Syon XLIII

Say what you will, the interim record
of preservation is awesome. First this,
then this, catches the affrighted eye.
Renegotiate the sleep-veil, admit
that other world this fantasizing world
conspires for and against us; our images
drawn out of cold fires: *Christ*
treading upon the Beasts, St Guthlac's
Psalter at Crowland, planted mid-fen,
dun scrolls, clay-moulded almost, basilisk
and cockatrice, creatures harmless enough
in small malevolence. As species
of reproduction far-fetched. Re-apply
Dies Irae with its scarifying
mnemonics to cleanse prayer. Range
how you will, anger, despair, are inbred
monsters: Nebuchadnezzar's crawlingly
bitter egress to gnaw grass; Cain's brood
busy at Heorot. Such startings-up,
slouchings, of self-hatred; a sullen
belch from the ice-maker in the small hours.
All honour to patience, but patience which
as *natural heart's ivy* – Hopkins – must
surely choke it: *it*, here, being the heart.

Geoffrey Hill's earlier poems are intricate and often astonishingly musical; his later work is notoriously even more intricate and as a rule far less musical, as though he is aware that the lyrical beauty of the early writing is in danger of becoming too fluent, so he must put obstacles in his own way to preserve the honesty of the poetry.

The Orchards of Syon was published in 2002; it represents – after the telegraphic abruptness of the two collections immediately preceding it – some retrieval, not of musicality but of engagement with deeply sensuous perception and experience: weather, soil, sky, the interior screen of imagining. In this poem, we begin with the durability of the dream-world, in particular our imagination of the *monstrous*. The world of fantasy that continues behind its 'sleep-veil' and is intermittently perceptible for us is one that works for another order of reality and works 'against us', works to unsettle us and make us strange to ourselves. The early mediaeval images of Christ treading on the beasts (trampling down 'the lion and the dragon', in the Latin version of Psalm 91) as seen, for example, in the eighth-century Ruthwell Cross or the marginal illustrations of legendary monsters in the later Psalter of St Guthlac, witness to the way that pictures of the forces arrayed against our humanity persist. They may seem almost 'harmless' in the grotesqueries of these mediaeval depictions, unconvincing as representations of what is actually going on inside; but we must revisit the vocabulary of demonic and hellish deformity 'to cleanse prayer'. That the monsters in the illuminated manuscript are called 'clay-moulded almost' sounds like an allusion to the language found in much mediaeval and early modern writing, of Adam being formed of 'clay': these powers are present in us from the first moment of our human formation.

Monstrosity is deeply ingrained in us: the story, from the book of Daniel, of King Nebuchadnezzar of Babylon being condemned to spend a year living as an animal to punish him for his pride is recalled, in lines of grindingly alliterative insistence ('crawlingly/ bitter egress to gnaw grass'), and the progeny of the first murderer, Cain, is identified as still active in the heroic culture of the great Anglo-Saxon poem of *Beowulf*. Our half-buried hostility to ourselves is what these dreams or nightmares manifest. Hill's 'slouching' echoes W. B. Yeats's famous image (in 'The Second Coming') of a 'rough beast' that 'slouches towards Bethlehem to be born' as the carapace of civilization cracks around us; and the 'sullen/ belch from the ice-maker in the small hours' is both a domestic image (the nocturnal grumblings of kitchen machinery) and an allusion to the ice-bound figure of Satan at the end of Dante's *Inferno*. We need patience with our self-hatred, the patience described by Gerard Manley Hopkins as clinging like ivy; but the poem ends with the fear that ivy not only clings but also chokes. Does patience simply immobilize us under a protective cover rather than prepare us for transformation?

Hill's religious sensibility is commonly a bleak one, and this poem is a powerful example. However remote the mediaeval images of diabolical threat, they catch our eye; there is something we shall recognize if we let ourselves be candid, the impulse to self-subversion or self-destruction, and its persistence is not to be domesticated as quaint and decorative folklore. The lion and the dragon, the basilisk and cockatrice, have to be trodden down, not just endured. Poetry has the task of making monsters visible without any immediate consolation or assurance; Hill's poems from the 1990s onwards approach this exposure of the false, the corrupting and the trivial – and of the self-disgust that the wordsmith must feel – with unsparing force.

Geoffrey Hill

The Orchards of Syon XLV

Listen, Meister Eckhart is here, ready
and eager to tell us his great news:
that we caught aright the revelatory
scream from the carrousel; that there's a divine
presence in destitution; that yes, we loved
bright Harry Heine and Frank O'Hara
as more than passing attractions when
I pass was the catch-phrase and they unheard of;
that the heavy residues from easy loving
render us breathless. Both you and I
who pray with the *dévots* yet practise
every trick in the book: our nuptials
are of the spirit entirely. The topos
of the whole is gratitude. Duino's
cliff-hanger we witnessed, and its consummation.
Wait, I've not finished. A radical
otherness, as it's called, answers
to its own voices: that there should be
language, rituals, weddings, and wedding-nights,
and tapes which spin fast forward, stop, reverse;
that there is even now hawthorn, this bush
pregnant with the wild scent and taint of sex;
that there are men and women, destinies
interlocked; and dying, and resurrection.

No consolations; but poetry also has to acknowledge what lives alongside the unconsoled. This poem from *Orchards*, following closely on the one we have just been reading, starts with what might be an ironic appeal to the 'great news' shared by the fourteenth-century contemplative Meister Eckhart: the intuition that something addresses or engages us in the moment of pain or extremity is not an empty one. But if the words are ironic, it is because this is in fact not news for any poet. The 'scream from the carrousel' is a difficult phrase to gloss. It seems to point to the Parisian 'Place du Carrousel', used as a site for executions in the French Revolutionary Terror; if so, the point of the lines is that chaos and bloodshed *show* something, if only in depriving us of the grim self-congratulations of humans who are satisfied with their history. The impact of poets like the German Romantic and radical Heinrich Heine (originally named 'Harry', surprisingly enough) and the innovative twentieth-century New York writer Frank O'Hara, was (for the speaker's developing sensibility) a lasting stimulus: the casual dismissal ('*I pass*') of prematurely cynical youth was impossible in the face of these writers with their mixture of scepticism and passionate embrace of the material and immediate. A youthful mind may find such enthusiasm comes 'easy', but the effect is heavy enough as we carry it with us through a lifetime, leaving us 'breathless' – struggling to speak. If we are indeed shown something in chaos, it is not something that allows us to be simply fluent.

Prayer and deviousness or ingenuity are woven together: 'every trick in the book' may have either a verbal or a sexual reference, or both. The reader is addressed and brought into complicity with the poet: the union between reader and writer may be 'of the spirit', but the entanglement of spirit with the complexities of desire as manifested in speech and sexuality is not to be denied. And the whole landscape is to be thought and spoken of in the context of *gratitude*. The reference to 'Duino's/ cliff-hanger' points us to the great Rilke and his *Duino Elegies* as a point of orientation; but the cliffhanging act of Rilke's poetry leads to a 'consummation' which is not that of this poem. 'I've not finished', says the speaker here: Rilke may have tied up his vision in the *Elegies*, with their eloquently and beautifully secularized theology, but this poetic voice here has more to say than that. The 'radical/ otherness' we glimpse in the revelation of our breathlessness and historical guilt is what draws out the joy and trans-rational excess of language, sex, ritual, the sense of narrative unfolding and doubling back, repeating and anticipating – of time as something more than mechanical succession. The strangeness of all this in terms of the world as it is habitually viewed is a mirror of the utter strangeness of what impinges from outside the imagination: this ultimate otherness 'answers/ to its own voices', the alien sensual festivity that surprises us. Our humanity is 'spiritual' in its sensuality, because this sensuality is the actual embodied form of 'destinies/ interlocked', the embodied form of what we could call *communion* between us, the drawing towards one another that can't be eradicated in us. And the possibility of communion is bound up with 'dying, and resurrection': the life that is lived in the presence of the other is one that cannot but confront its limitedness, and at the same time cannot but entertain the wildness of the hope of communion that proves to be indestructible.

It is a gruellingly complex poem to read, but it seems part of its purpose is to respond to the bleak picture of our inner monstrousness that is insisted on elsewhere. If we are able to respond in open, unprotected receptivity to what lies around us, we encounter not explanation or reassurance but a sort of 'grace of body', an awareness of desire, connection, rootedness, responsiveness. The whole sequence ends by affirming that the Orchards of Syon provide 'neither wisdom/ nor illusion of wisdom, not/ compensation, not recompense: the Orchards/ of Syon whatever harvests we bring them'. Whatever we harvest in our life and speech, there is an abiding place for these to be brought home.

John Hodgen

Visitation

Her name would have been Maria, had I asked,
her steps so light as she walked up behind me, her
braided hair,
her eyes, skittery, black as the sheep eyes I once
dissected.
She held out a yellow plastic cup and asked for
water.
Because it is so very hot, she said. She had seen the
garden hose,
coiled and green, me pruning the lawn. The water,
she said,
was for her two sons and her husband there in the
rusty Nova.
The father, silent as bread, refusing to look at me,
would have been Jose,
befuddled, always alone, the two sons, Juan and
Jesus.
It is so very hot, she said, and we have driven so far.

Sometimes the angels come. How slow we must
seem to them,
like people baptized, moving under water,
wobbling, weighted,
our voices softened when we are pulled into the
light,

our longings all foreseen, like shepherds struck
dumb,
throats dry, eyes turned to slits in the terrible sheen
of the night.

Tonight I know that sometimes families must run,
must put what they can into a car, quickly,
wordlessly,
leaving a table set for supper.
Tonight I know it must have been Mary who stood
beside me,
as surely as the time my mother as a child turned a
hobo away,
a man who could have been Jesus, her mother had
said.
Tonight I have given a woman some water, only that,
and she has given it to her husband, her sons,
and tonight they ride through the universe in their
rusty Nova,
like the disappeareds, the runaway children of the
stars.

The letter to the Hebrews in the New Testament encourages Christians to show hospitality, 'for thereby some have entertained angels unawares' (13.2) – alluding to the event in Genesis 18 where Abraham welcomes the three strangers who turn out to be messengers of God. This exhortation is in the background here, with the migrant family in their battered car, nervously interrupting the suburban routine of the speaker, recognized as angels – and indeed more than angels ('Her name would have been Maria . . . it must have been Mary who stood beside me', the Mary who with her husband and child has had to flee from the murderousness of King Herod).

There is quite a bit about water in the poem. The contrast between the water that is being lavished on the domestic garden and the water that is a necessity for the family is highlighted in the most economical way imaginable; this is not a poem of moral hectoring, but it is perfectly clear about the gulf between the speaker and the Hispanic woman who approaches him. However, the poem's second section takes this off in a different direction, with water imagined as what intervenes, like a veil or a pane of frosted glass, between the human and the angelic world – what makes it hard for angels to see or to recognize us, and vice versa. Do angels see us as if through water, or rather as if we were moving under water without realizing it, our movements – our responses of love and attention? – unnaturally slowed down? We are indeed 'people baptized', we have been pushed under the water of grace, and under the surface of the water we are clumsy and weighed down; we need pulling into the light which shows us what we truly want, what it is that our hearts are most drawn to. With the Christmas narrative again just on the edge of the poem, the speaker thinks of the shock experienced by the shepherds, faced with the 'terrible sheen' of the angelic glory filling the night in the fields near Bethlehem. If we can somehow be pushed through the veil of water, we shall see at last what matters to us – we shall see the desires 'foreseen' by God and the angels.

Water is all that the speaker has given or can give. The solidarity of baptism overflows at least to the extent of a shared cup of water. Jesus in the Gospels (Matthew 10.42) says that *even* as little as the sharing of a cup of water will count as establishing a life-giving connection between the 'little one', his vulnerable and homeless servants, and those among whom they live – the first-century equivalents of those who have enough water to tend their suburban lawns. The recognition and the relation are minimal, in one way, yet some willingness to share life or compassion has been fleetingly manifested. The longing to see and to serve the God who calls us out of the darkness of our comfort has been glimpsed, and there has been an intuitive grasp of something about the dreadful urgency of having to flee, 'quickly, wordlessly,/ leaving a table set for supper' (perhaps an oblique glance here at the Passover ritual, the Jews on the eve of their flight from Egypt eating in haste at their tables). The family as they set out again on their journey (where to?) can be seen for what and who they are – God's chosen, God's angels, God's Mother, God in the flesh. A vagrant turned away may indeed be Jesus; the request for water may be the divine summons, the 'burning bush' moment when God is visible even to our slow and waterlogged perception. The humble and awkward plea for help is a 'visitation' like that of the Virgin Mary to Elizabeth in the first chapter of Luke's Gospel.

So the family disappears on its way. Hodgen's odd word, 'the disappeareds', translates literally the term that has been commonly used in some Latin American countries, especially Argentina, for those who had been abducted by the security forces of a corrupt and violent government, the *desaparecidos* who vanished into cells, torture chambers and anonymous graves. The family on the doorstep has escaped this fate, but it stands for all those 'little ones' who are helpless before the violence of state power. The striking image that ends the poem, 'The runaway children of the stars', holds together the vulnerability of those whom God calls the baptized to identify with and their significance as manifestations of glory or 'epiphany' (like the star to the magi).

The more we read the poem, the more its layers of both biblical and contemporary allusion appear. As noted, it is understated in its moral register; but while it depicts neither a dramatic conversion nor a response of self-sacrificing solidarity, it leaves no doubt that the view from the domestic kitchen window will not be quite the same again.

Fanny Howe

The Angels

The lassitude of angels
is one thing
but how the gold got under their
skin I don't know

I met them
in the Fields of Mourning
where there is
no morning

only the end of night
the dull gold of
transforming suffering:

what is passed on –
as milk is pain –
passed on to those
we love, becoming
nourishment, good luck
for them

Some colors
imply an ease
with indirect experience:
in the Fields of Mourning

the point of each hour
is the dream it inspires

and there
the angels hang out
limp and gold
but suddenly anxious
if told

what trembling joy
their suffering has brought.

Angels appear in a good many of Fanny Howe's poems. The awareness of an elusive presence, announcing something, communicating from another level of seeing or understanding, is a strong image for the insight of poetry itself, trying as it does to persuade language to say more than it is ready to say, to trust its own indirection and uncertain focus to transmit truth. Angels belong in the realm of 'indirect experience', according to this poem. They are encountered in the context of grieving, in an atmosphere of pre-dawn greyness, in between the realities of 'mourning' and 'morning'. The tone is one of exhaustion after prolonged pain and effort, before any real light has dawned. But something is being shown and passed on in the 'dull gold' that suffuses these tantalizing presences.

What is passed on is the *narration of suffering*. The 'angels' are the powers that nourish a new generation with their capacity to speak about suffering without evasion. Just as the breastfeeding of a baby may be painful, so the feeding of those we love with our memories will reopen hurts from the past and prolong the pain that has been experienced; but by allowing the 'indirect experience' of that pain, something is transfigured and some gift is passed on. What matters about the past of suffering is 'the dream it inspires', the indeterminate hope that cannot yet, in this pre-dawn ambience, be seen in its proper colours, in its specific embodied shape. The drifting possibilities of seeing the story of suffering as something that generates wisdom, hope or even joy are like the half-formed images on the edge of sleep and waking, slow and vague shapes, but also transmitting a hint of subdued gold light. We would be startled, even panicked, to know just what will in fact be made possible by these intimations, these almost-phantom beginnings of bringing the history of human suffering into language.

It is a profoundly enigmatic poem. Who or what exactly are the angels? I wrote about them as 'powers' a few lines earlier, which is a bit of an evasion. The description – the 'lassitude' they seem to exhibit and the gold suffusing their skin – suggests the angels of Orthodox iconography, with the highlighting of the contours of their skin and (to Western eyes) languid posture. We might think especially, perhaps, of the angels of Andrei Rublev's great icon of the three angels who visit Abraham in Genesis 18, traditionally a symbol of the Trinity. Howe's angels are real agents: they are subjects worn down by pain; they are actual voices, however exhausted or faint. Perhaps they are the voices I hear in my own head and can't quite bring into focus; my voice and not my voice; the voices of real suffering persons, and also something else. Their very nature as possibilities in the making, not solutions, not finished work, is where the difficulty lies. The dim half-light before dawn is an appropriate time to become aware of them. And however indistinct they are, they say clearly enough that as soon as suffering is looked at, spoken of, even if that speaking is an inarticulate sound of pain, it becomes something that is brought into speech and so is stripped of its power to silence us. The voices are angelic, therefore, because they announce what we cannot realize for ourselves – a future in which suffering is recalled and narrated not just endured, a life/language 'breastfed' on this indistinct but unmistakeable awareness of the 'dull gold' under the skin of those who have suffered.

Fanny Howe's later writing and activism were deeply inspired by the liberation theology of 1970s Latin America. It is a context in which the imagery of this poem comes to life: it mattered immensely to name and go on naming all those who were rendered silent and anonymous by political repression, to celebrate those whose suffering had activated and inspired others to speak of them and for them – not just the figures of conventional heroism, but simply all whose humanity had nourished that of others, and whose insulted and denied humanity roused others to action and to the strange kind of celebration that insists on the nameless victims being given names and dignity. Their lives have made us dream of something. Yet if we try too glibly to systematize this, let alone use it as some sort of rationale for suffering and oppression, the angels are 'anxious': if we instrumentalize these voices, they may vanish; if we try to make them solve problems, they will fall silent. The poet's job is to find words that will transmit the 'angelic' intuition, the divine promise of the God who sat with Abraham, without false consolation.

Fanny Howe

The Descent

The descent has deepened
the interior lengthened

designated ending

Blind

pulled down inside and then
shot up again

to see east via the plateglass
a moon a monsoon an ashram

I used time almost wantonly
in that bald but sensual sky

to give me gusts
and more measurement

not to snap the stars shut
but Joseph said
you really ought

to tender how you sail by eye
your soul is just a length of baby

The plane tilts earthwards and the angles of the light inside shift dramatically. As the angle of descent sharpens, it is as if the plane's interior lengthens. This opening image calls up that other experience of moving towards a 'designated ending', the sense of approaching death: can we say of this that 'the interior lengthens', that there is more sense of depth or extension in the self?

The voice pauses significantly on the word 'Blind', inviting us to hear it for a moment in its normal adjectival meaning before letting us know that it is the window covering. What do we, what can we, see in the enlarged interior of ourselves? Have we learnt to see at all or does the adjective describe us as we advance towards our ending? Then the picture clears: the blind shuts out the external light, then snaps open. Do we see more if we shut our eyes for a season to what is outside, so that we see with new focus when we allow ourselves to look again? What the speaker sees – in a line that plays very effectively with both soft consonants and long vowels – is both the natural world, in its calm and its storms, and the space of meditative absorption that human beings create, the ashram (the line implies that the plane is coming to land in India). During the journey, the empty but somehow fertile and physically immediate sky has provided encouragement (the following wind suggested by 'gusts') in measuring time differently, 'wantonly', without anxiety (compare Ursula Fanthorpe's poem, p. 101, on the moments when we are delivered from 'timefors', the rigid punctuation of time by our worries about purpose and success). The syntax here, as often in Howe's poetry, is ambiguous, but the simplest reading is that the flight time, with its new sense of un-anxious temporal movement, has not been used to shut out the stars by which we navigate. But the unexplained 'Joseph' intervenes, to caution against even this measurement by the stars: we must learn to journey 'by eye', by the slowly educated instinct of the body adjusting itself as it travels. The unexpected verb 'tender' may be used in its usual sense of 'offer' – we must *show* or offer readiness to sail by instinct – or in the rare and archaic sense of 'acting with tenderness' – we must gently nurture our ability to do this.

And the poem ends with another of the tantalizing half-rhymes and assonances that are threaded through it, and with another unexpected turn, a phrase that could be read in several ways. The soul is a 'length of baby' – like a length of string or cloth? As if the soul were made of 'baby', as if it were a certain quantity of 'babyishness', or a series of baby-sized units, a series of 'infant' moments with the potential for growth. Or possibly: the soul is itself an infant, whose understanding needs always to be extended. Or again: the soul is always an extension, a lengthening, of the consciousness of the infant, always in the process of recovering that first synaesthetic encounter with its world. Whatever the exact meaning intended, it defines the soul's essence as something to do with the kind of consciousness that we lose in growing older; but as we grow towards our death, we have to recognize the soul we have lost in growing, and grow into a deeper kind of sensibility. The line seems to pick up the opening reference to the lengthening interior: as the inner life extends, it becomes more and more a continuation of the baby's receptive awareness. We must – you might say – be born again; and again.

Sally Ito

At the Beginning of Lent: Ash Wednesday

My mind is a brick and nothing gets through; the
  porous sponge
of my youth is desiccated into a slab of stone.

Painting the ashes on such a surface is an idle act
or a leap of faith by the bestower;
for the mind while receiving this mortal dust of
  sacrifice
is wandering through the temple maze of sellers
wondering what to buy, eat in the morrow.
Well, there'll be no sugar, caffeine, or even meat.
The beans will need soaking, and the fish bought
  fresh.

The sermon is about a recalcitrant camel
made to suckle its mutant offspring,
an oversized albino calf whose onerous birth
  caused the mother's
heart to harden, become indifferent. My mind is
  that heart.

The shepherds hire musicians, sing and rub the
  poor mother's neck,
and finally, teardrops glisten in that old *naga*'s eyes
  and she is made

to look on her child as if it were her own for the
  very first time.
The brick now sodden with tears
will keep in the moisture longer than you think,
and when through the doors of the church I slip
  into the world
the ash will be in me like salt in the sea.

Growing older is not necessarily to mature humanly: the poem begins with an evocation of the dry impermeability of the 'grown-up' heart, as opposed to the openness of a younger self capable of being invaded by a reality that will transform. The repeated actions of outward penitence, the annual smearing of ash on the forehead at the start of Lent, seem like a mere decoration of the surface of our lives, while underneath, the fussy, irritable self-protective fugues roll on uninterrupted. The significant pause for self-examination in Lent becomes a tiresome chore. The mind is stuck in 'market' mode ('the temple maze of sellers'), the world of bartering and haggling that Jesus encounters in the courts of the Temple; the preoccupations of 'what to buy, eat in the morrow' are close to those concerns that Jesus castigates in the Sermon on the Mount (Matthew 6.31: 'Do not be anxious, saying, "What shall we eat?" or "What shall we drink?" or "What shall we wear?"').

Ito, a Canadian poet of East Asian family background, is characteristically interested in how attention is rightly directed at the apparently mundane so as to catch the reflections of glory (the poem comes from a 2011 collection called *Alert to Glory*). *Rightly* directed: how to see the mundane world without anxiety or the distorting lens of possessiveness. The subdued worries of the mind here are not marks of real attention.

The mind has become hardened, unwilling to be soaked through or invaded (the reference to the beans that need soaking sounds like a mischievous hint that the human heart is much more resistant than the humblest of material objects). Ito gives us an unexpected image and an unexpected turn to the poem's flow – the camel that has given birth with pain and difficulty to a calf that looks 'abnormal', and seems to reject it. The herdsmen lavish attention on it, physically caressing and massaging it, softening its heart with music, until it is able to look with tears, love and acceptance at the albino calf. And the implication is that what we are not attending to, what we are resisting, is *what we have given birth to*: the self we have made ourselves to be, and so the history of the sad and unconscious mess we make of ourselves out of anxiety and fiercely defended idleness of spirit. The camel weeps lovingly for the calf; we are being prodded to weep for our damaged and diminished selves. The liturgy of Ash Wednesday is the music and the massage that softens us to our own need. We are to weep for ourselves and for our children, like the women who encounter Jesus on his way to the cross (Luke 23.28).

So one thing we can say about the traditional liturgy of the season is that it sets out to make us feel differently – not to have specific *feelings* (a kind of worship that can be simply manipulative), but to be more receptive to the unexpected inrush of a reality that we have not been used to admitting. This is both the truth of our own abnormality and also the abnormality or deformity of our refusal to look at it and accept it as our own. The gift that the Ash Wednesday ritual gives is the freedom to let this perception in and to let it change us.

The tears come, and soak through what seemed an impassable barrier of fearful defensiveness. The final metaphor is a skilful recapitulation of the images in the opening lines: the impermeable brick will retain water like a sponge; and the ash of repentant self-knowledge, self-acknowledgement, will become as imperceptibly pervasive in the once-hardened heart as salt in the sea.

Apart from anything else, Ito prompts us to see the apparently 'surface' action, the familiar routine of religious ritual, as potentially the means by which we are saturated in new possibilities. The liturgy does not have to give me ideas or sensations, but, given the chance, it will steadily make me more able to 'sense' who and what I am, and, like the reluctant camel, see my damaged self 'as if it were [my] own for the very first time'.

Mark Jarman

Unholy Sonnets 7

Reduce the proof of nature. So we tried
And still found that our bodies kept their faith.
Reduce the body, burn away the brain.
We tried and found the chemical debris
Inscribed with calculations of a mind.
Reduce the compounds, elements, all bits
Of matter, energy. Make all abstract.
We tried and met the idea of the act.
But what was that? Without prerequisites
Of . . . you know what I mean. We couldn't find . . .
What's the word for it? We couldn't see . . .
But any metaphor will seem inane.
Without the world, we met the death
Of God. And language. Both of them had died.

The allusion in the title is to John Donne's *Holy Sonnets*, posthumously published in 1633. There is no sustained attempt to echo or engage with the earlier work, but the twenty pieces in the sequence mostly reflect on moments of doubt and rebellion, and as such might be thought to earn the epithet 'unholy'. Some, however, double back and present an affirmative picture of faith, or at least a doubt about doubt. This is one such, tackling the reductionist world view that would exclude God from the intellectual landscape. Nature as a whole can offer no decisive proof of God, once we have emptied it of purpose; but we are still stuck with the oddity of the human body as the location of thought and imagining. So 'burn away the brain', re-describe human action in mechanistic terms; but then what remains is still a pattern of intelligible phenomena, a pattern that obstinately implies a mind to think it. Reduce this in turn to abstract mathematical functions; but then what is still left is the idea of an energy activating such functions, an energy without which we could not encounter anything that could be thought. And then?

The poem struggles for words ('you know what I mean. We couldn't find . . ./ What's the word for it? We couldn't see . . .'). Predictably enough, when we have in effect ruled the world out of consideration, there is nothing to say about anything; the very idea of a thing has vanished. Our obsessive search for a completely 'demythologized' environment in which no immaterial or formal shape can be allowed as a true presence leads us inexorably to this inarticulate stumbling. When we try to 'think away' from our material environment all trace of intelligent process, active mind, formal interconnection (the 'implicate order' about which the physicist David Bohm famously wrote), we don't end up with a tidy report on mechanical, impersonal transactions; we end up with nothing to say. A transaction remains an action, an exchange of information. Without this, we have no way to establish even the concept of an object: empty out the reality of intelligence and you empty out the notion of intelligibility. There is no *world* left; in the immortal phrase once used to describe Los Angeles, 'there is no *there* there'.

C. S. Lewis's dystopian futurist fiction, *That Hideous Strength*, has as its grotesque and bloody climax an event in which the Promethean scientists who have been so conscientiously labouring at removing from the world any suspicion of the reality of mind or truth find that they have been deprived of the power of intelligible speech. As the triumphant Christian magician who has triggered this denouement announces, they have renounced the *logos* of God, the divine wisdom encoded in the actual physical world, and so have had human *logos*, the capacity to make sense in common with other human beings, taken away from them also. The secularizing or disenchanting of the material world ends up in a denial of material reality itself, and the dissolution of material reality as a gift and a discipline for human understanding leads to the dissolution of speech into nonsense.

God and language die together; there are no metaphors to carry us over the gulf or beyond the brick wall of a 'real absence' in the world around, the absence of patterns that both nurture and resist our intellect, patterns that drive us to make connections and at the same time point us to connections quite other than we have made or could make. A secularized imagination, in this perspective, means a depthless world, and finally a world that dissolves around us because it carries no invitation to immersion in its solidity and mysteriousness. 'Be careful what you wish for' is one of the things this poem is saying; if you want a manageably mechanical world, be prepared for the end of language itself.

And the implication is that any act of resistance to this erosion of the world is not only a service to language but also a witness to God, whether this is acknowledged or not. An act of faith in metaphor, and in the connectedness it suggests, is incontestably an act of *faith*. If Jarman is right, writing itself is a religious act.

Mark Jarman

Unholy Sonnets 17

God like a kiss, God like a welcoming,
God like a hand guiding another hand
And raising it or making it descend,
God like the pulse point and its silent drumming,
And the tongue going to it, God like the humming
Of pleasure if the skin felt it as sound,
God like the hidden wanting to be found
And like the joy of being and becoming.
And God the understood, the understanding,
And God the pressure trying to relieve
What is not pain but names itself with weeping,
And God the rush of time and God time standing,
And God the touch body and soul believe,
And God the secret neither one is keeping.

Like George Herbert's famous sonnet, 'Prayer', this is a sequence of metaphors – or perhaps more strictly a mixture of metaphor and simile, since Jarman varies 'God is like . . .' phrases with a more direct kind of linkage. As the sonnet advances from octet to sestet, this latter takes over (no more 'likes' after line 8), an index of the growing urgency of the poem's movement, as though the sheer pressure of trying to find images for God were squeezing out the slightly distancing or detached effect of mere comparison. But the initial comparisons are forceful enough, for all that, and their force has a lot to do with their physicality. It is an unexpected physicality: the kiss and the welcoming or the touch of the hand are perhaps unsurprising, but 'the tongue going to' the drumming of the pulse is something different. It could mean both a literal caressing by the tongue of the pulsating skin or the tongue speaking or singing in step with the pulse's drum, and it eases us towards the image that follows, the sensation of humming on the skin, sound and touch inseparably fused.

The imagery broadens from these directly sensuous evocations to something rather different: God is encountered in the sense that there is in the world of something 'wanting' to be found, wanting to be born and grow, or to be understood; the sense of a pressure exercised by the world on our imagination, towards a depth beyond us that is actively drawing us to itself. And that pressure is then imagined as something that not only seeks to be recognized but also seeks to 'relieve/ What is not pain but names itself with weeping'. This seems to mean that the weeping in question is not the effect of any specific or localized human suffering but a general awareness of human longing and loss; in the reality that surrounds us, there is a movement towards this longing and loss, a silent pushing towards healing. And this may come through in the sense of time racing by, transient and transparent, or in the moment of stillness, 'in and out of time', in T. S. Eliot's phrase.

The two concluding lines bring together the sensuous resonances of the first section of the poem and the more elusive encounters of the second. Body and soul alike 'sense' God and trust what they sense (whether or not they are conscious of it, presumably); and what's more, they can't keep the secret, they show what they sense and trust in the actions they undertake. God is the showing-through, in both physical and spiritual or imaginative life, of that initiative of invitation, embrace, the call to recognition, that is active in all we encounter; a badly kept secret.

This holding together of the physical and the spiritual gives the poem its central energy. It is not that God ever appears or can appear as a physical object, yet encountering God is 'like' a certain kind of intensified awareness of and response to the body's own rhythms. And the recognition of one's own selfhood as always already being involved in recognition and being recognized, as well as the sense of unanchored loss or solitude – these are where God simply is, unarguably, not as some strange extra presence to be inferred. Perhaps that is where the poem is going: God is not an inference, a conclusion to any chain of reasoning, but (at the very least) a way of seeing into the centre of what we are, body and soul, or of registering in some way that we are seen and touched as we are, body and soul. The poem is about just that recognition of being 'touched'; and faith is the confidence that this touch is not our invention.

Elizabeth Jennings

A Childhood Horror

I have pretended long, in loyalty.
I had a childhood hurt for five harsh years,
I let it wound my good fragility
And over decades I've shed many tears
And sometimes wished that I were wholly free
Of faith because it was to me all fears,

Unhappiness and, yes, grief for a part
That should be left untouched in childhood till
There have been many blows upon the heart.
I listened to the words within that still
Confessional. 'You must not be a part
Of the communion tomorrow.' Frail

I was and still a child although fifteen.
My only fault was large uncertainty
Of my faith's tenets. I had not yet been
Close to grave sin. A dark shade stood between
Me and the altar. Gone was liberty
Yet absolution had just set me free.

The priest was twisted, sick. I felt no hate
For children think they cannot change such things
Or run from them. Of course it was too late
When later I could tell all this. Love sings

Now in my spirit but when black moods wait
For me I cannot launch them on light wings.

God, you meant terror once. But maybe this
Brought me close to your mysteries. I knew of
Unjust suffering. Deciding this
I sometimes now am filled with boundless love
And gratitude from which I've power to build
Music, the poem and all they are witness of.

There are several poems by Elizabeth Jennings about the violation of childhood – one ('A Child Destroyed') imagines in gruelling detail the rape and murder of a little girl. This poem is about the experience of a different kind of violation. As she says in 'A Child Destroyed', she has not known *this* extremity of terror and humiliation; her childhood fears were only 'imaginary' – but we are encouraged to think of the continuum between the atrocity of the rape and killing and the kinds of abuse or denial of childhood that we generally do not want to identify as such. Another poem, 'First Confession', describes the bewildering effect of making a sacramental confession at the age of seven and finding childhood misdemeanours suddenly elevated to the status of sin: something is being done that destroys 'the child's right element/ Of joy'. The healing promised by the sacrament turns into hurt.

The poem reproduced here speaks to both of the other two mentioned. What is being described is a renewal of the hurtful effect of the sacrament, this time in the context of a 15-year-old's experience of being denied Holy Communion because of religious doubts. Confession has clearly been consistently an occasion of demoralizing and frightening sensations. The kind of self-doubt and self-scrutiny that ought to come with the experience of maturing responsibility – knowing what it is to hurt others and be hurt by them – is forced prematurely on a vulnerable awareness, with the result that God becomes remote or worse. 'God, you meant terror once.' It is possible, as the poem's conclusion affirms, that this can be seen as part of what makes poetry itself imaginable, because of the painful awareness of injustice and the incomprehensibility of suffering, an awareness that is a central dimension of art. But the closing lines, resting on a moment of '*deciding*' what has been happening, do not quite settle the matter: 'deciding' has about it a feeling of deliberate, willed resolution, while the experience evoked is not truly resolved and perhaps cannot be.

The association of religious institutions with the abuse of children is now far more widely and clearly acknowledged than it generally was when Jennings wrote these poems, but the sense of an interconnection between different kinds of assault on childhood trust is inescapable. The child's helplessness in the face of violence, the child's assumption that things 'had' to happen in this way, the 'loyal' silence, even the absence of anger or hatred, all these will be familiar to anyone who has listened to the testimonies of children who have endured mental and physical abuse. But the poem, along with 'First Confession', raises the broader issue of how it is that a sacrament the purpose of which is liberation becomes a means of – effectively – enslavement: enslavement to guilty and anxious fictions about God. Instead of opening up a way to reconciliation (and confession is commonly called the Sacrament of Reconciliation), its effect is to erect a barrier.

Jennings was a committed Catholic Christian, and this poem offers not exactly a justification but a kind of interpretative structure in which the insult to both childhood and God can to some extent be made sense of. Readers will vary in their judgement of how far this convinces, psychologically or poetically. But she is a good and honest enough poet to embed the word 'horror' in the title, and to present with unconsoled clarity the effects of corrupt religious power. Any reflection on the range of experiences we call 'spiritual' is bound to reckon with this. The merging of the power of another human being with the power of God, the appeal to God to justify a distorted and dehumanizing exercise of human power, and the exploitation of the most vulnerable to gratify the agents of power are all disturbingly frequent features of how religious establishments work. Jennings begins by placing 'pretence' alongside 'loyalty', suggesting the cost of these betrayals in terms of a collective loss of integrity and the loss of any sense of faith as liberating or humanizing, as well as the obvious and appalling human damage to indviduals. 'I've . . . sometimes wished that I were wholly free/ Of faith because it was to me all fears': the question of whether the practice of faith and the existence of organized communities of belief is worthwhile in the face of such wishes provides a difficult and necessary lens for reading any poetry grounded in the traditions of collective spiritual discipline. That is why a poem like this, along with the other related poems mentioned, needs to be in a collection like this.

D. Gwenallt Jones

Sin

Take off the business suit, the old-school tie,
the gown, the cap, drop the reviews, awards,
certificates, stand naked in your sty,
a little carnivore, clothed in dried turds.
The snot that slowly fills our passages
seeps up from hollows where the dead beasts lie;
dumb stamping dances spell our messages,
we only know what makes our arrows fly.
Lost in the wood, we sometimes glimpse the sky
between the branches, and the words drop down
we cannot hear, the alien voices high
and hard, singing salvation, grace, life, dawn.
Like wolves, we lift our snouts: Blood, blood, we
cry,
the blood that bought us so we need not die.

Gwenallt's poetry includes examples of both highly disciplined verse in (Welsh and English) classical forms and, especially in his later work, pieces in looser and more informal style; this tightly constructed sonnet seems, in its brevity and concentration, to seek to embody something of what it describes, the sense of sin as a trap, an environment of close-woven pressures, inside which we can barely see the possibility of another world. Its opening lines enact a stripping away of all the dignities that we award ourselves, uncovering the pitiable and absurd primitive reality beneath; the language is redolent of self-disgust. We do not even understand the mechanisms of our own violence.

Like Dante at the beginning of the *Divine Comedy*, we are in the middle of a 'dark wood'; and the darkness encompasses our thought and imagination, however sophisticated we think ourselves. Hints of something else drift down to us through the close-knit branches of the forest, but we are unable to make sense of them. All we truly know is our inarticulate thirst for life; and in a concluding image, more stark even than the rest of the poem, Gwenallt presents us to ourselves as wolves howling for blood. The final line in the original Welsh is literally, 'baying for the blood that ransomed [or 'purchased'] us'.

It is a complex as well as a shocking image. Its violence accords with the general tone of the poem, bitter and uncompromising about human degradation: even our longing for redemption is a kind of animal greed. Yet there is a pathos in it also: even our animal greed is a longing for redemption, for which we can have no words. The hungry wolf knows instinctively that something has been done that breaks through the suffocating canopy of the forest, and sniffs it in the wind. It is not that we are baying for an impossible future; the blood has already been shed.

So the poem is both a stark account of what sin means and an affirmation that sin is already potentially overcome. Sin is the inescapability of our inarticulate instinctive violence, all that lies beneath the thin surface of self-congratulatory civilization. Gwenallt grew up in the wake of the First World War, in the oppressive conditions of the industrial valleys of South Wales (his father died in a horrific industrial accident), and he has no temptations to adopt either a secular or a liberal Christian optimism about human progress. His own move, as a young man, from revolutionary socialism to a rediscovered

Christian faith, had something to do with the sense that his early Marxism could not cope with the deviousness of the human heart and the tragic quality of human experience. The Calvinism of his family faith will have made him familiar with a harsh account of the extent of human fallenness, in which even our residual hope or love is bound to be shot through with the cravings and obsessions of the insane 'little carnivore' we have become (although his own developing religious convictions moved in a more sacramental and ecumenical direction). Yet God is not absent from this seemingly Godless world, and the redemptive act is already foreordained. Our thirst for blood, the very violence that shows how trapped we are in the terrors of the forest, is bound up with our longing for healing: in the shedding of the blood of Christ on the cross, our own violence is itself what unpredictably and paradoxically releases the pardon of God, and enables us to learn the alien words that filter through the thickets. God works with and through the most destructive compulsions of our nature so that they become the channels of grace: the blood we shed becomes the blood that gives us life.

Gwenallt is not, of course, elaborating a theology of the atonement, but in that condensed and even grotesque final image, he implicitly offers a bold model of divine freedom. God is that agency which can absorb and transfigure our passion for destruction, can move within the terrible outworkings of that passion to bring about the revolution of grace. We may still stand in the pigsty, in all our humiliating absurdity, but we are 'purchased' – our release from the trap is eternally paid for.

Brigit Pegeen Kelly

The Music Lesson

Collect of white dusk. And
The first epistolary drops
Strike sparks from the leaves,

Send up the sweet fragrance
Of the Far Gone. Where
The maple fell in another rain

Red and white umbrellas
Hold back the weather: sun
And moon and the seasonal

Displays the four hands
Keep time to: the telling
And the told. Back and forth:

Back and forth: the lesson's
Passion is patience. Through
The domino tumble and clutter

Of the pupil's untutored touch
The metronome keeps
A stiff upper lip, pays out

Its narrow train of thought,
While above, God,
Gold carrion in a lit frame,

Rehearses His reproach, one-
Noted. Final. The unnegotiable
Real estate of absolute loss:

Discipleship's cost. O hands,
Hands, doing their work:
The steeple hat of the dunce

Is stiff with recalcitrant
Notes, but still the ghost hammers
Leap. And luck makes an entrance

In this: See: lightning
Partitions the dusk – illuminating
Our brief lease – and with

A cocksure infusion of heat
Luck lays hands on
The boy's hands and prefigures

The pleasure that will one day
Possess this picture for good.
This is the stone the builders

Rejected. Pleasure. *Pleasure.*
The liquid tool, the golden
Fossil that will come to fuel

In lavish and unspeakable ways
All the dry passages
The boy does not now comprehend

Or care for. And then his
Stricken hands will blossom
Fat with brag. And play.

This is an exuberantly – but very coherently – image-packed poem about time and grace. Kelly gradually sets a scene, of early evening, rain just beginning to fall, and she does so with a teasing allusion to the liturgical sequence of the Mass. The Collect, the prayer for the day, is followed by the Epistle, a reading usually from Paul's letters; and so here, the emptiness of the 'white dusk' is a kind of prayerful clearing of space for the 'epistolary' communication to begin. As the poem unfolds, it is clear that this is not a casual reference.

The showers that were once kept off by trees are now held at bay with umbrellas; but the passage of time is the same as ever. The four hands of teacher and pupil have to keep the same rhythm, with each other and with the impersonal ticking of the metronome. 'The lesson's/ Passion is patience' – what the lesson teaches is patience, but also, perhaps, 'Passion is patience' is the lesson itself. The two words are intertwined in any case: we cannot but *suffer* the passage of time, and our most consuming desires are generated in and nourished in time passing. The sense of passionate engagement in the making of music is counterposed to the 'stiff upper lip' of the metronome, which has and can have only one 'thought', which is measurement. Our instinct is to imagine God as exercising similar 'metronomic' judgement: the gilded crucifix ('gold carrion' is a bold image) looks down to remind us of the risk of 'absolute loss' (notice the punning 'real estate' – a real condition, a real 'territory') if we engage in the work of 'discipleship' – which here seems to mean the task of serious and self-forgetting learning of a skill.

The awkward student piles up the mistakes; but the music itself, the formal substance of what is being enacted, doesn't falter ('the ghost hammers/ Leap'). And this steadiness in the background prepares us for the lightning flash in which the incomprehensible obedience of dull and regulated practice on the instrument becomes a moment of *joy*. 'Luck' seizes the student's hands and transforms the entire experience into what it will one day become, an experience in which the fact of pleasure will make sense of every note and every physical movement that realizes the notes. The 'dry' and incomprehensible passages will be suffused with the 'liquid' that brings them alive – like oil (fossil fuel) springing in dry places. The aching and uncomfortable hands will 'blossom', fuelled by this fluid in the veins, 'And play'. The poem ends with this triumphant word, which could be indicative or imperative here. The entire point of the dreary and error-laden practice is play, sheer enjoyment.

And this is identified by Kelly with 'the stone the builders/ Rejected': this image, originally from Psalm 118, is used in the Gospels to describe the destiny of Jesus, once rejected, now recognized as the 'cornerstone' that holds everything together (Mark 12.10 and parallels). Joy, it seems, is what will show itself to be the cornerstone. Here and now it is at best on the edge of our experience of the relentless passage of time and the struggles of learning. But even the present 'dusk' can be 'partitioned' by the unpredicted interruption of delight. There is in fact a 'sacramental' moment evoked here (which is why the liturgical language at the poem's opening is significant), a moment in which the future coming together of body and spirit is not only prefigured but also realized in the middle of the body's laborious journeying, marked as it is by mechanical slog and frequent error.

'Discipleship' is a word used here in connection with what we are attempting and failing at. And the voice of the poem announces not that the disciplined work of producing a 'musical' life is simply set aside by the uncovenanted moment of pleasure but that such a moment reminds and reassures us that pleasure is indeed what our passionate patience, our suffering of time's passage, is finally about. The reality of the music itself will one day truly and lastingly possess us, not by invasion but by transfiguration.

Sarah Klassen

Advent

We are waiting (again) for the One
who has already come
and gone, leaving us
bereaved.

One waiting in the wings
for the cue – political, apocalyptic
or dramatic – to step into view,
descend,

be finally revealed
to the bewildered crowd –
complicit or without guile.
And to a remnant, impatient

for the curtain to rise on some
anticipated vindication. As if
flamboyant entry to a final act
will finally untangle everything:

a flawless *denouement*. As if
(if you're not left behind)
a book will open up,
page after blinding page.

A prophet's alleged to have said:
we cannot believe in one for whom –
for reasons philosophical,
emotional or rational –

we do not
(cannot,
will not any longer)
wait.

Every year in the pre-Christmas season of Advent, Christian liturgy and hymnody concentrate on the theme of waiting – as if the end of the story had not already happened in the events of the birth and life and death of Jesus. Has the expected saviour then 'come and gone'? Who or what are we now waiting for?

Sarah Klassen's poem analyses the way in which expectation can work as we wait for someone or something to come 'on cue', to come at the moment we think appropriate, or to come with a clear proof that we who are waiting are at last to be proved right. This is a deliberately *theatrical* framing of our expectation: we look for a resolution of the sort that will send us out from the theatre satisfied that the loose ends have been tied up – the 'flamboyant entry to a final act', like the Duke shedding his disguise at the end of Shakespeare's *Measure for Measure*, or, even more spectacularly, the descent of Jupiter from heaven in *Cymbeline*. From now on, things will be clear – or, more specifically, the security of our position will be clear. Klassen makes a glancing allusion to the mythology popular in some extreme Protestant circles, especially in America, of a final 'Rapture' in which some are taken direct to bliss and some are 'left behind' (the title of a bestselling series of fantasies about the end of the world based on this scheme) – a particularly robust version of expectation orientated towards the manifestation of how right we have been. The book that opens up, 'page after blinding page', might well be a Bible now stripped of all ambiguity, infallibly telling us what we already think we know

But, the poem insists, waiting for vindication, waiting to be proved right, is something that is not easily compatible with actual *faith* – to the extent that such waiting is not really waiting at all, but an attempt to possess here and now the future we long for. The complicated concluding sentence warns that we cannot *believe* in one for whom we will not wait. There are all sorts of reasons for not waiting, personal or theoretical; but this impatience manifests a lack of trust. We shall always be lured back into the kind of 'staged' waiting where there are in fact no real surprises ahead. We know that there will be a solution in our terms – and in our favour.

So if in Advent we are sent back into a waiting room, even though we believe the promised saviour has come, it is because we have to learn to trust that saviour as one who will never simply deliver to us what we have asked for ourselves. His coming, past or future, is not defined by being a solution to the problems we can recognize, let alone by guaranteeing our triumphant vindication. It is itself, himself.

The lines of the poem grow shorter and the point is driven home: the very last line is grammatically part of the sentence we have been reflecting on, but the one isolated word invites us to hear it or read it as an imperative, not just an infinitive. We are to wait with the integrity and the risk of openness – not in confident anticipation of being proved right, but in trust that what we wait for will be beyond our imagining. The expected one has indeed 'come and gone'; that first coming should have shown us that we shall always be encountering him as ahead of us, as exceeding what we know. The very fact that he has gone, that we are still here, living in incompleteness, tells us that whatever lies ahead, it will not be the anticipated ('flawless') closure we might have designed. But we wait in trust because *we* cannot design our own liberation and our own lasting joy.

Avraham Yitzhak Kook

Sukkot: The Light in the Sukkah

On the *Yamim Nora'im*
the intensity compares
to almost unbearably dazzling light.

Sometimes eyes are narrowed,
aching at the strain
of seeking the Divine.

In the shelter of the *sukkah*,
fierce rays are filtered;
a softened glow shines steadily within.

And from this gentle light,
twinkling motes float up
drifting through the latticed roof.

Rav Kook, originally from the Baltic regions of the Russian Empire, was one of the most learned and creative Jewish teachers of the twentieth century, and his copious literary output included poetry as well as rabbinical scholarship and ethical teaching. He became the first Ashkenazi Chief Rabbi of what was then still called Palestine in 1921, exercising an immense influence on the Jewish communities of the Land, and is recognized as a spiritual teacher no less than a scholar and commentator. His poems on the great commemorations and celebrations of the Jewish year are of particular importance for understanding his vision of Jewish identity and calling.

The celebration of Sukkot – what English-speaking Christian readers will probably know as the 'Feast of Tabernacles' – is mandated in Exodus 23 and Leviticus 23: it is originally a harvest festival (hence one of its Hebrew names, the 'Feast of Ingathering'), but in Leviticus it is given added significance as a reminder of how the people of Israel on their journey from slavery in Egypt lived in 'booths', temporary shelters, as they journeyed to Canaan. The celebration reasserts the absolute dependence of the Jewish people on God; all that human ingenuity and effort can build is as temporary and fragile as the makeshift structures of their desert wanderings. So for a week, 'all that are native in Israel shall dwell in booths' (Leviticus 23.42).

The celebration begins five days after the Day of Atonement, Yom Kippur; and Rav Kook's poem opens with the contrast between the relentless intensity of Yom Kippur and the move outwards into the open air during Sukkot. The *Yamim Nora'im*, the 'Days of Awe', are the ten days of concentrated religious observance, the high point of which is the Day of Atonement: rabbinical commentary regularly stresses the overwhelming nature of the prayer and liturgy of Yom Kippur, a time when the spirit is on the very edge of a holy presence so all-consuming that it can feel as if it threatens to annihilate the human. The purpose of the prayer and fasting of the Days of Awe is to bring each person into the presence of the Holy One without excuse or distraction. But Sukkot represents a going out from this intense inner world. One ancient and influential rabbinical tradition sees the transition from the *Yamim Nora'im* as re-enacting the movement from the moment when Moses, coming down from Sinai with the Torah, declares God's commandments and promises to Israel, to the moment when he instructs the people in the building of the 'Tabernacle', the moveable structure in which God's presence accompanies the people of Israel in their journeyings. First comes the declaration of the covenant, bringing each and every member of the people into God's presence; and then the task laid on the people is the building of a place in the world for God to dwell – the Torah-directed community of justice and mercy within which God will be made known.

So Sukkot is both an easing of the 'strain' of the Days of Awe, the almost intolerable pressure of the divine presence (like the cloud of divine glory that descends on Solomon's Temple at its consecration and makes it impossible for the priests to keep their place in the building, as described in 2 Chronicles 7.2), and a sign of the calling to move outwards into the world so that the divine glory can be seen and released within the creation. Rav Kook evokes the way in which the temporary structures of branches and light materials and odds and ends allows the blinding flame of divine presence to be 'filtered', like sunlight through leaves. We cannot bear too much of the blaze of God's glory, and so we are mercifully given a time when we can be sheltered from it; but this is not a withdrawal either on God's part or ours. If God spares us the terror and ecstasy of divine presence, it is so that we can build a visible, communal sign of God's nature, God's calling, God's gift in the world.

The beautiful final image of motes drifting up to the roof, like sparks from a fire or dust caught in a beam of light, draws on the Kabbalistic doctrine that the divine glory has been fractured and dispersed within creation, and that the calling of the holy people is to unite in their lives the glory that is hidden in the world with the glory that abides in heaven (a theme that is utilized also in Celan's poem, 'Your Beyondness', on p. 62). Building the 'tabernacle', the temporary shelter in which God can move through the world and accompany those called to God's service, is not only a matter of creating a sign of God's fidelity; it is also active and effective in releasing the hidden sparks of glory. Sukkot speaks of a renewal and healing of the entire created order. The terrifying experience of God's proximity that has dominated the Days of Awe is one side of a picture the other dimension of which is the marriage of heaven and earth through the fidelity of the holy people to the everyday demands of justice and kindness.

Avraham Yitzhak Kook

Sukkot: The Sukkah of Peace

For seven days . . . all citizens in Israel shall live in sukkot [thatched huts]. (Vayikra 23:42). This teaches that it is fitting for all of Israel to sit in one sukkah. (From the Talmud, Sukkah 27b)

Can all Your people
dwell in one *sukkah*?
No well-built fortress, this,
with vaulted ceiling
and buttressed pillars to hold it up –
its gaping roof and fragile walls
expose us all: left-wing and right;
those who deny Your existence
and those who tremble before You;
those who would transmit Your word
and those who would renew it;
the native born and those
still searching for their place;
scions of the ancient tree
and later-grafted branches.
And yet spread over us
your *sukkah* of peace,
for as the walls sway in the wind
and star-lit rain seeps through the roof,
a song of unity may yet emerge.

The evening prayers for the Sabbath include a petition that God will spread over those who have kept the Sabbath a *sukkah* of peace – a shelter, a canopy. In this poem, Rav Kook connects this prayer with a text in the Talmud which argues that the injunction to 'all Israel' to dwell in booths during the week of the feast means that the whole people sit 'under one shelter'. But how can this be? Kook offers a bold answer to the question: just because the *sukkah* is fragile and incomplete, it leaves us all equally exposed – the 'righteous' and the 'unrighteous', the believers and the unbelievers, the insiders and the outsiders. The dwelling we build is not some kind of Gothic cathedral, the walls of which provide clear lines of demarcation. What is most deeply shared among the people called by God is the knowledge of our incompleteness; they are never going to be able to finish the building and determine who is inside and who is outside. This is why in rabbinical teaching there is no requirement that the *sukkah* be a tidy or complete structure; even the most ramshackle attempt, full of gaps and holes, with only a couple of makeshift supports, will count as kosher, because, according to the commentators, peace is of such value in God's eyes that even the smallest effort towards it is valid and pleasing to God.

There are themes in common here with Imtiaz Dharker's 'Living Space' (p. 79). But it is important to see how the poem also reflects the very specific history of Rav Kook's own labours in holding together a deeply and often contentiously diverse Jewish community, acknowledging the place within it of those who thought of themselves as wholly secular in their belief and motivation. But it goes deeper: the idea that the unity of God's people – perhaps the unity of the human family itself – is something to do with its shared exposure, the inescapable nakedness to risk and suffering that is involved in being human, is one that will resonate with an age in which we are having to confront shared fragility in all sorts of new and frightening ways – pandemic, environmental crisis, food security and water supplies. The imagery of this poem suggests that only when we acknowledge that the vulnerability we share is the ground on which we may come to recognize one another, to see our experience in that of our neighbours, will there be any peace worth the name. So when we pray that God will cover us with a *sukkah* of peace, we are in fact praying that God will protect us all by giving all of us a sense of our shared need – a strange prayer to pray, we might think, but appropriate if it is only in this sense of need that we are delivered from mutual hatred and rivalry.

It is hard for a Christian reader not to feel the irony (intentional or not?) of the language about 'scions of the ancient tree/ and later-grafted branches': Paul's letter to the Romans (11.17–24) famously compares the relation of Christians to Jews with the relation of a graft to the original stock. This has been bizarrely ignored or, worse, inverted by so many Christians as if it signalled the supplanting by the ingrafted branches of the entire organism from which they draw their life; if Rav Kook was familiar with this passage, the lines seem to imply that even the delinquent children of the Jewish family who have so abused and assaulted the parent stock might just conceivably have a place under the *sukkah*. It is at the very least a challenge to the Christian to revisit Paul's complex and laboured metaphor and to think harder about those moral fragilities and offences that have disfigured Christian history.

The concluding images of the poem, especially the evocative 'star-lit rain', point to the gaps in the structure as the means of blessing: the failure to finish the self-protective projects with which the human mind occupies itself, the projects that seek to consolidate higher and thicker divisions between us, is a mercy. We saw in the previous 'Sukkot' poem how the image of motes drifting upwards towards a latticed roof (a roof with openings) spoke of the hope for reunification between glory above and glory below; is the descent of the 'star-lit rain' a counterpart, glory descending through the same gaps in the structure we have tried to build?

Denise Levertov

The Jacob's Ladder

The stairway is not
a thing of gleaming strands
a radiant evanescence
for angels' feet that only glance in their tread, and
  need not
touch the stone.

It is of stone.
A rosy stone that takes
a glowing tone of softness
only because behind it the sky is a doubtful, a
  doubting
night gray.

A stairway of sharp
angles, solidly built.
One sees that the angels must spring
down from one step to the next, giving a little
lift of the wings:

and a man climbing
must scrape his knees, and bring
the grip of his hands into play. The cut stone
consoles his groping feet. Wings brush past him.
The poem ascends.

In Genesis 28, Jacob, fleeing from his brother's vengeance, lies down to sleep and dreams of a ladder or staircase extending between earth and heaven, with the angels 'ascending and descending on it'. This is the obvious starting point for the poem; but the definite article in the title (which is also the title of the collection in which it first appeared) directs us also to the family of plants known as 'Jacob's Ladder' (from the small leaflets springing out from the stem). Imagine the structure of the plant reproduced in stone: descending angels would need to be nimble in managing the angles at which the leaflets spring out. And to do this gracefully, they need 'a little/lift of the wings'.

The stone staircase looks deceptively 'soft', rose-tinted (the rosiness presumably nudges us to think of rose-tinted spectacles, but also perhaps of the 'rosy-fingered dawn' of Homeric verse); this, however, is because of the harshness of the sky against which it is seen. The grey and unresponsive heaven contrasts with what seems to be an open passageway between the divine and the human. In fact the passage may be open, but it is hard enough for angels to descend, let alone for humans to ascend; Levertov's 'sharp angles' recycles the familiar pun on angles and angels. The human who attempts to climb confronts the equivalent of a mountain face; the whole body is involved in scrambling up, and our skin is scraped. Yet we can feel something under our feet: the stone is 'cut' for us to ascend. In the background here is the biblical comparison of believers with stones cut or trimmed for the building of God's temple (1 Peter 2) and the metaphor of Jesus himself as foundation or cornerstone (1 Peter 2 again, and 1 Corinthians 3.11).

So the road between earth and heaven is at the same time harsh and angular and also grounded in something more than the individual energy of the human being struggling upwards.

The effort of the whole material self to climb this ladder is one for which there are footholds already cut, and one in which the fleeting touch of angels' wings confirms that there is a destination above the awkward, stony, indirect path upwards.

'The poem ascends': the poem's job is a theological one – not to build the ladder but to climb it, knowing that the way, for all its difficulties, is prepared. There is a sort of three-stage process implied – the deceptive sense that ascent will be 'soft', something sharply distinct from the effort to penetrate the 'doubtful' sky; then the uncompromising and all-encompassing demands of the actual engagement; then the discovery of the unexpected foothold (with the multiple pun in 'consoles'). The descent of the angels is something that is going on in parallel to the upward movement: we don't *meet* angels going about their business of communicating heaven to earth, but we sense the rush of their passing, and so know that the path between earth and heaven is indeed open for words to ascend and descend.

Denise Levertov would not have identified herself as a believing Christian at the time she wrote this poem, though her upbringing had made her familiar with both Jewish and Christian thought and imagery (her father was a Jewish convert to Christianity, immensely learned in rabbinic literature). But, like all her work, it is deeply rooted in convictions about the sacredness of the physical cosmos and the poet's obligation to refresh the springs of vision (it is worth looking at some of her poems from the same early 1960s' collection about the 'holy presence' of the animal world, and also the piece called 'The Thread', which is to do with the hidden forces drawing her as a poet towards this holy depth in things). In the 1960s, she became increasingly involved with political activism – protests against racial injustice and war – and her poetry moves towards a more unconsoled world view, a more blunt moral calling-to-account, and ultimately a more explicit allegiance to Catholic

Christianity. But 'The Jacob's Ladder' remains (appropriately) a step on this journey, a declaration of faith in the language she is using in her 'ascent' that is based in the awareness of some kind of descending grace. Poetry is bruisingly difficult; but something has always already *enabled* it.

Denise Levertov

A Place of Kindness

Somewhere there is a dull room
where someone slow is moving,
stumbling from door to chair

to sit there patiently
doing nothing but be,
enjoying the quiet and warmth,

pleased with the gradual
slope of day's light
into his corner. Dull

illiterate saint, never imagining
the atrocious skills his kin
devise and use,

who are avidly, viciously active,
refining quality, increasing quantity –
million by million –
of standardized Agony-Inflicters.

Somewhere there is a dull room
no phosphorescence of guile illumines.
No scintillations
of cruelty.

Imagination could put forth
gentle feelers there.
Somewhere there must be

such a room, and someone dumb
in it, unknown to cruelty,
unknowing.

One of Levertov's poems ('In Mind') in her 1964 collection *O Taste and See* imagines two rival identities within the poet: one that is innocent, dignified and kind but with no imagination, the other 'a/ turbulent moon-ridden girl/ or old woman, or both', who 'knows strange songs –/ but she is not kind'. As Levertov became more and more deeply engaged in public and political witness, this particular duality is rethought. In the present poem (from the 1970s), the 'Dull/ illiterate saint', contemplating the way that the light falls in his dull little room, is set against the brilliance, 'the atrocious skills', of his fellow human beings. In the unexciting surroundings of the saint's environment, kindness is still possible; the dangerous blaze and sparkle of cruelty is utterly unknown.

Thus far, the 'saint' is like the first of Levertov's personae in the 1964 poem, innocent and benign; but this second poem interrogates the conclusion that innocence has no imagination. In the quiet room described, 'Imagination could put forth/ gentle feelers'; the implication is that kindness and imagination may after all belong together, that to be a stranger to the endlessly inventive brutality of human beings to one another is not a deprivation. There is an authentic use of the imagination for the sake of compassion.

To realize this requires us to resist the 'scintillations' of inhumanity. There is a superficial glamour to the complexities and shocks and apparent energy of evildoing that needs some demythologizing: inhumanity is not at heart creative or imaginative; it reduces rather than enhances or enlarges the world. Imagination may not in and of itself be 'kind' – the earlier poem is not wholly astray by any means – but it is not fully itself without the capacity both to understand the other (human and non-human) and to be drawn to the *affirmation* of the other. The subtlety of cruelty is skin deep, because it cannot break out of the self's desire for its own gratification, its lust for sensation. It does not move towards a new world; it only manipulates the unequal power reactions of the world that is already known. C. S. Lewis in *A Grief Observed*, his autobiographical reflection on bereavement, writes about the temptation to think of God as a 'divine Sadist', deliberately brutal to his creation; what delivers us from this temptation, says Lewis, is considering the sterile nature of cruelty. It cannot *make* or *generate* anything different from the ego.

The dull and wordless saint turns out to be less a prisoner than the ingenious torturer; cruelty is unequivocally evil, but it is also boring, the work of 'standardized' agents who have no real individuality. Ironically, it is the slowness and stillness of the dull saint that is the ground on which the gentler and truer imagination grows. The freedom to enjoy, to be 'pleased' with the movement of light across the floor, is more than the dramas of a greedy self.

We know from Levertov's life that she did not and could not have interpreted this as a recommendation for withdrawal from public life into the monastic cell. But if we need to be kind in a manically cruel world, we must start by bringing the greedy self to the 'dull room' of the physical, the everyday, silencing its cries for attention and gratification. Ultimately, kindness goes along with *seeing more*, inhabiting a larger world. Kindness of some sort, in other words, belongs with art – whatever short-term impressions may suggest otherwise – because if it does not, art will not bring us into the new world we need to discover for our healing. Levertov is not saying don't be angry about atrocities, but watch for the way anger can open the doors again to drama and glamour and, ultimately, to a shrunken and subhuman world. First, learn to be dull. That is where authentic imagination starts, in the 'stumbling from door to chair', in the absorbing of the warmth of a place in the world, in 'unknowing'.

Gwyneth Lewis

How to Read Angels

Yes, information, but that's never all,
there's some service, a message. A lie dispelled,
something forgiven, an alternative world
glimpsed, for a moment, what you wanted to hear
but never thought possible. You feel a fool
but do something anyway and are filled
with delight as you unfold

like a wing in a thermal. If it's peace
you're left with after your left-of-field
encounter, that's angels. If you feel less fear
and trust yourself less. But beware
of other voices, easier to bear
which sound more like angels than angels do
but leave you in turmoil, saying 'More. More.
  More.'

This is one of a sequence of twelve short poems about angels, understood specifically as whatever it is that speaks to us in moments of pain or bewilderment from completely outside ourselves (they can be read illuminatingly alongside Fanny Howe's poems on angels, including the one in this collection (p. 134), or Olga Sedakova's 'The Angel of Rheims' (p. 269). But Gwyneth Lewis recognizes that what seem to be voices from outside ourselves can't be taken completely on trust: in another poem in the sequence, she writes, 'demons are us in disguise/ as angel voices'. How do we learn discernment?

Well, here are some rules of thumb. Truthfulness, forgiveness, hope – these are reliable signs that whatever has been sensed or guessed at is more than just the contents of our own mind; even if what we hear is what we actually long to hear 'but never thought possible', this does not necessarily mean that we are telling ourselves consoling stories. What is convincing is the surprise that something we wanted might after all be thinkable; the other poem already mentioned suggests that one tell-tale feature of 'demonic' communication is that it never surprises us, only amplifies what we already know. To be surprised and then to be at peace with the new look of things is a good test. And the initially surprising linkage of being less afraid and trusting yourself less makes sense if you can think of the angelic message or service being something that draws you away from the habit of seeing yourself at the centre of everything. We learn not to be afraid partly by loosening our passion for control, by recognizing the inescapable riskiness of the world we're in; and if we can indeed let go of the obsession with shaping the world to our own requirements of safety and reassurance, we shall also learn a saving scepticism about our capacity to organize or understand where and what we are. If we are ready to live with risk and act with hope, something will 'unfold/ like a wing in a thermal', a wonderful image for the release of knowing that you can let yourself be carried.

So authentic angelic voices are those that enlarge and release – though that enlargement and release come at the cost of accepting that we are not, cannot be and (most liberating of all) *need* not be omnipotent. The paradox is that angels help us to live within our limits by showing us what can come to us from beyond our limits: once we face the truth that we are finite, we open the door to the real life of what is not ourselves.

If we don't face that truth, we shall not be able to encounter the other as really other to us, and so can receive nothing from them. The deceptive voice that can sometimes sound uncannily like an angelic visitation urges us on to extend our boundaries in an unlimited process of acquisition. But the growth we need as humans is not this build-up of what we possess but the increasing receptivity to the nourishment that the strangeness of the world and other people and God have to share with us.

The service of angels to us is to remind us that joy has to be received, not constructed or seized on for storage. As with other poems about angels, Lewis's sequence does not speculate about what exactly angels 'are': the focus is on what it is that acts to enlarge us so that we have more room to be hospitable to the reality before us, and so acts to check and expose our manic longing to inflate what we are and occupy more space. As the last poem in Lewis's sequence suggests, we look to a time when we no longer need such reminders but have become real natives of the painful and dangerous place we actually live in: when we can forego angelic messages because we see the healing Christ 'bringing cool dock leaves of mercy'. But meanwhile: we are still learners in the school of joy, surprised into new perception by the messages that break through into selves that are both deeply frightened and ludicrously self-confident.

Saunders Lewis

Prayer at the End

It's an experience everyone has that nobody else
  will know.
Each on his own in his own way
Owns his own dying
Through the millions of years of the human race.
You can look at it, you can sometimes recognize
  the moment;
You cannot empathize with anyone at that moment
When the breathing and the person stop together.
And then? Nothing reaches out to the then but a
  prayer groping.
Such a sorry creature is man, such a baby his
  imagination:
'In my Father's house there are many mansions',
As poor as our own, just as much earth-bound,
His intuition too in the days when he emptied
  himself.
And only this way can we ourselves picture hope:
'He is seated on the right hand of God the Father
  almighty' –
A general hailed with jubilation through the city of
  Rome
After the hazardous enterprise in a Persia of creation
And crowned as Augustus, Co-Augustus with his
  Father –

How laughable, the supreme assertions of our faith.
And around us remain silence and the pit of
annihilation
Into which our universe will soundlessly fall some
night.
Our words cannot trace the borders of silence
Or say God with meaning.
One prayer remains for all, to go silently to the
silent.

How to translate the title? The original Welsh is *Gweddi'r Terfyn*, and *terfyn* (like its Latin parent, *terminus*) can mean quite a few different things – 'end', 'goal', 'limit', 'boundary', 'frontier'. Perhaps 'Prayer at the Limit' would capture something of its bleak extremity – the limit not only of language but also of endurance. But the poem opens with an unambiguous reference to death, the one thing that has to be experienced in absolute solitude, in the sense that it can never be talked about *as* an experience; you cannot 'empathize', because there is no other human subject there for you to identify with. 'Nothing reaches out to the then', the 'afterwards' of death. And our imagination balks at this brick wall and responds with the crudest of metaphors.

Saunders Lewis was (and remains) a controversial figure in modern Welsh literature. Founder of the Welsh nationalist party, Plaid Cymru, imprisoned in 1936 for political protest (arson at an RAF bombing school in North Wales), advocate of neutrality in the Second World War (and, unfortunately and more than tangentially, a fascist sympathizer in the 1930s), a brilliant critic and innovative dramatist in the Welsh language, he was at once the most original and the most troubling Welsh literary figure of the twentieth century. As a Catholic convert, he was a rarity in Welsh-speaking circles and not a very welcome one. This poem, published in 1973, did nothing to soften his reputation as someone who relished shocking his public. The casual statement that Christ's language for the mysteries of eternal life was as childish as that of any other human being, the mockery of the formula of the creeds about Christ being seated at the Father's right hand, like a Roman general promoted to the status of co-emperor after a successful campaign in Persia – these led some readers to think that Lewis had virtually abandoned his faith.

But the poem's angry intensity really depends on taking orthodox theology seriously rather than otherwise. If Christ did indeed 'empty himself' in the Incarnation, if he truly became human, he *could not do other* than speak our limited and hopelessly inadequate language about God. If he has indeed gone before us to clear a place for us in the loving presence of the eternal Source of everything, that hope will always be inflected by our unredeemed fantasies of what 'victory' means. What we say as humans – even what Christ says as human – cannot articulate anything about God that is adequate, anything that is not, ultimately, ridiculous. The tension lies in the fact that something has been done, revealed, transacted, that is unequivocally the divine act of identification with us for the sake of our healing and salvation, whether or not there are words for it. It doesn't matter that we can't help talking crudely and childishly about it; but once we have seen what we are doing, once we have heard the absurdity for what it is, then it is time to be silent.

It is not a passive or resigned silence, though, not a sort of resentful abdication of the search to know and be known by God. The silence that Lewis points to is itself *prayer*, feeling its way into what cannot be described, feeling its way towards the wordlessness of God. The recognition that we are always on the verge of talking trivial nonsense about God, because the gap between reality and language here is so absolute, can and must coexist with the recognition that our nonsense is nonsense *because of* the scale of the sovereign reality that it tries so pathetically to show us, a reality apprehended by a sheer trust in a 'then' or a 'there' beyond our failure and our dying, a level of reality impenetrably silent so far as the life of our ideas goes, but entirely directed towards us in the form of saving and life-giving care. We all die alone; in the last analysis, there is nothing to talk about where death is concerned because no one can 'own' their dying in retrospect as we 'own' the experiences of our lives. But the very paradox of this universally shared isolation can be seen as a shared prayer of silence, the one thing that can finally hold us together and that we can long for together; the one thing poetry can appeal to and for.

Maitreyabandhu (Ian Johnson)

The Postulant

He felt himself to be the painful intersection
between two blissful worlds – a water splash
or knot of air. He'd closed his eyes on this world –
the sun just rising in the east, the fret of birds,
his frown from where two circles overlapped –
and where no flowers grew, his heaving breath
was chain-link or the figure of eight rotating.
When night fell, the space between two worlds
was all the shape he made, an empty dark without
moons or badgers while some piston pressure
or odd exertion was pushing the spheres apart
as if a great machine would move the aching stars.
What he thought to be himself he didn't know:
his pain was all that stopped the worlds unite.

For Buddhists, there is no such thing as the self. It is a proposition guaranteed to produce alarm and resistance in most non-Buddhists; and anyone endeavouring to write poetry out of such a perception might be thought to be aiming at the impossible. Maitreyabandhu is manifestly unbothered by this. He writes – as he does in this sonnet – very explicitly out of his Buddhist convictions, but he also writes poems of quiet, acute observation that might well be read as showing what a disbelief in the substantial self looks like in action. It is not coldly impersonal; but it has something to do with clearing away the kind of autobiographical agenda that makes you look at the poet, not at what the poet is seeing.

This poem, however, addresses a central theme in Buddhist thinking and devotion. A postulant is someone making the first steps towards monastic commitment; so we can expect that what is being explored is the early stages of the recognition that arises in meditative practice. Start imagining yourself as simply a place where processes converge and briefly tie themselves together (the splash, the knot). Step back from the immediacy of the world you can see, attend to your breathing (the references to 'chain-link' and 'figure of eight' have to do with particular techniques of following your breath around the body); you are making a hollow space within this world, making your physical presence a zone of overlapping realities – the specific sense experience you have closed your eyes on, and the uncaused, unborn, unending thereness that surrounds. The only thing that gives you shape and substance is the fact of overlapping – like the shared segment of two circles in a Venn diagram. The shape is only there because two circles share territory. Maitreyabandhu evokes the formless dark ('without moons or badgers', a wonderfully memorable, surprising and precise characterization) in which all that you are aware of is the rhythmical movement of breath, the 'piston pressure' coming and going, pushing the circles away from this overlapping territory so as to dissolve the shape they have created.

But the paradox is that as the worlds are pushed apart and the overlap shrinks away, the worlds *cease to be separate*. The meditating 'you' is still conscious of the stress of living between worlds, but it begins to grasp that the painful sense that you belong in neither world is itself what makes the worlds different or even suggest that they are in conflict. The more the meditating breath is 'pushing the spheres apart', the more the pain is recognized as the very substance of the self – and so as that from which deliverance is being sought. Instead of being the painful place between two realms of joy or at-homeness, the self can let go of its defensive obsession with its solidity and durability. The wholeness of the world, experienced without egotistical distortion, and the wholeness of what is simply 'there', can now map on to one another. And this is the bliss of enlightenment: the 'extinction' of which Buddhists speak is not the cancellation of some vital principle but the dissolution of a fiction that imprisons us in crises, dramas, sufferings, all of which take it for granted that each of us contains a solid core of identity beyond all relationship that is always being threatened. If this is not the case, what can threaten? If we can live without feeling threatened, we can live in the relatedness to all other life and process that is actually natural to us. The sensual world we see and feel is not separate from the 'thereness' of unborn and everlasting reality, nor is it swallowed up in it: we live not in between two worlds but simultaneously in two perceptions that are in fact not two – not rival perceptions, each trying to crowd out the other – but in a material present that is saturated with the uncaused and unbegun.

Noticing and attending to the pain is where this starts; meditation begins not with a flight to some transcendent realm but with sitting and breathing, simply existing as a breathing body within the world – stepping away from *engagement* with the senses, yet not denying them, letting the imageless, unconfined depth expand in the mind. Pain is what arises from the self's restless hunger to be stimulated and gratified, whether by experience of the world or by some imagined 'mystical' experience of the Beyond. So sit in the darkness until this hungry, fearful, grasping activity is nowhere to be seen or sensed. The 'not-self' moment is not a destruction but a reconciliation, unimaginable and indescribable from this side of the moment: emptiness and fullness, self-forgetting and homecoming together.

Paul Mariani

Holy Saturday

A dream the old song has it, just
a dream. I was driving the old beige
Camry going round and around
and around searching for the Jeep
I was sure I'd parked or would have parked
near the decaying wharfs down by the sea
the day before but unable now
to find it though I kept circling back
and forth and back alley after alley
without any luck then finally thought
to press the panic button on my key
fob and yes I thought I could just
make out the beep beep sound
so that I had to believe my car
was waiting out there somewhere
as now fog and night descended.
It was then I remember seeing two
middle-aged women sitting in an old
van one at the foot the other at the head
so I rolled down my window to ask
if they could hear the beep beep
and if they could would they please
please be good enough to tell me
where the signal was coming from
because as I explained my hearing

wasn't very good now and I couldn't tell
if I was even headed in the right direction.
They were friendly enough and both
smiled back at me and asked if it was
a pizza truck or an ambulance
I was looking for or if the thing
was red or white the whole time
these pleasant smiles fitted to their faces
until it dawned on me that I would have to
keep on searching by myself though by now
everything was dark and the signal I was sure
I'd heard I think kept growing dimmer
though it had to be out there oh God
it had to be out there somewhere
still waiting for me to find it.

Dreams are often about loss or lostness: we don't know where we are; we have somehow forgotten something all-important; we are pushed into a context where we have no idea what needs to be done or for which we have failed to prepare; our lives are suddenly and dramatically at risk. Mariani's poem, with its lack of punctuation, brilliantly evokes the way in which dreams seem to unfold in unbroken sequence, even when their images and their narrative are random and discontinuous when thought about; and it depicts the fearful and tantalizing sensation, familiar in dreams, of being just on the edge of grasping what's happening only to find another round of disorientation.

'Holy Saturday', the day between Good Friday and Easter: a good many Christians have found it a day of confused or muted emotions, a day when nothing seems quite right or appropriate. After the tragic bleakness of Good Friday, this day is simply empty: drab, subdued, even embarrassed. Teasingly,

Mariani weaves in a few little details of biblical and liturgical imagery. Searching through the streets and alleyways is reminiscent of the Bride in the Song of Songs, searching 'in the streets and in the squares' for 'him whom my soul loves' (Song of Songs 3.2), asking others whether they have seen the beloved – imagery that has long been applied in the liturgy to Mary Magdalene in her questioning where the Lord has been laid. The women sitting in the van, 'one at the foot the other at the head', evoke the angels at the tomb of Jesus in John 20.12. The question of whether the lost car is 'red or white the whole time' might echo the words of Isaiah 1.18, 'though your sins are like scarlet, they shall be white as snow'; or perhaps the 'robe dipped in blood' worn by the conquering Word of God in Revelation 19.13?

But the central image is that of the 'signal', the sign coming and going, not where we thought it was, fading away, not giving directions that we can follow – 'the signal I was sure/ I'd heard I think', the punctuation-free onrush of the words capturing skilfully the poise between certainty and doubt. Something is there, waiting to be found, we know that (don't we?); where is it, where do we even begin to look? On this unique day of the year, when the symbols (signals) of Christian art and liturgy are muffled or muted (decorations are removed from churches, images veiled, there is no reserved sacrament on the altar), we can't fail to be aware of loss. Good Friday has left the world denuded, but at the same time has left the world haunted by the echo of a signal – a sound that seems to come from nowhere identifiable simply telling us that what has been lost has not vanished but is waiting for us to find it.

The faith that Mariani's dream articulates is – by the end of the poem – coming close to the limits of what we can live with, close to a note of desperation ('it had to be out there oh God/ it had to be out there'). But there is no waking up just yet. We are held in the waiting, the confusion of knowing we heard something, saw something, knew something 'the day before' when the car was parked (or was it?). There is a hint of Eliot's magi: 'Were we led all that way for/ Birth or death?' – and also perhaps of Auden's 'Compline' poem in the *Horae Canonicae* sequence, where the speaker, escaping at the day's end into the darkness and chaotic symbolism of dreaming, cannot recall 'A thing between noon and three' – but is haunted by 'a sound', a rhythm, a feeling of altered motion.

What exactly *has* been seen or heard? And is Mariani's lost vehicle 'a pizza truck or an ambulance', a source of food or a source of rescue? This question from the women in the van, like their other question about whether the car is 'red or white the whole time', links the lost object firmly to some confused recognition in the dream that what's been lost is something of life and death importance. It is rather as though the actual moment of rupture or loss is too enormous and too painful for *thinking* and has to be approached only through the roundabout paths of dream (as Auden implies). Holy Saturday, with all its muffled grey silences and its veiling of clear signals, is nonetheless the moment when we sense the first stirrings of what Good Friday means. And we know at some inarticulate, subconscious level that the mystery is both more than we can bear and more than we can hope for.

Thomas Merton

The Fall

There is no where in you a paradise that is no place
and there
You do not enter except without a story.

To enter there is to become unnameable.

Whoever is there is homeless for he has no door
and no identity
with which to go out and to come in.

Whoever is nowhere is nobody, and therefore
cannot exist except as unborn:
No disguise will avail him anything

Such a one is neither lost nor found.

But he who has an address is lost.

They fall, they fall into apartments and are securely
established!
They find themselves in streets. They are licensed
To proceed from place to place
They now know their own names
They can name several friends and know
Their own telephones must some time ring.

If all telephones ring at once, if all names are
shouted at once and
all cars crash at one crossing:
If all cities explode and fly away in dust
Yet identities refuse to be lost. There is a name and
number for everyone.

There is a definite place for bodies, there are pigeon
holes for ashes:
Such security can business buy!

Who would dare to go nameless in so secure a
universe?
Yet, to tell the truth, only the nameless are at home
in it.

They bear with them in the center of nowhere the
unborn flower of nothing:
This is the paradise tree. It must remain unseen
until words end and arguments are silent.

Merton had a modest but solid reputation as a poet before he entered the monastery of Gethsemani in Kentucky in 1941, and he continued to write poetry during his years as a monk. His style changes markedly from the late 1950s onwards: he often turns to the surreal, fragmented manner characteristic of much of his imaginative prose, especially when addressing the social issues that preoccupied him more and more in the late 1950s and early 1960s, but he is also during this period much influenced by his reading in East Asian spiritual traditions, especially Buddhism and Taoism. The poem here reflects his exploration in this religious world, which was to continue with increasing intensity up to his death in 1968.

It is difficult to date the poem precisely, but it echoes the preoccupations of the early to mid-1960s, when Merton often wrote about the various ways in which both Christianity and other traditions spoke about the *point vierge*, the untouched centre of human reality in which or from which a vision of reality was possible that would be uncorrupted by the cravings and concepts generated by the ego. This 'no where' is accessible only to those who forego the story that solidifies our images of the self. Our 'fall' from the primordial non-duality and selflessness of awareness into the destructive habits of routine consciousness is the acquisition of a place to settle that is clearly mapped and clearly protected: 'he who has an address is lost'.

The poem sketches the different kinds of 'address' in which we are trapped, depending for our sense of ourselves on the licence given to us by others and our availability for communication (the ringing telephone; a Merton writing today would no doubt have included the social media account). We can always be sure that we exist because our names and numbers are secure: there will always be someone else to tell us that we are real, up to and including the moment when we become labelled and numbered bundles of ash (and Merton is presumably thinking not only of the neat disposal of cremated remains in a columbarium but also of the ash left after the firestorm of nuclear attack, another major preoccupation for him in these years). And the paradox on which the poem insists is that this secure identity in which our names are known forever 'freezes' a massive alienation between us and the world of which we are part. We are never at home in the world so long as we need to be named by others; 'only the nameless are at home', only those without an address, the 'homeless' who have no door for going out and coming in, are grounded in the world as it is. While words and arguments survive, the silent centre remains a secret.

A Christian or Jewish reader may wonder how this is to be reconciled with the biblical language of God knowing the names of those who are summoned into the new life of transfigured community – and indeed with the significance of names and naming ceremonies in these traditions. But the idea that God alone knows my true or eternal name (cf. Revelation 2.17) is not as alien as one might think to Merton's language. What is toxic for us is to trust in the 'security' of knowing we are locked in to the speech and imagination of others in the world, insisting that we are safe because we have a place in the systems and languages of human power. To believe that we are named or recognized by God is ultimately to say that neither we nor any other finite subject have access to what is at the heart of our existence; our identity can never be a possession, not even for the ego. Dietrich Bonhoeffer (see pp. 16) wrote a poem in the prison camp articulating his bewilderment as to who he 'really' was and concluding with a bald expression of trust that God held the answer. As against the common caricature of Buddhist or Taoist thinking, the point is not that human relations are simply illusory or that the deepest reality is 'impersonal', but that the root from which we live is not an object for inspection. Our compassionate engagement with one another is the fruit of this radical acceptance that no human identity is a 'thing' to be owned. Recognizing this is the way back – or forwards – to the 'paradise tree' we have lost in word and argument and the stories that we ceaselessly tell ourselves about ourselves.

Larissa Miller

It was on the Very Last Day of Creation

It was on the very last day of creation
that speech rose into rhyme,
when the Lord looked at
the work of His hands and suddenly something
sang in Him, as though a string was touched
in the soul and began to sing all at once:
it trembled and caught fire
and all the words, that had lived apart,
prayed through tears: 'O Lord,
O make it so that all can come together,
fuse, interweave.' From that time forwards
rhyme trembles like a flame,
born of two words,
at the height of the Divine game.

The climax of God's creative work is not simply humanity – so this sonnet argues – or even human speech, but *rhyme.* God finishes the work of creating and there is something like a firing of neurons: a connectedness suddenly appears in all things, a fiery thread weaving apparently discrete, diverse things together. God's own inner reality is activated anew in song, and the created soul sings in response.

The imagery is rich and has strong affinities with various traditional metaphors and mythologies. The idea of the human soul/spirit as a string to be touched by God is one that looks back to early Christian writers like Ephrem the Syrian and Augustine (and it is used by George Herbert in the seventeenth century also). But the notion of a divine 'harmonic' echoed in creation evokes a distinctive Russian Christian interest in the divine Wisdom, Sophia, existing in both uncreated and created form. This is, in its way, a 'Sophian' poem. But, like the theological speculations about Sophia that flourished in nineteenth- and early twentieth-century Russia, it also owes a good deal to the Jewish Kabbalistic world and the mythical model of creation as a dispersal of the divine glory into the diversity of the material world (compare Celan's poem, 'Your Beyondness', p. 62). The names of all things cry out to be reunited in the primordial flame of connection.

Two things that no translation of the poem can easily bring out are the use of *half*-rhymes in the first few lines (*tvoren'ya/ govoren'e, zapelo/ zadelo*), and the assonance in the sequence of words, 'come together, /fuse, interweave' – *soslosh'*, *slilos'*, *splelos'*. It is as though the poem is itself straining towards rhyme, embodying the tearful frustration of human words or names as they try to find a way back to one another through the long story of creation. There is a moment of possibility at the very beginning of things, but creation already exists in a condition of differentiation, and has to find a way of honouring that *difference* without being frozen in *disruption* or disharmony. So language itself cries out for healing as soon as it finds its voice.

Poetry – rhyming poetry – is what God makes possible in language, so it is implied. It is not itself a complete healing (the tantalizing assonances and not-quite-rhymes suggest as much), yet it gestures in a unique way towards this hope. Two words are linked in the firing of a rhyme, and this reflects the divine 'game' – *igra*, surely referring to the 'playing' of Wisdom in the presence of God that is spoken of in the great hymn to Wisdom in the eighth chapter of the book of Proverbs. In other words, it is not just that poetry (or human creativity in general) is a kind of sharing in God's creative act because it produces what is new; the specific thing about poetry that makes it a reflection of the divine flame of connectivity is the way in which words, the sense and references for which are so different, may be held together in a verbal pattern.

Russian is a language exceptionally rich in possibilities for rhyme; other languages – English and German, for example – are less well blessed, but may find other vehicles for displaying this connectivity, alliteration, assonance of vowels and so on. The point is that a poetry which embodies what Miller sees as the primordial possibilities of language must be one that somehow allows uncontrolled, unexpected links between words to emerge in a way that suggests the song at the beginning of the world is shared by God and what God has made. All good poetry, we could say, is invested in puns and 'chance' echoes, in wordplay and the unexpected, almost absurd, resonances that run through all our speech, joining things up behind our backs. Language, Iris Murdoch wrote, 'makes jokes in its sleep'. And that is one reason for seeing language itself as a vehicle of grace.

Larissa Miller

I'm on about My Own Stuff Again, and Again

I'm on about my own stuff again, and again,
but you see, You too, O God, repeat yourself,
and Your subjects are not new,
and Your pictures are hopelessly similar:
sky, drizzle, rustle of grass . . .
You have Your own, I my own, how could it be
  otherwise?
The rain falls – together we merge in the crying.
We have coincided – how could we not?
I am in Your likeness and my failures
are only an unnoticeable part of Yours.

If poetry is some kind of embodying of God's pervasive wisdom within the created order, it might seem that it was obliged to be constantly renewing itself, discovering new subjects, new worlds to conquer verbally. In this teasing little piece, Miller wryly observes how our writing returns repeatedly to the writer's ego; the opening words in Russian could be rendered 'Me again'. But God evidently has the same problem of repetition: nothing new in the subjects of God's art, but the unbroken processes of the world constantly recycled. God and the poet alike can only deal with what is theirs; God's 'Me again' is the bare fact of God's steady presence at the heart of all action and process; God can't help being unoriginal.

The poet's 'failures' or 'setbacks' or 'misfortunes', the poet's inability to break out from the familiar, are in fact a sign of the divine image in the human imagination – a reflection of God's 'failures'. It is a striking and rather mischievous turn of phrase. God's 'failure' is simply the fact that God can't stop being God; so our failure is perhaps likewise our inability not to be what or who or where we are. If we are indeed doomed to such failure, what this means for our poetry is that it can never escape its rootedness in what we actually and physically are and in the regularities of our shared world. There are no new worlds to conquer, only the same one over and over again – and not to conquer, but to re-enter and re-present. And our faithfulness in returning to the familiar in the hope of finding the new within it is the point at which we as artists 'merge' or 'coincide' with God: when the rain falls, our perception of it as weeping slips into the inexhaustible range of meanings that have been woven into the phenomenon from the beginning by the hand of God.

The poem is in part a protest against a hyper-romantic view of poetry (and, by implication, other arts too), a concept of creativity that demands constant revolution. But constant revolution is unthinkable, simply because the world we are encountering is a world the reality of which is founded on the faithfulness of its creator; we are never going to be able to escape repetition. Miller's insight might be compared to that of Euros Bowen (p. 43), when he writes about how poetry is pulled back inexorably to the same old themes, despite the protests of those who want it to be topical or relevant. The themes are made new *in* us, not by our efforts to become what we are not. So part of what's required of the poet is the modesty not to try to escape. The massively ambitious claim that humans are made in the divine image turns out to be a signpost back to the most ordinary and routine realities, the grass and the rain, and the real creative gift of poetic representation is the freedom not to find this stultifyingly dull – to see the routine landscape freshly each time we look. If it really is God who is recycling or repeating God's self in and beneath it all, there will always be more to see and know.

Miller has written about the aspiration to 'wordless' poetry, a poetic response to what there is that does not seek to interrupt the world but to 'flow' with it. It is always within this that we find renewal. As another brief poem from the 1990s puts it, we move from the common heritage of birth and growth towards 'somewhere/ where it's all fresh'; but that 'somewhere' is not a timeless paradise, it is the localized reality of physical experience as time moves on, experience that produces (in a very striking phrase) 'blood, pain and anecdote'. We go on living through the same environment of fragility, sustained by the same rhythms of the world around; and those rhythms are made new for us and in us as we plot our location again and again in a landscape that does not alter in itself but which we learn to see from countless new angles, often with cost and struggle, which in turn we must learn to narrate with honesty and patience – 'pain and anecdote'. And we keep on resisting the seduction, the short cut, of fantasizing a different world. 'Me again' may not after all be such a bad thing if it is grounded in a recognition of and a responsive attunement with the 'Me again' of the Creator.

Les Murray

Poetry and Religion

Religions are poems. They concert
our daylight and dreaming mind, our
emotions, instinct, breath and native gesture

into the only whole thinking: poetry.
Nothing's said till it's dreamed out in words
and nothing's true that figures in words only.

A poem, compared with an arrayed religion,
may be like a soldier's one short marriage night
to die and live by. But that is a small religion.

Full religion is the large poem in loving repetition;
like any poem, it must be inexhaustible and
  complete
with turns where we ask Now why did the poet do
  that?

You can't pray a lie, said Huckleberry Finn;
you can't poe one either. It is the same mirror:
mobile, glancing, we call it poetry,

fixed centrally, we call it religion,
and God is the poetry caught in any religion,
caught, not imprisoned. Caught as in a mirror

that he attracted, being in the world as poetry
is in the poem, a law against its closure.
There'll always be religion around while there is
  poetry

or a lack of it. Both are given, and intermittent,
as the action of those birds – crested pigeon, rosella
  parrot –
who fly with wings shut, then beating, and again
  shut.

There is a lazy way of comparing poetry and the language of religious faith, often working on the assumption that both are examples of language when it is not 'on oath' – not obliged to be exact but licensed to be impressionistic and non-'literal'. Les Murray is very definitely not a lazy poet in any sense, and his comparison of poetry and religion is far more searching and surprising. He begins by telling us what religions actually *do*: they bring together all our diverse levels of thinking and imagining and all our engrained habits of negotiating the world around us; and in doing this they show themselves as essentially poetic. And this in turn tells us something about poetry: that it is not simply an arrangement of words. It is part of an engagement with truth that must extend beyond the words alone, yet the words are still crucial.

Murray turns away from the cliché that the truth of either poetic or religious utterance is 'beyond words' or 'beyond definitions'. Poetry aims to do in a small space what religion does in a large, communal and historically extended space: to hold a mirror to a formidable range of shifting, threatening, exhilarating 'givens' that require us to adjust to their presence and make sense of them. Poetry is necessarily occasional and local; it dances around between these 'givens' and catches a reflection where it can, perhaps as if holding a mirror beneath a leafy tree with the sunlight darting and quivering through at different angles, while we shift about, trying to find the angle at which to slant the mirror so as to reflect a beam. Religion is found in 'loving repetition'; we have learned at least some of the moves of the dance, we know a bit how to deploy our words, what angle to hold them at – though there are unexpected or disorientating moments when we can only wonder why we are nudged to turn *this* way rather than that.

'You can't pray a lie, said Huckleberry Finn;/ you can't poe one either': the reference to Huckleberry Finn is very much Murray, appealing to the unvarnished earthy honesty of Mark Twain's fictional young roughneck, a kind of holy fool. And as for the otherwise unknown verb, 'poe' – Murray is mischievously tossing out at us a possible verb for the action of poetry which is the same as a familiar word of schoolboy smut, the kind of innocent profanity that a Huck Finn sort of character might use. Whether praying or 'poeing', the action is about holding the mirror: we can't choose what the mirror will show.

And what the mirror does is 'catch'. In one of the most memorable phrases of this poem, Murray says that God is 'caught, not imprisoned' in the language of faith, as a fleeting image is caught in a mirror. The truth of religious language, you might say, is neither that it is an exact description, a 'capture' of its object, nor that it is an effective but non-literal evocation. It is a fleeting gleam of what is real. Murray is an idiosyncratic but fundamentally orthodox Catholic; he is not interested in religious language as well-meaning uplift or edifying noise, but in the truthfulness of what is said and the sacramental reality of what is done. But both the truthfulness and the sacramental presence are as vivid and as elusive as the truth of the poem.

God inhabits the world as poetry does the poem – that is, as a presence that pushes us further than what we have already said or grasped. The poem we have read and mastered once and for all is not much of a poem; the world we have mastered once and for all is not much of a world. The two discourses of poetry and faith are inseparable; and they both alike come and go. Religion is there implicitly both in poetry and in its (felt) absence. And the poem ends with the wonderful image of birds in flight clenching their wings and gliding, then flapping them again and then closing them, a rhythm of action and surrender interwoven, the strenuousness of the beating wings, the yielding to a current carrying the bird forwards. As in the work of poetic writing, we work *and* we depend, we struggle *and* we coast on the currents of grace.

Les Murray

The Chimes of Neverwhere

How many times did the Church prevent war?
Who knows? Those wars did not occur.
How many numbers don't count before ten?
Treasures of the Devil in Neverwhere.

The neither state of Neverwhere
is hard to place as near or far
since all things that didn't take place are there
and things that have lost the place they took:

Herr Hitler's buildings, King James' cigar,
the happiness of Armenia,
the Abelard children, the Manchus' return
and there with the Pictish Grammar Book,

The girl who returned your dazzled look
and the mornings you might have woke to her
are your waterbed in Neverwhere.
There shine the dukes of Australia

and all the great poems that never were
quite written, and every balked invention.
There too are the Third AIF and its war
in which I and boys my age were killed

more pointlessly with each passing year.
There, too, half the works of sainthood are
the enslavements, tortures, rapes, despair
deflected by them from the actual

to beat on the human-sacrifice drum
that billions need not die to hear
since Christ's love of them struck it dumb
and his agony keeps it in Neverwhere.

How many times did the Church bring peace?
More times than it happened. Leave it back there:
the children we didn't let out of there need it,
for the Devil's at home in Neverwhere.

A robust pushing back against one kind of secular polemic: how effective has the Church been in realizing what it talks about? We can't know, says Murray, and it's the devil's work to make us focus on might-have-beens. We can't know how much worse our history might have been without the presence of the community of faith; we can't know (in effect) just how bad our situation is, how vanishingly unlikely any kind of moral success might be in our world.

Murray builds up a witty succession of counterfactuals, on both the public and the private stages, from a Hitler who continued training as an architect to the human loves you never pursued and the great poems you never got around to writing – and also the wars in which you would have died. 'Sainthood' is not quantifiable; but what if 'Neverwhere', the land of counterfactuals, were populated by all the possibilities that the lives of holy people averted, in ways that are completely inscrutable to us? How many outrages have been 'deflected . . . from the actual' (a memorable phrase) by sanctity? The syntax of the last two stanzas is complicated, but the argument seems to be that, in our history, the pressure is always on to revert to human sacrifice as the default mode; we solve problems by killing, one way or another. But in the great central act of 'deflection', which is the life and death of Christ for whom all lives are equally loveable, the drumbeat urging us to slaughter is rendered inaudible. Christ's saving 'agony' keeps the idea that pain and terror are inevitable for all firmly in the land of counterfactuals. And what was actually needed to avoid slaughter and atrocity is there in 'Neverwhere', a potential never realized; don't try to excavate it, leave it there with all those lives trapped in unfulfilledness. They are going to need it; and it will be there for them in the mysterious economy of healing that the fact of Christ has brought into being.

'It might have been worse' is often a feeble and unconvincing response to the facts of suffering or failure. I don't think Murray is offering any such bromide. He is doing at least two things. First, he is inviting us to remember the massive seriousness of human pain and disaster, what seems to be the omnipresence of destructiveness in our world, and reminding us of what has been called 'the problem of good'. It is not just that the presence of evil in a world created by a benevolent God is a problem; it is just as much a problem that there is unpredictable and incalculable holiness, generosity and mercy in a world where every kind of pressure pushes us towards the abyss of cruelty and despair. And, second, he is defining our task as attending to what is actually in front of our eyes. Eliot at the beginning of 'East Coker', the first of the *Four Quartets*, tells us that 'What might have been is an abstraction/ Remaining a perpetual possibility/ Only in a world of speculation'. Murray is bolder, naming the world of speculation as the devil's territory, the unreal world where we long to settle down in a reality that accords with our wishes and projections.

It is not that the historical failures of the Church are being minimized or whitewashed here, simply that the Church's overall effectiveness in its mission is not something that can be available for some kind of global scrutiny, with metrics that would allow us to say whether its existence had been worthwhile. The job of Christians, including Christian poets, is to keep their eyes on the real; if the real includes some indication that holy lives deflect the curse of our condition – and the real certainly includes the life and death and resurrection of Jesus – that is what we need to hold on to. And holding on to it allows us to see 'Neverwhere' not only as the repository of lost dreams and hopes but also as the rubbish heap of horrors stillborn and tragedies averted. None of us has the perspective that would allow us to draw up a balance sheet. Stick to what's there; always good advice for poets.

Paul Murray

The Rock

First, it blocks your way
then opens it, an amazing,
improbable grace, but actual.

And the force of its weight
when it hits you – if
it hits you – marks you for life.

And there is no escape
from its hurt, though its force
weakens even as its weight

holds. And you are
struck so hard, at first,
and remain so stunned

that nothing in the world,
it seems, can protect you
from its curse: that jagged

fate, that rock
against which the heart's wave
rises, live and crystalline,

and falls
and breaks most powerfully
into the foam of the spirit.

Murray's poem belongs in a collection that appeared after a long gap, many of the poems in it dealing – more or less obliquely – with the experience of profound inner pain and disorientation. This poem takes up a familiar cluster of biblical metaphors and applies them to that experience. The image in Psalm 118.22 of the stone cast aside and then retrieved to become the cornerstone is used many times in Christian Scripture, as is the language in Isaiah 8.14–15 of God as a stone over which human beings will stumble; Matthew 21.44 in some manuscripts develops this further, with Jesus saying that 'he who falls on this stone will be broken to pieces; but when it falls on anyone, it will crush him'. Jesus is both the rejected and rescued cornerstone and the God whose rock-like sanctuary in the midst of the chosen people is also a cause of wreckage to the enemies of that people. So the language here of the rock that both blocks the way and opens it, that both resists the pressure of your advance and falls on you, builds on this set of metaphors for the manifold effect of Jesus' presence: protecting us, grounding us, resisting us – and crushing us.

The impact of the holy one cannot but hurt us and wound us lastingly. But Murray says enigmatically that 'its force/ weakens even as its weight/ holds': the inescapable solidity of the impact and the burden it drops on us is not always experienced as a blow or an assault. The weight *holds*: it settles on to us so firmly that we cannot imagine ourselves prised away from the rock face to which we are pinned.

And then the metaphor changes key, to a rock in the middle of the ocean, with waves breaking over it (did Murray have in mind, even tangentially, the focal image of William Golding's novel *Pincher Martin*, in which a dying man is left isolated on a solitary rock in the sea while he struggles to refuse the painful mercy being offered to him by a God he does not believe in?). We may be pinned inescapably to the rock, but the tidal flow of the heart is not immobilized: waves rise and fall, broken, and the spray of their breaking is 'spirit'. The rock breaks us open, but not in the way we first thought: it breaks up the movements of the heart so that they are – what should we say? – 'refined' is hardly the word; but certainly made light, made mobile and diffused, by the unchanging solidity of the rock.

That final twist – very reminiscent of the kind of metaphorical resolution we often find in R. S. Thomas – affirms that our encounter with the rock of divine action or presence does not leave us simply hurt, crushed, passive; something still moves towards and around this presence, only to be transformed by the uncompromising reality of the divine. The life of 'spirit' is what happens when the heart's movements are shattered and reconstructed in the foam thrown up in this collision. Spirit, it seems, cannot be brought to life except when what we (think we) are is confronted with the unyielding weight of the holy – of Christ's presence in Murray's context. We cannot take for granted that the life of spirit is something simply 'given' in all human experience, something that can be expressed in terms of a gentle attraction to the sacred, a magnetic lure. We are always already 'broken', which is why we experience God as 'curse' or 'fate'. But to let ourselves break or be broken on *this* rock is to be open to the birth of spirit, that spirit which, in Christian Scripture, connects us with one another and with God. Something is blocked, denied – but what is denied is our *denial*, the power of our resistance to truth, so that the blockage itself is the moment of opening, the 'improbable grace' that changes us.

The encounter with what seems a harsh and hostile presence – in suffering, doubt, inner darkness, self-hatred, revolt against the God we (think we) have known – is what makes our movement forwards possible. The stone falls on us and crushes – not ourselves as such, but the illusory unity we have made of or for ourselves. We must be loosened from the grip of this, dispersed into 'foam', if we are to be at one with reality, inside and outside.

Dorothy Nimmo

The Pottery Lesson

Why do you break your pots as soon as you have
made them?

Because they are not right.
Because I don't like them.
Because they don't satisfy me.
They are not the way I want them to be.
They are all crooked.
I am ashamed of them.
I am ashamed of myself.

Those are good answers
but they are not the answer. Why do you break
your pots as soon as you have made them?

Because I have made them.
Because they show too much.
And I don't want to look and
I don't want anyone else to look
because I recognise them
because they are mine.

Those are good answers.
But they are not the answer. Why do you break
your pots as soon as you have made them?

Because when the clay is broken,
soaked in water, wedged on the board
and returned to its original state
it can be used again.

That is a good answer. Still, it is not
the answer. Why do you break your pots
as soon as you have made them?

I can't answer your question.

When you can answer that question
you will no longer be broken.

Dorothy Nimmo's poems are balanced and economical, verbally inventive, metaphorically startling, the work of an intelligence that is sceptical, vulnerable, compassionate and sensitive to the absurd. She writes with special insight and warmth about the language and behaviour of early childhood. Her Quaker affiliation meant that she was reticent with regard to any kind of doctrinal language, but there is an unmistakable moral and spiritual seriousness in all she wrote. This poem is a rare instance of her addressing something like a 'spiritual' theme head-on, with its echoes of one of the recurrent images of Hebrew and Christian Scripture: the relation between potter and pot is used by the prophet Jeremiah (Jeremiah 18) and St Paul (Romans 9) to describe the relation between God and creation or, more specifically, God and God's people. The potter has the freedom to break the pot and start again, and this is seen as a sort of rationale for what appear to be the arbitrary aspects of divine choice or divine favour. But Nimmo turns this image of the potter's sovereign freedom around and applies it once more to the processes of *human* making (including, we must assume, the making of art and the making of sense): why do we break what we have made?

The question and answer unfold with more than a touch of the semi-ritualized quality of a master–disciple exchange from some repository of Zen-like wisdom. What I make is not good enough and tells me that *I* am not good enough. What I make exposes me, tells others what I don't want told. What I make can be cancelled so that I may start again. The one thing I learn in this cross-examination is that destroying what I have made is *not* in fact an arbitrary action, to the extent that it is rooted in who I am, what I fear, what I want. What I have made is not separable from who I am. The work 'gives me away', in more than one sense – that is, it 'betrays' and exposes me, and it puts me into the hands of others. My urge to destroy is born from the fear of being given away.

So long as my explanation for the destruction simply rehearses versions of this fear, nothing will change. The question pushes inwards towards the more fundamental invitation to recognize that I break what I have made because I am *myself* already broken: I cannot bear to see myself or to be seen truthfully and so look constantly for the possibility of a fresh, self-created start. The Zen-like tone of the poem is at its most marked in the last two lines, a sort of *koan* – an apparently contradictory or at least paradoxical summing-up of the exchange thus far, not a resolution but an invitation to further silence in which the challenge can settle (and unsettle). We stop being radically broken when we find an answer to the question of why we break what we make; we can answer the question of why we break what we make only when we see our brokenness. The fear of being seen, the fear of being imperfect, the fear of being trapped without the hope of starting again, all these are symptoms of the fact that we are not at one with ourselves. The fear is a symptom not an explanation.

And the final admission that 'I can't answer your question' is the beginning of insight: the list of reasons we can identify falls short of the truth of our basic fracturedness. Indeed, listing reasons like this both manifests this fundamental fracture and keeps us from seeing it for what it is. Not knowing what to say means we begin to see why our answers aren't enough; seeing that our answers aren't enough stops us from forgetting or ignoring the question. The fresh start of recycling the clay for a new piece of work is going to be futile if we fail to see what we are repeating, what wheel we are bound to (to exploit the pottery metaphor a bit further). Our human work, our human creativity and meaning, is always the product of a divided heart (think of W. H. Auden's lines about loving your crooked neighbour 'from your crooked heart'). Admit what you can't say; look at the inner breakage. Sit with it. Perhaps the urge to break yourself once again will be stilled.

Naomi Shihab Nye

Fundamentalism

Because the eye has a short shadow or
it is hard to see over heads in the crowd?

If everyone else seems smarter
but you need your own secret?

If mystery was never your friend?

If one way could satisfy
the infinite heart of the heavens?

If you liked the king on his golden throne
more than the villagers carrying baskets of lemons?

If you wanted to be sure
his guards would admit you to the party?

The boy with the broken pencil
scrapes his little knife against the lead
turning and turning it as a point
emerges from the wood again

If he would believe his life is like that
he would not follow his father into war

What generates religious extremism? There are various kinds of sociological explanation, no doubt valid as far as they go, but here Naomi Shihab Nye, a poet of American and Palestinian family, looks at the deeper imaginative and emotional lure of fundamentalism before moving to the poignant concluding picture of a child somehow failing to connect the ordinary experience of breaking and starting again with what it is like to lead a human life.

'Fundamentalism' may appeal because of the hunger for advantage. 'The eye has a short shadow': we may hear behind this, 'the "I" has a short shadow' – the ego does not cast a long enough shadow to reinforce its sense of its significance. And the 'eye' is limited by its own range: if it is turned earthwards, it will miss the wider view it longs for; if it shares exactly the same ground as others, it will not be able to see more than others, over heads in a crowd. There may be an appeal that lies in the conviction of being in privileged possession of truth that others don't know – particularly seductive when you are beginning from a position of perceived inferiority. It may have something to do with the fear that nothing you do could satisfy God, so a system that promises an exact definition of what *would* satisfy God is compelling. And if your heart is more stirred by images of power than by the everyday, and if you want to make sure that you have access to the privileges such power brings, you will want to know the passwords that guarantee you access.

This is not only a succession of vivid images; it is an implicit portrait of a psychology – anxious, unhappy, resentful, desperate to be recognized as special, recognized even by God. And whether or not this amounts to a scientifically exact portrait of the individual extremist, it sums up a set of assumptions and a variety of psychic wounds without which extremism would not take root. Perhaps the deepest insight is in the words, 'If one way could satisfy/ the infinite heart of the heavens?' – the key word being 'satisfy'. Is faith about *satisfying* God, earning the right to say that we have done what needs to be done and said what needs to be said with regard to God? A great deal of religious language is indeed about this kind of 'satisfaction'; a whole strand of Christian theology about the world's redemption flirts dangerously with this temptation to aspire to a tidy balance sheet, whether in the form of a wooden moralism or a crude account of how Christ pays off our debts to God by his suffering. Other religious traditions have their own versions of this. It is a language that is inherently backward-looking, as if the state of belief in which we now find ourselves had nowhere else to move, no territory into which to grow. All there is left to do is to insist on the privilege that true belief has brought, and to avenge the refusal of others to accept their own inferiority – the refusal to recognize their error and their unpayable debt to the truth they have scorned.

The final section gives us a homely image for what another kind of faith might look like: the 'little knife' which might in other circumstances be a weapon, is here the means of patient and repeated work on the broken pencil. Pencils break time after time, *so long as we need them to write with*. That is to say, we go on writing and rewriting, telling and retelling our story. The tragedy is to repeat the patterns we have inherited instead of finding new words. For the boy not to 'follow his father into war', he must be confident that new words can be written, new narratives constructed. There is a continuity in the repeated working on the same pencil with the same knife: the boy does not have to start from scratch, to make up a faith, a world view, from nothing. But he has to make the leap of imagination which will tell him that scrutiny, questioning and new beginning are woven in with the living of a human life lived in time.

We do not have to cast a longer shadow or find some way of seeing over the heads of others. And most importantly, we have to leave behind the fear of not 'satisfying' a God who is nothing but an infinite demand for compliance. We have to discover a God who is the infinite enabler of new beginnings, new words to write, new ways of sharing with others that possibility of new, sharper, humbler and more compassionate insight.

Naomi Shihab Nye

The Words Under the Words

for Sitti Khadra, north of Jerusalem

My grandmother's hands recognize grapes,
the damp shine of a goat's new skin.
When I was sick they followed me,
I woke from the long fever to find them
covering my head like cool prayers.

My grandmother's days are made of bread,
a round pat-pat and the slow baking.
She waits by the oven watching a strange car
circle the streets. Maybe it holds her son,
lost to America. More often, tourists,
who kneel and weep at mysterious shrines.
She knows how often mail arrives,
how rarely there is a letter.
When one comes, she announces it, a miracle,
listening to it read again and again
in the dim evening light.

My grandmother's voice says nothing can surprise
her.
Take her the shotgun wound and the crippled baby.
She knows the spaces we travel through,
the messages we cannot send – our voices are short
and would get lost on the journey.

Farewell to the husband's coat,
the ones she has loved and nourished,
who fly from her like seeds into a deep sky.
They will plant themselves. We will all die.

My grandmother's eyes say Allah is everywhere,
  even in death.
When she talks of the orchard and the new olive
  press,
when she tells the stories of Joha and his foolish
  wisdoms,
He is her first thought, what she really thinks of is
  His name.
'Answer, if you hear the words under the words –
otherwise it is just a world with a lot of rough
  edges,
difficult to get through, and our pockets full of
  stones.'

We know through our bodies, our skins, not only our minds: Nye's celebration of her grandmother begins with this simple truth – the recognition that we learn in touching the stuff of the world around; and the 'knowing' hands that cover the speaker's head are 'like cool prayers' because they signal a connection that is deeper than speech or ideas. We are already being told implicitly that the grandmother's knowledge of God is like her knowledge of grapes or goatskin, a familiarity of ordinary physical contact. Surrounded by alien and incomprehensible things – including the piety of the 'tourists . . . at mysterious shrines' – and cut off from the apparently friction-free connections that modernity takes for granted, she is able to see the arrival of a letter as a miraculous gift. Nothing is taken for granted; and so, strange as it sounds, nothing is unexpected either. Each moment arrives with its own particularity, its own unique presence, even the moments of pain and trauma – the kinds of moments that we can imagine a Palestinian grandmother of a certain age having to confront. She does not need to be constantly 'in touch' with her scattered family because she is so unselfconsciously in touch with the immediate world she inhabits; when her family members leave her for far-off new homes, she acknowledges that they will grow and move and put down roots somewhere and eventually die.

'Allah is everywhere, even in death.' And so whatever she talks about, she is actually talking about God, 'her first thought'; she has heard 'the words under the words', words that simply say that this is a hard world if you are not able to see it and sense it as *giving God* to you. If that is how you know the world, you know God in every touch and speech.

Nye is not saying that we should simply aspire to such a condition – a more or less impossible hope for the poor banished children of the modern mind; but she is inviting us to acknowledge what kinds of loss or lack we are habitually involved in. We can read the poem as a diagnosis of what imprisons and diminishes us – how we have forgotten what it is to 'know' with our hands, how we are on edge for the constant reassurance that we are in contact with others who reassure us of our reality and significance, how we lose the capacity to receive the ordinary as a gift. Recognizing all this is part of learning to live with our inevitable dying. How far we are able to grow into the discernment of the words under the words is an open question, but we can perhaps learn to see more clearly what we don't know. And what we don't know is not some transcendent spiritual truth; it is the working of our own bodies, the way in which our own physical organism learns to negotiate its environment and absorbs the moves, the ways of handling, that allow the 'rough edges' of the world to be managed with intelligence and grace.

Much has been written in recent decades about the irony that a supposedly materialistic age is so strangely illiterate about how the body learns and responds in a bodily environment – even as the sciences force us to a fuller recognition of how 'pathways' are shaped in the brain in and through physical habit. Nye's grandmother is a figure who has lived her way into an instinctive, receptive adjustment to whatever life presents – not in passivity but in a deep bodily intelligence; and in that intelligence, God is as much a 'given' as the grape or the dough. God is what is known in the body's wisdom, in the 'apt' and fluid responsiveness of the organism to the environment. The final image of 'pockets full of stones' suggests both a kind of primitive arsenal – pockets full of elementary missiles to throw at one another – and those committing suicide who (like Virginia Woolf) fill their pockets with stones to weigh down their drowning body. Without the grandmother's almost imperceptible but ever-present sense of God as the subject of all that is happening, we are at risk both of violence and of despair and self-destruction. Is it possible still for bodies that have been nourished in the habits of modernity to learn at least something of the skills of shaping daily bread?

Alice Oswald

Seabird's Blessing

We are crowds of seabirds,
makers of many angles,
workers that unpick a web
of the air's threads and tangles.

Pray for us when we fight
the wind one to one;
let not that shuddering strength
smash the cross of the wing-bone.

O God the featherer,
lift us if we fall;
preserve the frenzy in our mouths,
the yellow star in the eyeball.

Christ, make smooth the way
of a creature like a spirit
up from its perverse body
without weight or limit.

Holy ghost of heaven,
blow us clear of the world,
give us the utmost of the air
to heave on and to hold.

Pray for us this weird
bare place – we are screaming
O sky count us not as nothing
O sea count us not as nothing

How would the non-human world pray if it had words to do so? Various poets have meditated on this – with varying levels of seriousness: Alice Oswald's poem is a particularly rich imagining of this, entering into the place occupied by the seabird in flight and also inviting the reader to allow this imagined place of non-human thought and feeling to cast light on the human 'place' and the human world.

The life of the seabird is an 'unpicking' of the invisible currents of the air, finding a path through the impenetrably complicated and tightly woven lines of force that both resist and support the bird in flight. Movement is in 'crowds', yet each one has to face the wind as a single organism. So the first prayer is that 'the cross of the wing-bone' will hold against the gale for each bird. It is as though this bone cross is what lies at the centre of the bird's living flexibility and responsiveness. But God, for the bird, is first and foremost the one who gives the power of flight itself – 'God the featherer' (a neat echo of 'God the Father'), who can always lift, and who gives and sustains the furious energy of flight. Christ is invoked to clear the way from body to spirit – a body that is already close to spirit, a 'perverse' body from our point of view, accustomed as we are to earthbound solidities; and the Spirit is (as in the original Hebrew and Greek) indistinguishable from the force of the wind. But it is a wind that can be leaned on and gripped in the act of flight, something that carries us through the criss-crossing forces of the air towards an 'utmost' that remains undefined. And the prayer that finally emerges in the endless scream of the seabirds is not to be counted as nothing: almost weightless, fragile, flying in and around a force that can be annihilatingly destructive, the bird still begs to be itself, to be seen as real.

A vividly simple evocation of what we can think about the experience of the bird; but also prompting questions for the human imagination. Are we also negotiating invisible lines of force that are both potentially destructive and potentially life-giving, weaving a pattern or at least a line of survival through the already densely patterned environment we inhabit? How do we journey from body to spirit, and can we understand that it is not a matter of simply stepping from one world to another, from solid stuff to pure immaterial energy? How does bodiliness itself become spiritual, able to rest on the wild turbulence of the air ('to heave on and to hold')? Is the whole of our life, too, a continuous cry not to be counted as nothing? We also learn to move and negotiate by moving in groups, in the shared world of language and symbol that make up the life of our minds, yet we have to face the wind alone; we might pray as well that the bony armature of our identity does not break under the assault. And a certain kind of praying person might connect that bony structure with the cross of salvation, which (in the mediaeval monastic epigram) 'stands still while the world turns'.

I certainly don't think that Alice Oswald is deliberately writing an 'edifying' poem that boils down to a long metaphor for human experience: the poem occurs among a number of others in which the very specific reality of both sea and birds is the focus. But when poetry connects worlds by imagining the utterly strange, it allows the utterly strange in turn to build a bridge back into our own thinking. Imagining the bird's prayer is inevitably imagining our prayer; imagining the bird is imagining the self. Pondering what is not native and familiar to me is one way of discovering about myself what I can never know by egocentric introspection. Alice Oswald has written a poem that is, among other things, about how poetry works and how metaphor – seeing the familiar in and through the alien – is a means of discovery, not a decorative comparison. And the discovery is something to do with how we learn to be *held* by the tumultuous energy that surrounds and carries, not shattered by it, and how we come to imagine a wind, a gale of force, that is always lifting us in and along the journey deeper into our own bodies, towards where spirit works most freely.

Ruth Padel

Learning to Make an Oud in Nazareth

The first day he cut rosewood for the back,
bent a sycamore into ribs and made a belly
  of mahogany. *Let us go early to the vineyards*
  and see if the vines have budded.
The sky was blue over the Jezreel valley
and the gilt dove shone
above the Church of the Annunciation.
The second day, he carved a camel-bone base
  for the fingerboard.
I sat down under his shadow with delight.

The third day he made a nut of sandalwood,
and a pick-guard of black cherry.
  He damascened a rose of horn
  with arabesques
as lustrous as under-leaves of olive beside the sea.
  I have found him whom my soul loves.
He inlaid the sound-hole with ivory swans,
each pair a valentine of entangled necks,
  and fitted tuning pegs of apricot
to give a good smell when rubbed.

The fourth was a day for cutting
high strings of camel-gut. *His left hand*
  shall be under my head.

For the lower course, he twisted copper
pale as tarmac under frost.
He shall lie all night between my breasts.
The fifth day he laid down varnish.
Our couch is green and the beams of our house
are cedar and pine. Behind the neck
he put a sign to keep off the Evil Eye.

My beloved is a duster of camphire
in the vineyards of Engedi
and I watched him whittle an eagle-feather, a plectrum
to celebrate the angel of improvisation
who dwells in clefts on the Nazareth ridge
where love waits. And grows, if you give it time.
Set me as a seal upon your heart.
On the sixth day the soldiers came
for his genetic code.
We have no record of what happened.

I was queuing at the checkpoint to Galilee.
I sought him and found him not.
He'd have been in his open-air workshop –
I called but he gave me no answer –
the self-same spot
where Jesus stood when He came from Capernaum
to teach in synagogue, and townsfolk tried
to throw Him from the rocks. *Until the day break*
and shadows flee away
I will get me to the mountain of myrrh.

The seventh day we set his wounded hands
around the splinters. *Come with me from Lebanon,*
my spouse, look from the top
of Shenir and Hermon, from the lions' dens.
On the eighth there were no more days.
I took a class in carpentry and put away the bridal
rug.
We started over
with a child's oud bought on eBay.
He was a virtuoso of the oud
and his banner over me was love.

Israel, Eretz Yisrael, Israel/Palestine, IOPT, the Holy Land – how we speak about this strip of land in the Eastern Mediterranean is going to be a major clue to our political and religious orientation. Using the wrong name can end a conversation abruptly, can send signals of threat or betrayal. In her 2014 collection, *Learning to Make an Oud in Nazareth*, Ruth Padel tries to capture the imaginative world of this territory, where Jewish, Christian and Muslim languages, perceptions, traditions mix and migrate, where suffering and exile are part of everyone's story but differently told. The title poem of the collection is an intricate meditation on a woodworker carving a traditional musical instrument; the detail of the poem takes us through eight days, describing at first the variegated crafts needed to shape the different components of the instrument, and then – 'On the sixth day the soldiers came/ for his genetic code'. The craftsman disappears.

Throughout the poem, the depiction of the making of the oud is woven in with quotations from the Song of Songs in the Bible, that overwhelming celebration of physical love: the sixth day is marked by the haunting words of the Bride in the Song – 'I sought him and found him not.' The disappearance of the instrument maker is linked with the gospel narrative of the efforts of Jesus' fellow townsmen in Nazareth to kill him. On the seventh day, the Sabbath, 'we set his wounded hands/ around the splinters'. Is this a ritual of burial or of restoration or both? As the new week starts, or the world that is beyond weeks and days, the speaker of the poem has to take up the responsibility for making the instrument, beginning to learn the crafts and using a child's instrument as a model. The old craftsman has made something possible: 'his banner over me was love' – another of the resonant and strange images of the biblical Song, used to suggest that the whole narrative is about both creative love and breakthrough by way of suffering and violence endured. Not coincidentally, some of these texts from the Song are associated in Christian liturgy both with the pain of longing that is experienced in contemplative prayer, and with Mary Magdalene and her plea to be told where the body of Jesus has been laid.

Padel – without insisting on a neatly orthodox Christian interpretation – constructs a subtly layered perspective. Behind or beneath the immediate picture of a local craftsman (Christian? Jewish? Muslim? Historical or contemporary?) is the sequence of the events of Holy Week, especially Good Friday and Easter Eve (and later in the collection there is a remarkable sequence of poems connected with the seven 'words' of Jesus from the cross). This in turn opens out on to the seven-day creation story, the narrative of the emergence of a 'musically' coherent and beautiful cosmos. The sixth day, when human beings are created, is both climax and tragedy; human presence means loss and conflict, and (echoes of Bonhoeffer; we could read this poem with Auden's elegy for Bonhoeffer (p. 16) alongside it) human 'maturity' is the moment when God appears to give no answer. The 'open-air workshop' of divine art is empty, and the speaker waits in the checkpoint queue, the crushing and humiliating border between two territories, two worlds. Somehow the traumatic disruption is not the last word: the hands grasp the shattered wood again, and – although something has unmistakeably ended – something also begins as the 'child's oud bought on eBay' serves as a model for a new act of art, of making.

The history of the Land is one of disruption and of the murderous violence that follows it – the tearing away of the Christian community from the Jewish people, now destined to carry a projected guilt created by the Christian story, the Muslim revolution against Christianity (and Judaism) and the setting up of a new claim to universal inclusion in a community of faith that in practice excludes and divides. The story of the creation, of the Land, of the focal figure of the crucified Jesus, of the victim of some unspecified act of revenge or terror or institutional repression, is always a story of breakage and continuity: the seven days of creation seem to be a record of tragedy, yet there is an 'eighth day' (early Christian commentators often use this as a designation for Easter Day itself), in which human beings discover they have a creative liberty that is still not destroyed, even if it has to learn its lessons with and from children. The music is not silenced, the sensuous beauty of what is evoked in the first few sections of the poem is not lost. Hands around the splinters, including the splinters that are ourselves.

Sylvia Plath

Mystic

The air is a mill of hooks –
Questions without answer,
Glittering and drunk as flies
Whose kiss stings unbearably
In the fetid wombs of black air under pines in
  summer.

I remember
The dead smell of sun on wood cabins,
The stiffness of sails, the long salt winding sheets.
Once one has seen God, what is the remedy?
Once one has been seized up

Without a part left over,
Not a toe, not a finger, and used,
Used utterly, in the sun's conflagration, the stains
That lengthen from ancient cathedrals
What is the remedy?

The pill of the Communion tablet,
The walking beside still water? Memory?
Or picking up the bright pieces
Of Christ in the faces of rodents,
The tame flower-nibblers, the ones

Whose hopes are so low they are comfortable —
The humpback in his small, washed cottage
Under the spokes of the clematis.
Is there no great love, only tenderness?
Does the sea

Remember the walker upon it?
Meaning leaks from the molecules.
The chimneys of the city breathe, the window
  sweats,
The children leap in their cots.
The sun blooms, it is a geranium.

The heart has not stopped.

Sylvia Plath is seldom thought of as a poet with any marked interest in the religious, but this poem stands out as both a poignant and a searching exploration of the 'mystical' experience – poignant because it was written just over a week before her suicide. The setting seems to be the wooded New England coast in holiday season: an atmosphere of deadness and sterility ('fetid wombs'), but haunted by the awareness that God has irrupted into the scene, into the speaker's world. The air is crowded with questions – the 'hooks' milling around like insects, catching in the flesh and hurting it – that push at this awareness, the consciousness of something that has embraced and in some sense consumed the speaker's entire identity, soul and body. Once that sense of transforming contact has occurred, what can possibly make the rest of life bearable? It is – in a very different idiom – the question that Eliot poses at the beginning of the *Quartets* about the 'waste, sad time' that extends before and after the moment of insight. With a characteristic intensity and tension of metaphor, the consuming experience is both one of being burned in the sun and of being 'stained' by the dark shadow of what religious vision has generated and built, the 'ancient cathedrals'. Whatever exactly has happened – and some have associated her language here with the sense of something like 'possession' that characterizes her voice in the *Ariel* poems – the visitation of the holy feels in retrospect uncomfortably like a violation, a pushing aside of the person, both opening up an ecstatic hyper-awareness and 'using' or using up the actual human sensibility involved.

What makes this close weave of trauma and loss bearable? The use of 'remedy' just might echo the phrase in Shakespeare's *Measure for Measure* where Isabella reminds Angelo that the God who might have claimed the right to punish 'forfeited' souls is the one who 'found out the remedy'; but this may be a chance resonance. The 'remedy' that is sought here is whatever might enable us to live within the boundaries of the everyday again. Is it the routine of the Church's sacraments (the image of the consecrated eucharistic bread as a 'pill' goes back to the second Christian century; had Plath somehow encountered the phrase of Ignatius of Antioch, referring to it as the 'pill' or 'medicine' of immortality?)? But Plath's own experience of 'pills', medication for her mental state, included an earlier suicide attempt; the eucharistic host as pill is an unpromising prospect. Is it the practice of finding inner quiet and rest 'by still waters' as in Psalm 23? Or simply holding on to the recollection of the lost intensity? Or is it the discipline of looking for the dispersed reflections of Christ's face in the most humble and vulnerable of creatures, those with the lowest hopes? Should we be learning from them how to live with expectations too low ever to be seriously disappointed, like the 'humpback' in the cottage – a faintly grotesque, folkloric picture, inviting us to hear a touch of irony in it?

The wry thought that the answer is perhaps to be found in lowering our expectations to a 'comfortable' level suddenly becomes serious. What if the most significant level of our experience were not after all the intensity of vision or passion but simply 'tenderness'? Commentators have noted that Plath more than once draws on a comment made by a therapist to the effect that what attracts women to women, which they do not find in men, is 'tenderness'. The implication is that we should in fact suspect the overwhelming erotic violence of the momentary 'possession' of the self by God; or, to put it rather differently, the sea abides, even when the miraculous and dramatic event of Christ's walking on it has passed. Something continues when the drama is over, and that something may be not a storm of cosmic passion but a fathomless kindness at the heart of the world. We have to return to the humble expectation of the animal, the 'disabled', to pick up the clues of meaning.

'Meaning leaks from the molecules' might (so some critics have argued) signify that meaning is draining away from the stuff of the world; but it could equally be that meaning is seeping out of the most elementary particles that make up the world – that meaning is inescapably to be discerned in the bare material reality of things. The imagery of breathing and blossoming – the sun, which previously was a 'conflagration', is reimagined as a flower – suggests that some abiding rhythm in the world has quietly come into focus. The moment of possession and ecstasy has served its turn in bringing life into the dead landscape we began with, but it is not to be clung to or idealized. 'The heart has not stopped.' The pulse of life is there, not destroyed or swallowed up or incurably damaged by the moment of vision, and not silenced or buried by the return of the everyday. The poem remains full of uncertainties about the possibility of life in the wake of intense awareness and intense suffering; we can hardly read it without remembering Plath's own impending decision to end her own life. But it is still a deep probing of how we think about the advent of comprehensive meaning in our troubled imagination; and 'tenderness' – something of which Plath came to see she had so little experience – is at the centre of this enterprise.

Michael Symmons Roberts

On Easter Saturday

Hell is being harrowed as we speak,
ten thousand leagues below us a colossal fish
with xylophonic teeth is filleting the deep,

and in its wake comes all this:
blossom pulls from orchards, streams from peaks,
the sun – though weighted by the days

it freights inside – is drawn into a lake
and hauled down to the darkest ocean trench,
since depths are being harrowed as we speak.

And though I know it makes no sense,
I feel – if I stand still – its tinfoil scales, the blinkless
eye, the muscle of its tail, and all that I once

took as mine is flensed from me, a thankless
healing, leaves me wondering if I am sea, or fish,
if harrowed hell is me, if I am cursed or blessed.

Michael Symmons Roberts' 2013 collection – or, rather, sequence – is (as the title hints) a sort of Psalter. The title teases the reader with this echo, though, as the epigraph tells us, a 'drysalter' is 'a dealer in drugs, dye-stuffs, gums, oils, etc.'. It is a series of 150 brief poems in strict form, all of 15 lines; there are groups with the same title, representing different takes on a recurring theme; there are evocations of the psalmist seen in different modes or under different kinds of light; there are brilliant metaphorical transformations of familiar scenes, with the entire collection flowing back and forth between sacred and secular focus – though it would be more accurate to say that sacred and secular are not easily distinguished here.

This piece for Easter Eve (which you might read alongside Paul Mariani's poem (p. 193) for the same day) addresses the theme of the 'harrowing of hell' (the descent of the crucified Jesus to the depths of the realm of the dead and lost) by way of a single bold metaphor. The depth of the ocean is being threshed and stirred by some immense presence, stirred so violently that it creates a kind of whirlpool into which the visible world is being inexorably drawn – the blossom sucked from trees as if by a fierce gale, the streams pulled down from mountain tops to the sea, the sun itself and all the future days that it contains 'hauled down', despite its weight. As the tumult shakes the deepest trenches of the ocean bed, the whole world is stripped, poured into a crucible.

And the speaker senses this in his own depths: what seemed to be his, what seemed to be securely possessed or understood, is 'flensed' – a word most at home in the whaling industry, where it means the stripping of skin and flesh from the bones of the whale (and this imagery is echoed and developed further in another poem, 'Wetsalter' – 'he flays you first, then rubs it [salt] in'). The harrowing of hell is not about something that is happening elsewhere, the upheaval of the ocean bed is internal as well as external. The uncertainty as to whether 'I am sea, or fish' is a recognition of the double truth of the poet's position – and of the believer's position too. What is being 'harrowed' is me; the chaos is what happens as my own internal deadness and lostness is traumatically disturbed. But also, I am the harrower:

it is the Christ-haunted consciousness that registers and moves with the trauma and upheaval, that pushes it into language and image and recreates that scouring and 'flensing' in words. The poet's job is a reflection of Christ's descent into hell, it seems; but this is only possible, it only makes sense, if the poet's own hell is harrowed by a grace beyond the poet's imagining.

So, 'cursed or blessed'? The poet faces the acute pain of stripping away what has been clear, so as to let language reshape itself after the vortex of descent into turmoil: a blessing, despite the pain. The poet is given the tools to 'harrow' the depths of a reader: a curse, despite the gift, because it comes with the weight of responsibility and the reality of risk. And 'the poet' is of course an abstraction (poets shouldn't be writing about poets, or if they are it is so that the poet's sensibility can be grasped as an acute version simply of *human* sensibility): the reader is invited to recognize the close weave of curse and blessing in the whole business of searching for language that is both truthful and transforming. The 'as we speak' of the first and ninth lines appears not just as a conventional marker of simultaneity ('even as we speak') but as a reminder that *in our speaking*, especially the intensified speaking of art, depths are being disturbed, with consequences we cannot control.

Part of what gives this poem such energy is how it evokes intense activity just 'off-screen', just around the corner of perception. We can see the effects of the oceanic turbulence, but what actually goes on in the depths is not for us to chronicle or chart. So one of the things the poem leaves us with is the understanding that the language of faith and of poetry alike are distant tremors from an earthquake that we can't confront directly; evidence of more than language can manage, but still the unmistakeable impact, 'as we speak', of what the *action* of truth or reality is in us and on us, a 'harrowing' of what is most deeply buried.

Michael Symmons Roberts

A New Song

Sing a new song to the Lord,
sing through the skin of your teeth,
sing in the code of your blood,
sing with a throat full of earth,

sing to the quick of your nails,
sing from the knots of your lungs,
sing like a dancer on coals,
sing as a madman in tongues,

sing as if singing made sense,
sing in the caves of your heart,
sing like you want them to dance,
sing through the shades of your past,

sing what you never could say,
sing at the fulcrum of joy,
sing without need of reply.

Why do we praise? Where do we find the resource to 'sing'? This is a poem that could be read alongside Olga Sedakova's two poems in this volume (pp. 269 and 273), especially the second, 'Chinese Journey 18', as an affirmation that praise is as inescapable as lament in the human world. The singing evoked here is not a full-throated self-indulgent performance;

it is what manages to escape from choked and knotted insides because it can't be contained; and it *names* or at least points towards what can't be named ('what you never could say').

Another poem in Roberts' collection ('Portrait of the Psalmist as Ultra-Singer') warns against singing in order to avoid the 'still small voice' or to fill up an interior void ('to make my skull full'). But the singing in this poem is precisely the opposite of any kind of *choice* being made to sing in order to avoid a menacing silence. And it is the tension itself that somehow sparks the song (like George Herbert's great Easter poem in which the 'stretched sinews' of Christ on the cross teach us 'what key is best' for praise).

'Sing as if singing made sense': we utter our praise as if it were the natural thing to do (compare Sedakova (pp. 269 and 273) once more). And perhaps we should read the phrase as meaning 'sing as if it were singing that created meaning' – literally *made* sense. Praise is not a reasoned judgement on how things are but the creative spring out of which meaning arises. The choking and stress of our experience drive us to 'collect' ourselves in a new way, to bring inner darkness into unfamiliar focus. And praise is by definition a kind of speech that doesn't expect a reply: it is sheer acknowledgement.

In the Psalter, psalms of praise, songs that call out for cosmic celebration, stand alongside bitter testimonies to protest, anguished isolation, unconsoled torment and lament for collective trauma. There is no attempt to balance the books. What is said by the psalmist is what the psalmist has to say – in both senses: what there is for the psalmist to communicate, and what the psalmist is *bound* to give voice to. At this point of utterance, there is no interest in creating a comprehensive scheme of meaning, there is only the extraordinary fact that singing creates sense. It does not have to be a form of words that corresponds to what is there in the world; it is enough that the world irresistibly draws it out. 'The fulcrum of joy' is a strong metaphor for the place from which this singing comes: there is a still point about which human language swings, praise or protest or whatever, and that is the joy to which the heart returns; or the unarguable and non-reasonable presence we call joy is the point of leverage on which we can be raised beyond where we begin.

In other words, it is not that praise could be a means of gaining anything; it is the sign of a gift already given. It is gratuitous, outside the economy of payment or earning, and it is also natural or even necessary, the product of simply being human in the world. The poem is an exhortation not to be afraid of this surprising gift; like Sedakova, Roberts is telling us to be ready for the excess that our reality pushes up to the surface, in the face of all the pain and failure that seems to occupy the whole of our human territory. Art and faith belong here: never explanatory or systematic discourses, but expression of and witness to a 'fulcrum' that we can't lay hold of.

Tadeusz Różewicz

Unrecorded Epistle

But Jesus stooped
and with his finger wrote on the ground
then he stooped again
and wrote on the sand

Mother they are so dim
and simple I have to show them
marvels I do such silly
and futile things
but you understand
and will forgive your son
I change water into wine
raise the dead
walk the seas

they are like children
one has always
to show them something new
just imagine

And when they approached
he covered and effaced
the letters
for ever

In the well-known story of Jesus' encounter with the 'woman taken in adultery', preserved in John 8.1–11 (although it is certainly not part of John's original text), Jesus bends down to write with his finger in the dust. Why? And what does he write?

Interpreters have speculated since the earliest days of the Church; Różewicz, whose poetry often includes ironic and unexpected variations on the Catholic world view he had grown up with and never completely rejected, imagines that the one thing Jesus cannot say to the crowds around him – and so must address to his mother who alone knows his secret, and must write in the sand, where it can be instantly erased – is that he can attract hearers for his teaching only if he performs miracles. The miracles in themselves are an embarrassment, almost a vulgarity, 'silly/ and futile things'. It echoes what Jesus *does* say openly in the Gospels – as in John 4.48, where Jesus complains that people will not believe without 'signs and wonders'. And the point was developed by Dietrich Bonhoeffer (look again at Auden's poem about him, p. 16) in his groundbreaking lectures on the doctrine of Christ in Berlin in 1933: a first-century West Asian spiritual teacher would naturally have been remembered as performing wonders; but this is not what is important or abidingly significant about Jesus. In one sense, the historical accuracy or otherwise of these reports of miraculous events is neither here nor there for faith. The uniqueness of Jesus for Christian belief lies elsewhere, in the events of cross and resurrection, and in the underlying reality of his divine identity.

But Różewicz is doing more than echoing this quite orthodox theological insight. The 'Unrecorded Epistle' is addressed to Mary, whose forgiveness is sought by Jesus; Mary will understand and pardon the fireworks of miracle, because she knows both who her son is and how the world needs proof before it will believe. She is herself invited to believe what has been said to her by the angel about the child she is about to conceive, but there could never be simple public proof of the child's divine origin and redeeming destiny. It is not that miracles are impossible or irrational; it is that they will never do the real job of prompting faith. They may serve the limited function of capturing attention, as they would with children eager for exciting novelty.

'Just imagine', says Jesus to his mother: it is an expression of headshaking exasperation, or at least frustrated surprise, at the dimness of his audience; but it is also an imperative. Just *imagine*: don't look for proof but let your imagination free to work on and in the world. Imagine a world in which the miraculous presence of healing and mercy was tangible, as tangible and perceptible as changing water into wine or raising the dead. The story of which the original incident is a part is a story of Jesus exercising a plain and radical mercy, delivering the condemned woman from those eager to punish both her and Jesus. As Jesus bends to write in the dust or sand, it is as though he puts side by side the casual physical wonders he regularly performs in the gospel story and the real miracle of divine forgiveness, and desperately needs to say to someone that it is the latter which is important. Yet he knows the childish mind to which he speaks, a mind that can only 'imagine' the new life by being shown new wonders.

In the Gospels we catch another glimpse of this in the story of how Jesus heals the paralysed man who is let down through a hole in the roof (Mark 2.1–12): Jesus challenges the hostile onlookers as to whether the physical miracle of healing is in fact harder than the forgiveness of sins. The implication is both that the point of the healing is to persuade people that Jesus does in fact have authority to forgive sins, and that this forgiveness is a matter of costly labour, the labour of the whole of Jesus' life and death. The lapsed Catholic Różewicz does not declare a decision about whether or not the greater miracle of redemption has actually been achieved, but he gently pushes us back to critical reflection on our own self-gratifying urge for what is visibly new and exciting – and how such an urge can stifle the deeper impulses of imagination unless it opens up on to that greater miracle.

Tadeusz Różewicz

Thorn

I don't believe
I don't believe from morning
till night

I don't believe from the one shore of my life
to the other
I don't believe
as patently deeply
as my mother
believed

I don't believe
when I eat bread
drink water
love a body

I don't believe
in his altars
signs and priests

I don't believe in town
in the field and the rain
in air
or the gold of annunciation

I read his parables
simple as an ear of corn
and think of the god
who did not laugh

I think of the tiny
god bleeding
amid white
sheets of childhood

of the thorn which tears
our eyes lips
now
and in the hour of our death

A beautifully poised expression of standing at the threshold of faith. We begin with the straightforward statement that the speaker doesn't believe as an older generation might have (doesn't believe in the way Naomi Shihab Nye's grandmother did, for example; see p. 227), with a faith that extends unproblematically through life and is present in the ordinary acts of life. More aggressively, the speaker refuses to believe in 'his altars/ signs and priests'. But then the emphasis shifts. When the speaker says that he does not believe 'in town', it seems like a continuation of the previous statement about not believing in the daily routine of life; but the text skilfully traps us with the double sense of 'believing in'. The speaker no longer has any belief in the environment he inhabits, town or country, any more than in the supernatural radiance of the promise of the Incarnation. The loss of belief in the inherited faith produces not a world of clear and positive perception but the experience of an environment without depth or hope, disenchanted, an experience of alienation from the elemental life around (rain and air).

The Christ whose 'altars/ signs and priests' have been rejected is a teacher of fruitful parables, nourishing and generative, 'ears of corn' (alluding to the various parables of sowing and harvesting in the Gospels), but no more. 'The god/ who did not laugh' implies a sense of the God of tradition as somehow oppressive, at odds with human joy; the phrase recalls the apocryphal mediaeval account of Jesus, purporting to be by a contemporary, which states that the Saviour 'sometimes smiles but never laughs'. But this leads immediately into a more serious recognition that the god who is without laughter is indeed a god who is, in the traditional narrative of faith, familiar with suffering from his birth onwards. Why should he laugh to reassure us in a world where the suffering is more obviously the common currency of human experience?

And it is this which makes faith something that cannot be forgotten or excised. Like St Paul with his 'thorn in the flesh' (2 Corinthians 12.7) to remind him of his human insufficiency, our imagination is pierced by the image of the bleeding child as an embodiment of God. What we see and what we say will carry the marks of this memory; the thorn has indeed snagged in our soft flesh and will stick there until death – and that phrase, 'now and in the hour of our death', cites the Angelus, the prayer of that luminous moment of annunciation that we have turned away from.

As in Vernon Watkins' poem, 'Adam' (p. 335), there is a challenge to the claims of a completely secularized imagination. It is impossible, we are told, to believe in the old way; yet, as St Paul is kept humble by the thorn in his flesh, so our ambitions are chastened by our inability to forget the metaphor of God as the wounded child – even when we cannot see it as more than metaphor – and by the disturbing anxiety that, when we cease to believe in God, the world itself becomes 'incredible', a place where trust and hope are extinguished: 'I don't believe . . ./ in the field and the rain.'

Różewicz is not venturing an *argument* for returning to faith; there is perhaps no way back that we can devise from the loss we have come to take for granted, the loss of the faith of our parents' or grandparents' generation. But this cannot be all that there is to say. We may not have the resources to carve out a way back, even if we wanted to. But what if the object of that inherited faith is still involved with our own bleeding and mortal humanity, whether we like it or not?

Gjertrud Schnackenburg

A Gilded Lapse of Time 12

For you the earth was motionless, silent,
Suspended, except that it gaped with hell,
With a distant reverberation underfoot,
A din you heard rising from the world's
Shattered insides where those without hope
Rave and beat on the ground.

But stranded on the cliff's edge
Of your death mask, and older than you were
That morning when you began to take the way down
Into hidden, gigantic dimensions,
Over the sides of diminishing terraces
I can't bring myself to peer from –
Here on earth, in the room above
The temple they built on your tomb,
I circle around

And reappear, an apparition in midair
In the glass case where your death mask shows
The likeness of a man who, closing his eyes,
Holds still in order to discern
A very faint sound.

This poem belongs in a sequence about Ravenna in north-eastern Italy, with its unique complement of churches in which sixth-century mosaic decoration survives in splendid abundance. Schnackenburg devotes several poems to the imagery of these mosaics, but then moves on to the tomb of Dante Alighieri, the foremost religious poet of the European Middle Ages. We have already in the earlier poems of the sequence been reminded of the cosmology of the mediaeval period – spheres within revolving spheres, to some of which the planets are attached, and at the centre the earth, not moving like the heavenly bodies the music of which surrounds us: 'motionless, silent,/ Suspended'. The belief that the earth stood at the centre of the universe was not – as superficial accounts still sometimes claim – a mark of belief that earth was the most important location in the cosmos; on the contrary, it was a place in which heavenly harmonics were difficult to hear.

But it is not completely silent. Dante describes a hell that is literally a pit opening up within the earth; and from that pit of suffering and abandonment, 'reverberation' can be heard, a kind of shuddering distant noise that disturbs the ear of anyone who pauses and listens for it. Dante begins his great *Divina Commedia* by starting to journey down into the inverted cone that is the *Inferno*, the terraces gradually shrinking to one point (the silent frozen figure of Lucifer). The speaker thinks back to a viewing of Dante's so-called death mask (likely in fact to have been made more than a century after the poet's death), displayed in Florence: a 'cliff edge' for the observer in the sense that we are looking at a face that has looked over the edge of the world into the pit. It is not a journey that the poem's speaker feels any inclination to join.

So the observer circles the silent mask, rather as the planetary spheres circle the silent earth, intermittently reflected in the glass that encloses Dante's face. The contrast drawn seems to be between the listening silence of the mask, striving to 'discern' the buried sounds of hell, and the smooth motion of the observer who declines the task of attending to the Inferno. The poems that follow bear this out, as Schnackenburg reflects both on Dante's ultimate silencing and blinding in the *Paradiso* before the vision of God, and on the grotesque and horrifying moment in the *Inferno* when he tears a branch from a tree and the tree discharges blood and cries of pain. The trees are the metamorphosed souls of suicides. Is poetry a matter of tearing words and blood together out of human extremity, a kind of giving birth to something better left unspoken/unborn? So we might think if we imagined 'poetry was love'; but this leaves us bored and disgusted with poetry. What if something entirely other is at work? What if we need to look over the cliff edge if we are to look into the face of God?

So poetry is not simply 'love' in any straightforward way, and certainly not if love prevents us from attending to what is there to be seen. If we stop ourselves seeing and hearing the reverberation of suffering in the circles of hell, we may avoid the radiance of eternal love. Dante's mask shows the face of someone who has been still enough to hear the sounds of hell, but also still enough to imagine the immense irresistibility of God's presence. The reflection of the observer's face in the glass case may or may not map on to a face like Dante's; poetry has to decide whether or not to look for that still point. A high risk and a high 'reward' (wrong word, of course). True seeing, hearing and speaking grow from that risk and make us think again about what we mean by 'love', and how easily we can make it serve our reluctance to look over the edge.

David Scott

The Friends' Meeting Room

I have known silences between
breaks in conversation, agonisingly
searching for the next word. I remember
the silence of exams curdling in my stomach;
and the silence of aloneness filled
with small domestic noises,
a kettle clicking off and distant traffic.

I've even known a silence bring me
to my knees, in an ancient church, held
through the regular deep ticking
of a mechanism in the tower
when everything that summer afternoon
had slowed right down. But this,

in a room of many windows
and much light, is another silence
palpable, gathered by life's long haul
attempting to do the right thing,
silence waged with thought, and moral.

Poetry regularly tries to conjure silence, in one way or another; to discover when and how to stop and make room. David Scott here itemizes different sorts of silence, beginning with the silence that makes the wrong kind of room, a space that cries out to be filled because it is exposing gaps in understanding or sympathy. The silence of the exam hall is one filled with mute anxiety; the silence of plain physical solitude somehow amplifies the small or far-off noises we would not otherwise notice. Neither of these makes the room we need. That can happen in a building where silence is habitual, engrained in the material environment, underlined by the slow rhythm of a clock on the church tower: time lengthens and allows for something more than was planned or expected. We might at this point expect a reflection along the lines that R. S. Thomas so often develops, about waiting and watching, as if for some elusive bird in the thicket or on the seashore.

But the poem – without denying this perspective – moves on to the silence of the Friends' Meeting; a plain, light-filled room, in which silence is not – so to speak – inherited in the very form of the building, nor imposed by something external, nor accidental. It is 'gathered by life's long haul/ attempting to do the right thing'. The Quaker commitment to listening before action, the commitment of the 'long haul' of ordinary human experience, is what produces this shared silence. It is, in other words, born out of a particular sort of human struggle, a silence that is achieved by this unswerving search for action that has integrity. 'Silence waged with thought' is a skilfully challenging and ambiguous phrase. Normally we 'wage' war; so the silence may be itself the struggle *against* thought, the struggle to silence thought of a certain kind. This is reminiscent of the way in which the great ascetical teachers of the early Church write about the battle against *logismoi*, chains of obsessive mental activity, forged out of fantasy, memory, desire, fear and so on, and the battle also with concepts and images of God that keep us from the radical challenge of divine infinity, the ultimate 'space' we are drawn to inhabit. But the 'waging' of silence might equally be a conflict pursued *thoughtfully* – 'with thought' in another sense: thoughtful silence is effective as a means of waging the war against various kinds of violence because it makes us hesitate and look at our impulses. The thoughtfulness creates its own 'room', a gap of time without pressure to act so that action when it comes will be more than just *reaction*.

Scott calls such silence 'moral' because it both grows out of and feeds into a particular mode of behaviour, the characteristic Quaker search for reasoned consensus and the refusal of violent means of pursuing conflict in any circumstances. The thrust of the poem is thus not simply that a creative and spiritually significant silence is more than a cessation of speech; that is a fairly familiar point. It goes further by seeking to pinpoint a specific kind of spiritually charged silence, the silence that comes from moral patience and persistence, the habit of not just reacting, not just acting on instinct.

And this implies that silence can be something we practise in the details of daily life, not something we wait to overtake us; the 'long haul' of patient self-examination and reflective pausing is what makes the shared stillness of the Friends' Meeting so distinctive for the poet here. The ambience that invites and intensifies silence is not the architectural space hallowed by prayer but the awareness of a shared commitment to honesty and struggle. It is not by any means that this somehow pushes out the idea of silence as openness to grace; but such openness must be invited and nourished in all personal and collective decisions, not only in Eliot's 'unattended moment'. Somehow we must learn to 'make room' in the very heart of our actions.

David Scott

Canon Fenton, Theologian

There was something defiant about his funeral,
as if he had decided from the start
to resist the eulogy.

No one more fascinated than he
by the ending of St Mark's Gospel,
refusing the milliner's itch, to stitch
just one more bit onto the story.
For him the story was of faith,
and how faith narrows down the power
of most things, this side of the future.

The eulogy would be merely what he did
in the waiting room: life's see-sawing
of one foot onto the other, which is
nothing, in comparison to the light
so bright we can only see it
through the negative. That is the light
that brooks no eulogy.

The outer life is burnt or buried on a particular
date,
but faith flies away from there, to become something
suddenly other. No one I know has been so firm on
that.

John Fenton was a distinguished New Testament scholar and an exceptionally forceful preacher; he would be hard to classify as either a liberal or a conservative in any conventional way, as he defended some radical views on various issues of biblical interpretation, yet held passionately to a profoundly orthodox view of God's freedom and the human need of grace. Above all, he resisted any systematizing of belief that would domesticate the strangeness and inexhaustibility of God's reality.

David Scott – who had been a pupil of Fenton's – pays him tribute in this poem, while recognizing that Fenton himself would have fiercely resisted being eulogized. The ending of Mark's Gospel to which Scott refers is the enigmatic statement that the women discovering the empty tomb of Jesus 'said nothing to anyone, for they were afraid'. For the poet, this is what Fenton would have seen as an exemplary theological moment. A less inspired author would have given way to the 'itch' to elaborate, to provide a satisfying ending. But what if the ending is and should be inconclusive? Not inconclusive in the sense that we are left simply with a vague impression about the resurrection, but in the sense that some immense fact has been disclosed about which we do not know what to say. It unveils the future, you could say; it affirms God's faithfulness to the divine promise. But by doing so it tells us how little we can know or do here in this world, how little human capacity amounts to in itself.

Hence the image of the 'waiting room'; this is not where the ultimately significant action happens – or, perhaps more accurately, it is not where *we* have the job of performing the sort of significant actions that merit eulogies. We manage this life as best we can, and it is not a matter of indifference (Fenton would certainly not have thought that); but it is not a theatre for us to do great deeds and accumulate honour. Fenton in this regard is close to St Augustine's scepticism about the obsession with honour and status, 'glory', that human beings display, and his preaching often returned to the necessity of puncturing our self-importance (he liked to challenge the dictum ascribed to St Teresa of Avila, 'Christ has no hands on earth but yours'). What is significantly active, in and beyond the world alike, is the unbearable light of divine presence, which 'we can only see . . ./ through the negative'. Our denial, our negation of our own power to be significant or honourable or whatever, is one way of glimpsing just what it is that acts and matters. And the wording here evokes also the image of the photographic negative in which light and dark are reversed: we see the light of God in stark, black contrast to the light we think we have generated by our actions.

Faith is, the poem says, a narrowing down of what we think we can do, not by means of abusing or undermining our actual bodily and historical reality but by putting it into a relentlessly realistic perspective; and so, when 'the outer life' evaporates, as it is bound to do, faith is free to step into the unimaginable future that has been so paradoxically and tantalizingly shown to us in Jesus. What lies beyond the life we now live is more different than we could think: the promise of that difference lies in the very fact that we have no proper images of it in what seems to matter to us now, in our pictures of ourselves, our scales of values and so on. Eulogy is impossible in this perspective – except for the modest eulogy at the poem's end: no one else saw this so clearly.

Christian faith and other kinds of faith are often rebuked for being too preoccupied with heaven at the expense of earth. That is not what Scott celebrates in John Fenton. To be 'preoccupied with heaven' in that way has often meant only that heaven has become a fictionalized version of earth, with all our follies and vanities absolved and sanctified. The challenge here is sharper. Looking to heaven is looking determinedly away from the follies and vanities that smother us day by day; the enigmatic promise of life eternal is simply the glimpse, the hint, that we must be ready for a transformation more total than any system or any image can capture (look at Olga Sedakova's 'The Angel of Rheims' poem, next). And because of this we can act in this life not with success and acclaim but with freedom and honesty. To know what that looks like, you need to know someone like John Fenton.

Olga Sedakova

The Angel of Rheims

for François Fédier

'Ready?'
The angel asks, smiling –
'I'm asking; though I know quite well
you're ready, sure to be;
you see, it's not just anyone I'm talking to,
it's you: you,
human being, whose heart just can't survive
knowing that you've betrayed even your earthly
  king –
the one they used to crown here on this spot to
  rule the nation –
let alone that other Lord, of course,
the King of Heaven, our slaughtered Lamb
who dies in the hope
that you'll hear me asking, again
and again and again,
as every evening
the bells conjure my name
here in this country of overflowing wheat
and shining vineyard,
where the ears of wheat and the vine clusters
soak up the sound of me.

But all the same,
in this rose-pink and crumbling stone,
with my raised hand
that some World War has broken off,
all the same, let me remind you: are you
ready?
Ready for plague, famine, earthquake, fire,
foreign invasions, surges of aggression?
Well, yes; all that's important, obviously, but it's
not what I'm asking about, not what I'm under orders
to remind you of, not what they sent me for.
What I'm saying is:
are you
ready
for more joy than you'd believe?

The 'Smiling Angel' is a thirteenth-century sculpture on the West front of Rheims Cathedral. It was severely damaged by German shells in the First World War and restored – though still with one hand missing – in 1926. This quizzical poem is a sort of translation into words of the angel's quizzical smile. The angel teases and tantalizes the reader.

It is clearly the angel of the annunciation: the angel's voice is what we hear echoing in the Angelus ringing from church bells across the countryside, a peaceful, even sleepy, northern French pastoral setting that has absorbed, 'soaked up', the sound of the angelic 'Hail Mary' for centuries. But angelic voices are not just comforting echoes in a glowing rural landscape; they also announce change, and change may be threatening and destructive. The angel glancingly reminds us of the horrors of war, draws attention to its own 'wounds' – and then turns the tables once again. 'Are you ready?' We hear it as a warning to gird up our loins for coming to terms with the terror and pain of history; and then the angel smiles and shakes its head. We're not invited to think about anything so obvious as suffering and catastrophe: in a world like ours the truly revolutionary fact is *joy*.

In some sense we don't need reminding to be 'ready' for tragedy; it's too close and familiar. We don't need an angel to tell us that the world is terrible. In St Luke's Gospel, it is not, after all, the angel of the annunciation who tells Mary that her soul will be run through with agony as if with a sword; that is the message she hears from the old prophet, Simeon. Mary would only have had to look around her in Galilee to see the signs of the military occupation, the routine violence, which Sedakova's angel casually catalogues, the experience the angel has witnessed directly at Rheims. But the angel's first word to Mary is literally 'Rejoice', in the Greek of St Luke. What we are not ready for is the possibility of ecstatic fulfilment, heaven and earth united in extravagant celebration.

It has been said that if there is a 'problem of evil' in the world (how can a good God create a world in which such anguish is possible?), there is equally a 'problem of good': if the world is so dark, how is it that there is a promise and a delight that seem to outshine the darkness even for those who have known the worst of human loss and agony?

The daring question posed by Sedakova's angel is whether it is not sometimes more comfortable, paradoxically, to settle down with the expectation of failure or suffering or hopelessness, so that the possibility of something quite other is as traumatic in its way as suffering itself. As usual, Shakespeare captured it, in the depiction of the death of Gloucester in *King Lear*: his son Edgar reveals that he is still alive and has been accompanying the old man, blinded and cast out, in his despairing wanderings, and 'his flawed heart/ . . . Twixt two extremes of passion, joy and grief,/ Burst *smilingly*.' The knowledge of forgiveness and restored love can be too much for us – especially in the nightmare world of greed, venom and inhumanity that Shakespeare's play depicts. The smile of recognition is both a consummation of reconciled joy and the final burden that the heart ('flawed', both weak and guilty) can't manage to carry.

'Are you ready?' asks the angel. Can you brace yourself for a discovery that your own emotional resources may not be able to cope with? The discovery of an infinity of delight? Human beings, says the angel, feel a kind of guilt about betraying or forgetting the memories of prosperity and stability associated with the ancient coronation ceremonies that used to take place in Rheims cathedral; perhaps it is time that we thought about what we may have betrayed or forgotten in losing sight of the revolutionary promise of a grounded, lasting, transfiguring joy, the promise of Mary's Son.

Olga Sedakova

Chinese Journey 18

Let us praise our earth,
  let us praise the moon on the water,
praise what is for no-one and for everyone,
  what is nowhere and everywhere –
big as a swallow's eye,
  or a crumb of dry bread,
or a ladder of butterfly's wings,
  a ladder let down from heaven.
It's not just tragedy and pity
  that steer my heart like a bridle,
it's everything that smiles
  in the miraculousness of water.
Let us praise branches, dark, beyond all price,
  bathed in live crystal,
and all the spirits keeping watch, unsleeping
  over every seed in soil,
and that there is reward
  and warding-off of evil,
and that, as gardens have gardeners,
  earth has praise.

This piece is part of a substantial sequence of poems with Chinese associations – the first collection that Olga Sedakova published, establishing her as a poet with profound religious themes but capable of articulating them at a bit of an angle to the Christian language she would later use more directly in her work. The poems evoke characteristic features of Chinese landscape and traditional art. We should read it with Chinese painting and calligraphy – and poetry – in mind: the spare, fluid lines, the depiction of cloud and mountains, broad and still rivers and moonlight. Just as in her poem 'The Angel of Rheims' that we have just been reading, Sedakova draws us away from any exclusive imaginative concentration on suffering: what breaks open the heart is not just tragedy but also beauty – and not just beauty in a conventional sense, but the kind of beauty that seems to say to the viewer that it really doesn't matter whether she's there or not.

Not an easy idea to get your head around; but there is certainly a dimension of recognizing beauty that goes beyond just finding something that speaks to *you*. Sedakova is pointing to the moments when we simply forget that we are looking. The object, the scene, just holds us. It isn't 'ours', it is simply there, something we drop into and out of, something that is what it is because of its rootedness in something immeasurably beyond my own perception and presence. This is beauty as 'sacred', as having a depth that we don't fathom, far beyond what relates to us as passing observers – a face that is turned away from us, we might say.

Once we have registered that there is a dimension of reality not determined by us, a perspective to which we are not central, we can recognize that there are agencies, processes, call them what you will, that sustain the continuities of things, around the corner of our vision. The memorable concluding image about gardening helps make further sense of this. 'Gardens have gardeners' – not the other way round. The garden is already a working convergence of natural processes, and among those processes is the conscious involvement of human gardeners – who will soon be in trouble if they imagine that they can treat the garden as a possession that they control. And the earth itself 'has praise': the acknowledgement of the beauty that is purposeless and free of its 'audience' is part of earth's own life. Our conscious recognition, representation, celebration of beauty is one of the things that 'earth' does, creating intelligent, receptive images of itself in the eye of human observers and speakers. Poetry is neither an arbitrary and rootless exercise in word-spinning, nor a slavish reproduction of what is 'out there'; it is a way in which the whole complex of reality mirrors itself in human speech and thinking and feeling, it is reality coming to a rebirth in word and image.

Praise, then, is not just what we *add* to the world, a dutiful acknowledgement of its order or beauty. It is something that the world actively makes possible and brings to birth. Like the gardener in the garden, we have real initiative and agency here; but like the gardener in the garden, we are engaging with an active environment of which we are genuinely part. Seeds are sown in the world and human speech is one of the things that come up from the soil. Pushing it further, it's as though Sedakova is saying that poetry itself is a natural thing even before it is a cultural phenomenon. We 'praise', we stand in conscious and grateful recognition before our world, because the world's processes have brought to life a humanity whose nature and instinct is just that act of glad recognition.

So we are left with a fruitful tension. The moment when we recognize a beauty that in one sense has nothing to do with us – the ice coating the tree's bark, the moon reflected, these perceptions that have nothing to *give* us in the way of usefulness or profit – is the moment when we might just grasp that our humanity itself *is what it is* in this act of recognition. We are most deeply in tune with the truth of our participation in the world around when we are most radically detached from the urge to exploit it and 'make something of it'. The 'detachment' of poetry from ordinary human usefulness is essential to our being human at all.

Martha Serpas

Poem Found

New Orleans, September 2005

. . . And God said, 'Let there be a dome in the
    midst
of the waters' and into the dome God put

the poor, the addicts, the blind, and the oppressed.
God put the unsightly sick and the crying young

into the dome and the dry land did not appear.
And God allowed those who favored themselves

born in God's image to take dominion over
the dome and everything that creeped within it

and made them to walk to and fro above it
in their jumbo planes and in their copy rooms

and in their conference halls. And then
God brooded over the dome and its multitudes

and God saw God's own likeness in the shattered
tiles and the sweltering heat and the polluted rain.

God saw everything and chose to make it very good.
God held the dome up to the light

like an open locket and in every manner called
the others to look inside and those who saw

rested on that day and those who didn't
went to and fro and walked up and down

the marsh until the loosened silt gave way
to a void, and darkness covered the faces with deep
sleep.

Hurricane Katrina struck the south-eastern seaboard of the United States in August 2005, and the city of New Orleans in particular suffered massive damage. The Louisiana Superdome, a large sports venue, was used as shelter for those who had been forced to leave their homes and had no alternative accommodation; overcrowding, structural weaknesses in the building, failures in power supplies and lack of medical and sanitary facilities rapidly made this a nightmarish environment. Several people died (at least one by suicide).

This is the starting point for Serpas (a native of Louisiana, whose work often deals with local culture and issues), as she picks up the language of Genesis 1 about how God in creation extends the dome of the sky ('the firmament of heaven' in older translations) over the earth to separate the 'waters above' and the 'waters below' – the chaotic ocean out of which the order and stability of life on earth is summoned by God's command. The poem uses various phrases from the Genesis text – and later from the book of Job – as a savagely ironic framing for the appalling (and avoidable) plight of those confined in the Superdome. In contrast to the Genesis narrative, the dry land is nowhere to be seen – literally, as the flood waters rise around the building, metaphorically as the order of created life breaks down in chaos and squalor. Predictably, those who had to take refuge in the Superdome were the least secure and prosperous in the community, the very old and the very young and the left behind, those incapable of protecting themselves for whatever reason, those without resources; the wealthier parts of the population had various escape routes. For them, being made in God's image means the freedom to take charge and decide the fate of others; God, it seems, permits them a liberty not granted to those imprisoned in the dome.

Yet God, 'brooding over' the mass of suffering people (like the Spirit 'brooding over' the chaos of the first stages of creation), sees his face reflected in the wreckage of the Superdome (damage to its roof and soaring temperatures were among the factors that made conditions unbearable) and the suffering of its inmates. God holds it up to the light and invites the secure and powerful to look – presumably to recognize the divine image that God's self sees there. Like creation itself, the disastrous situation can be made 'very good' (Genesis again) if it opens the eyes of the powerful. But those who look do nothing (they 'rested on that day', like God at the conclusion of his creative work); those who refuse to look go 'to and fro and . . . up and down' in the earth, as Satan describes himself doing in the first chapter of the book of Job – an earth that is reverting to watery chaos, undergoing a sort of de-creation. The darkness that covers the face of the deep in Genesis 1 is restored in the 'deep sleep' of indifference, and the primal void opens up once more.

A poem of controlled anger and a brilliant, unsparing reworking of scriptural imagery; the question it poses is, 'Where do we think the divine image is to be seen?' In our own comfortable liberty to buy off the threat of suffering and danger, or in the damaged and insecure humanity held for a precarious moment in the space between the waters above and the waters below? It is a poem that poses questions of the utmost urgency as the environmental crisis worsens: the intolerable injustice of the New Orleans situation is a picture of the kind of imbalance that is threatened by climate crisis, where the least protected carry the heaviest load of risk –and 'those who favored themselves' continue their perambulations by jet and their discussions and endless deferrals of action, or else walk away.

These spectators, 'the others', become complicit in de-creation, in the work of the 'Opposer', the literal meaning of 'Satan'. The refusal to acknowledge the divine image is not simply a moral failing, it is also an unpicking of the fabric of the created world, a vote for chaos. The ultimate irony is that the self-protection of the powerful accelerates the tilt of history towards a chaos that will extinguish the human world. St Paul wrote to the Romans that 'it is full time now for you to wake from sleep' (Romans 13.11); the psalmist (Psalm 95.7–8) urges us to listen *today* and not harden our hearts.

Vikram Seth

This

Hearts-ease, hearts-bane; a balm that chafes one
  raw;
  The soul in splints; graph with no grid or gauge;
  A fort, a house on stilts, a hut of straw;
A tic, a weal, the flu, the plague, the rage;

Bug swept in through the net; moth with a sting;
  Two planes in fog jammed blind; a mailed kid
  glove;
  A dance on coals that makes us yelp and sing;
A rook or roc or swan or goose or dove.

A beast of light; a blaze to quench or stoke;
  Bread burst and burnt; sweet wind-fall;
  storm-cloud-milk;
  Hope raised and razed; skin-ploy; sleep-foil;
  steel-silk;
Hands held in lieu of breath; our genes' sick joke;
  The sea to drink or sink in; the gods' sty;
  What we must have or die; or have and die.

For some time, the novelist and essayist Vikram Seth has lived in the Old Rectory at Bemerton in Wiltshire, where George Herbert lived in the seventeenth century for the three years before his untimely death. He has written about the experience of Herbert as 'a tactful host, who never tried to bully me into his philosophy or style'. But he was moved to compose a short sequence of poems the style of which was indeed shaped by Herbert's writing, poems modelled on a handful of the older poet's most distinctive works, playing with rhymes and line-lengths and complex patternings of sound and shape on the page. They are as a group entitled 'Shared Ground' and were designed for musical setting.

Seth admits to not being a religiously committed writer, and his background is not Christian but Hindu, yet the poems – simply by their formal echoes of Herbert's music – prompt some lingering on the frontier of 'sacred' and 'profane' experience, some questioning about how porous those boundaries are. Herbert, after all, is a master of finding his way Godwards in conversational speech about everyday things. This poem is based on Herbert's well-known sonnet on prayer – a string of metaphors with no grammatical connection, simply a flow of constantly shifting insights about one central experience that is not to be pinned down once and for all.

What, then, is 'This'? In Herbert's prototype, the subject is announced in the first line but not repeated; here it is not even announced. The title does not tell us either, but what is being explored in this dense and wonderfully allusive poem is love. Like all good metaphorical speech, the succession of images sets out the contradictions that push us into poetry (that 'hurt us into poetry' as W. H. Auden says in another context). We are healed and we are wounded; we are in a landscape with no coordinates, we are supported and guided, we build a house that is fragile and well defended. We hurtle towards one another like planes flying blind. We 'dance on coals'. The experience is the grating cry of rooks, the predatory descent of the giant bird of Arabic folklore, the swan's grace, the goose's absurdity, the dove's traditional gentleness and fidelity. It is fire that needs either feeding or smooring (covering with ashes). The verbal nimbleness intensifies as the poem moves on, the assonances getting tighter (burst/burnt, raised/razed, the intricate sequence of 'skin-ploy/sleep-foil/steel-silk'). Just as Herbert dares to construct a deliberately clumsy three-word adjectival compound ('Christ-side-piercing' – prayer as the spear thrust into the side of the crucified Jesus), so Seth gives us 'storm-cloud-milk'. Love is genetically determined, mocking our pretensions to seriousness; and it is also where the gods go slumming. It is 'The sea to drink or sink in' – a harsh choice, between drowning and the insatiable thirst produced by salt water; both mean death.

Death is where the poem appropriately concludes, with an echo of Auden's poem, 'September 1939'. The last line of that poem was originally, 'We must love one another or die'; Auden later recoiled from what he came to see as sentimental illusion and substituted, 'We must love one another *and* die' – and eventually declined to reprint the poem at all. Seth simply presents the two wings of the paradox; we shall die without love, and love will kill us.

Part of the skill of this sonnet is the way in which it sustains throughout the tension between the creative and the destructive in love. The old Elizabethan association of death with sexual consummation (Shakespeare is constantly making use of the double sense of 'die', in the plays as well as the sonnets) is very much in view, but so is something deeper still: what if that which we most desire is indeed what will 'kill' us? What if, to be where we need to be, to be 'in the truth', something of us must be consumed and vanish? Herbert would have grasped what was behind all this, understanding as he did how a love that is finally at one with truth might hurt us out of our protective masks.

Karl Shapiro

The Alphabet

The letters of the Jews as strict as flames
Or little terrible flowers lean
Stubbornly upwards through the perfect ages,
Singing through solid stone the sacred names.
The letters of the Jews are black and clean
And lie in chain-line over Christian pages.
The chosen letters bristle like barbed wire
That hedge the flesh of man,
Twisting and tightening the book that warns.
These words, this burning bush, this flickering pyre
Unsacrifices the bled son of man
Yet plaits his crown of thorns.

Where go the tipsy idols of the Roman
Past synagogues of patient time,
Where go the sisters of the Gothic rose,
Where go the blue eyes of the Polish women
Past the almost natural crime,
Past the still speaking embers of ghettos,
There rise the tinder flowers of the Jews.
The letters of the Jews are dancing knives
That carve the heart of darkness seven ways.
These are the letters that all men refuse
And will refuse until the king arrives
And will refuse until the death of time
And all is rolled back in the book of days.

Jewish tradition sometimes speaks of how the actual Hebrew words and letters of the Torah, the five 'books of Moses' that begin the Hebrew Scriptures, pre-exist in heaven, to be contemplated from the very beginning of creation by the angels. The imagery of the poem is of written words that are 'strict', 'clean', that chain and confine humanity and at the same time are on fire; they are a spiky hedge for human flesh, but their sharpness can also 'carve the heart of darkness'. What we are shown is – we could say – the very idea of divine language, an utterance that splits and maps and makes sense of the chaotic dark of the world we inhabit; or, turning the image in a different direction, as Shapiro briefly and starkly does, an utterance that makes shocking and unwelcome sense of the chaotic blankness, the false innocence, of 'Christian pages' (significantly rhyming with the 'perfect ages' through which the black 'flowers' of the Hebrew text obstinately push their way). The white space of the page is scribbled over with the black, burnt letters that declare Christian guilt for the atrocities of two millennia. The absolving death of Christ is undone by these letters; there has been no atoning sacrifice for Christian murderousness towards the Jews. And so, at the same time, the actual suffering of Christ the human being, the *Jewish* human being, is pressed more relentlessly than ever on our sight, the crown of thorns is plaited afresh.

Shapiro's imagery is brilliantly dense and closely woven, 'Twisting and tightening', like the words he is writing about. He is reversing our perspective as readers and speakers. One of our favourite illusions is that we can *use* words to mean what we please, wiping them out when it suits us. But what if words confine us, what if they tell us of what we can't do and can't forget and can't erase? These 'black and clean' embers from the fire of human bigotry and cruelty, these 'tinder flowers' (and notice the teasing verbal echo that tempts us for a moment to think we are reading or hearing 'tender' flowers and harshly pulls us back), represent the truths we have no power to destroy: ultimately they stand for the truth of God's own moral stability, for all that the Law, the Torah, declares. But they communicate this simply by their persistence – blackened remains from the flames, irredeemably staining the page of a history we have tried to expunge and rewrite. This is what 'all men refuse': the acceptance of historical guilt. And this is what Christianity colludes with, pretending that the end has come and the letter of the Hebrew text is absorbed into a nebulous world of the spirit. The Jew, in contrast, is still waiting for the king to come. The Jew does not pretend history is over or healed or redeemed.

This is more than just a 'Holocaust' poem. It puts to the Christian reader a fundamental question: is the redeeming death of Christ an alibi for the evils of Christian history? Do Christians speak of the mystery of the cross in such a way as to pretend to an innocence that is wholly false? And does the Christian claim to bear witness to a point on which human history finally converges mean that the angular realities of suffering – and, more particularly, the suffering inflicted by Christians – can be regarded as invisible, stowed away in the past? For the Jewish reader, this is a poem that echoes the prayer, 'O earth, cover not their blood', which so many have prayed at the site of the death camps. Over against the hazy dishonesty of pagan hedonism, the religious dramas of Gothic piety, the comfortable blandness of nationalist romanticism, the charred fragments of the Hebrew script continue to rise up and spell out the unchanging divine Name. Paganism, religiosity, romanticism may help us to believe that the crimes of history are 'almost natural' (there is a world of irony in that phrase); the Jewish alphabet denies us any such comfort.

C. H. Sisson

Steps to the Temple

What is belief? A recognition?
Who knows of what? If any say
He knows, he lies.
Who knows what never was begun
And will not end? God is a way,
And a surprise.

And in that way we cannot choose,
For choice deceives us, as it must.
We live in sense,
Certain at least that we shall lose
That urgency, for we are dust.
Our recompense,

If any, cannot be to find
That beauty and that bitterness
Again. A new
Perception must await the vanished mind
– Or none, and which of these we cannot guess.
That much is true.

So here, we who are fallible
As shifting sands, may feel the tide
Flow over us, or in, or out.
If in, then all will then be well;

If not, then we should feel no pride
Even in doubt.

A sympathetic commentator described Sisson's version of Anglican Christianity as 'pagan' – in the sense that it was grounded less in doctrine than in an overwhelming awareness of locality and belonging, a religious affirmation of the relations that define any individual here and now. Sisson, a formidably intelligent essayist on a variety of topics as well as a poet and critic, defended a very idiosyncratic kind of conservative politics, in which the monarchy and the professional civil service played a central role as maintaining a pragmatic local order with no claims to transcendent rightness in its decision but with a sustainable degree of stable, trustworthy capacity to keep daily business flowing. The Church functioned as a reminder that the life of the individual had meaning only within the inherited community and that its highest end was an intelligent loyalty to the life of that community as the only place where a solid identity could be found through a shared consciousness coming alive in each physically separate human being. 'Our thoughts are not our own', he wrote, and a public tradition of corporate religious practice was essential to recognizing this and living it out with dignity. Sisson will write of 'incarnation' as fundamental to his understanding, but in a somewhat unusual sense: it is a divine assumption of humanity as such. It almost does not matter what the detail of the story of the Incarnate One is, because the point is that God has taken on the 'kind', the human race as such. Whatever the complications that arise from determining exactly where the limits of humankind can be found, the point remains, only as an instance of humankind could the 'individual' be thought of – let alone redeemed.

'Pagan'? Perhaps not quite, though not precisely orthodox Christianity either. What stops it being the plain sanctifying of a national status quo or a purely 'given', unthought attachment to place and heritage is the recognition that the substance of the Christian story does have moral consequences. If this myth is in any way true, it points us to seeing one another differently from how we should otherwise see people. From one point of view, all we can say is that if God is real, incarnation is possible and the morality of Christians corresponds with what most truly exists; and if not, we shall certainly not find any more adequate representation of truth by exerting our individual imagination.

This terse and elegant poem articulates something of Sisson's austere religious sensibility. Unsurprisingly, given his admiration for the seventeenth-century English poets and divines, its style is reminiscent of the cadences of some of George Herbert's verse – and the poem's title surely refers to Herbert's collection, *The Temple*. If we have faith, it is an acknowledgement of something that we absolutely cannot know in itself. 'God is a way,/ And a surprise': what we know is the path of behaviour, ritual and moral, by which we acquire a practical wisdom to hold us steady in the world. Whatever else must be wholly unexpected because literally unimaginable. Individual choice about faith is neither here nor there: what prompts or leads us is the life of our senses, in a deeply paradoxical way. It is sense experience itself that tells us that the life of the senses will pass. The 'urgency' of that life cannot persist, and so what there is – if anything – that will not pass must be other. Ahead of us, therefore, is either oblivion or a totally unfamiliar kind of perceiving or knowing – the surprise of God. No guarantees, no proofs; and so we can have no objective certainty about how the tide actually flows over our 'shifting sands', whether bringing us to an eternal home or sweeping us out to a featureless ocean. The arrogance of the unbeliever needs chastening as much as the triumphalism of the believer.

There are some parallels with Betjeman's approach to faith (though neither would have relished the comparison, I suspect). 'And is it true? For if it is . . .' Sisson approaches this not with Betjeman's vaguely optimistic wistfulness but with a more clinical lucidity: if we believe, it is because we have recognized something that by definition is not an object for the ordinary experience of the senses – recognized either by some obscure intuition or simply by thinking through what sense experience can and can't deliver. Our belief is never compelled (or defended) by knock-down argument, but neither is it based on our choice. We recognize, if we recognize at all, a path into which we are summoned, in which, once we have begun to walk, we have no choice about the direction we are taking. Faith is both a drastic openness to the most radical surprise and the acceptance that this path has no defence, no rationale, beyond itself. Like a good many other philosophers and poets (Wittgenstein, for example; worth looking at Jan Zwicky's poem in this collection), Sisson stands poised between scepticism and contemplative absorption. Not a bad place for poets and philosophers to live – though not the only one.

Dana Littlepage Smith

Thoughts Without Order Concerning the Love of God

The kingdom of my kitchen invites one snail
to measure a carrot peel with the full length

of her body. Of Christ and necessity this snail says
nothing. The celery shines. By morning, my
countertops,

my floor will glisten with the star road of her
meanderings.
It measures a universe of dark and light in silence.

The fleshed heart of the strawberry, the skirts of
daffodils:
each in its turn holds this snail's antennaed
attention.

To fold into the curve of time and space, exactly
as things are is this creature's genius and my intent,

daily in the kingdom of my dark kitchen
where life arrives with its glorious abandon.

Somewhere in the background are the philosophical reflections of Simone Weil, whose various essays on 'Forms of the

Implicit Love of God' and similar topics (collected in the posthumous volume, *Waiting on God*) do have something to say, unlike the snail in this poem, about 'Christ and necessity'. But the shining trail that the snail makes in its nocturnal progress through the kitchen is a kind of embodiment of what Weil writes about: the need for an attention to the immediacy of the world around that will displace the fretful, self-directed activities of the self by simply adhering to what is there and conforming the intelligence to its shape – the discipline we acquire in studying mathematics or in learning a language, as she spells out in some of her best-known essays. The love of God, so far from being an intensified emotional state enjoyed by the soul in private, is ultimately just this adherence to what is there, enabling us to act in freedom from self-preoccupation.

The snail is a model of 'attention', we are told here: it tracks with exactitude the contours of all that it encounters, 'folds into the curve' of what is there. The use of the word 'attention' points us towards Weil's inspiration for the poem: and the speaker describes her goal as precisely this kind of attentiveness. The snail carries it through by its own native 'genius'; the human subject has to discover it intentionally. Yet the catch is, the more deliberate and conscious that intent, the harder it is to attend – a theme Weil's notebooks discuss more than once. We are not told in the poem how our intention can lead us to the snail's level of fidelity to the line and contour of things as they are.

But the 'dark kitchen' is a place where 'life arrives': it is not that we are simply struggling to move and grow in a vacuum. Life comes with 'abandon' – once again, a charged word, often used in French spiritual writing for the determined acceptance with which the human self approaches the matter of everyday living once the fantasies and cravings of the ego have been quieted. 'Glorious abandon' is a conventional enough phrase for natural exuberance, but in this context it is also the glorious unselfconsciousness of the life around us which we must learn to respond to with a self-forgetting that will hold us close to God, an adhesion to our trust in providence as close as the snail's to the carrot, the celery, the flowers and the floor.

The snail has 'measured' a whole world in the silence of the night. The words imply that it is in such dark and silence – and the kitchen, we must remember, is 'dark' – that we learn to practise this slow, adhesive movement, slipping slowly over the tangible surface of things and absorbing the feel of each contour; like the snail, we have no map of the whole territory and no short cuts that will help us in this travelling. It takes the time it takes. Simone Weil writes about the 'labyrinth' we enter once we have been drawn in to the world's life and beauty, and how it pulls us towards a centre that is a sort of black hole into which we disappear: we are 'eaten' by the magnetic reality of God at the heart of things, and although we emerge from this labyrinth, it is as radically altered beings, beings changed by the love of God. That love is constituted by the following of the labyrinthine path, by the time taken. These may be 'thoughts without order', but the order they invite us to follow is the step-by-step feeling our way along the territory of our world that we learn from the snail – not a presence many would be glad to see in a kitchen, but a welcome teacher for all that.

Stevie Smith

The Airy Christ

After reading Dr Rieu's translation of St Mark's Gospel

Who is this that comes in grandeur, coming from the blazing East?
This is he we had not thought of, this is he the airy Christ.

Airy, in an airy manner in an airy parkland walking,
Others take him by the hand, lead him, do the talking.

But the Form, the airy One, frowns an airy frown,
What they say he knows must be, but he looks aloofly down,

Looks aloofly at his feet, looks aloofly at his hands,
Knows they must, as prophets say, nailèd be to wooden bands.

As he knows the words he sings, that he sings so happily
Must be changed to working laws, yet sings he ceaselessly.

Those who truly hear the voice, the words, the
 happy song,
Never shall need working laws to keep from doing
 wrong.

Deaf men will pretend sometimes they hear the
 song, the words,
And make excuse to sin extremely; this will be
 absurd.

Heed it not. Whatever foolish men may do the
 song is cried
For those who hear, and the sweet singer does not
 care that he was crucified.

For he does not wish that men should love him
 more than anything
Because he died; he only wishes they would hear
 him sing.

In 1952, the classical scholar E. V. Rieu published a translation in modern English of the four Gospels. Stevie Smith, an agnostic with a strong and persistent interest in Christianity – and a love for the traditional liturgy of the Church of England, a theme that recurs in her poetry – was intrigued and clearly challenged by Rieu's version, and her response reflects a very characteristic blend of scepticism and religious seriousness. The Christ of the new translation is 'he we had not thought of' – a figure detached from the structures of doctrine, especially doctrines of the atonement, about which Smith had some stringent things to say. The Jesus of the Gospel she reads is aware of his fate, even aware that what he says, does and suffers will be transformed – at best – into a system of law and compulsion and – at worst – into a dramatically distorted mechanism that sanctions atrocities. But he speaks, or sings, on: 'the sweet singer does not care that he was crucified'.

On the face of it, this is a strange reading of Mark's Gospel, in which the presence of the cross is so clearly signalled from early on, and the radical turning upside down of familiar values, familiar definitions of life and death, risk and safety, success and failure is so deeply woven into the narrative. 'Airy'? The modern biblical interpreters who have emphasized the austerity and abruptness of Mark's Jesus might find it an odd adjective, but the 'airiness' Smith evokes is not exactly the light, even bland thing that the word might at first suggest. It is an aloofness, a detachment that frowns in – what exactly? Puzzlement? At the distance between the song and the bleak destiny, not only of suffering but also of betrayal and corruption. The compelling authority of this Jesus is that it *does not matter to him* that he will die in anguish, any more than it matters to him whether he is loved and adored or not. The airiness is a disconcerting liberty, a distance from any kind of concern for ordinary measures of effectiveness and popularity.

So Mark's Gospel of the cross turns out to be a very paradoxical matter indeed. The cross, the humiliating defeat of Jesus in his agonizing execution and in his betrayal by his followers from the first century onwards, is central and all-important precisely because it does not matter to Jesus. The song (and is Stevie Smith being at all ironic in calling it 'happy'?) is presented as that which is incommensurably more real and powerful than the horror of execution and betrayal. The dark fate awaiting Jesus simply belongs in another universe from the song; and the Jesus who sings it sees his fate from the vantage point of this other universe.

What we are to make, on this basis, of the harrowing accounts of Jesus' suffering in the garden of Gethsemane or his cry of abandonment on the cross is a bit opaque, to say the least; and also the repeated theme in Mark of Jesus' deep frustration at the obtuseness of the disciples. But Smith has highlighted something that any reader of Mark – and indeed any orthodox Christian – might well want to ponder. Even granted the agony in the garden, and the different kind of suffering represented by the knowledge of being misheard and misrepresented, the focal point of Jesus' speech and action in the narrative is the truth that the kingdom is here and now, never mind what may happen to the one who announces it; and what enables him to announce it with absolute authority is absolute freedom from concern about whether anyone is going to listen or even love.

It's worth reading this poem together with the one that comes immediately before it in the *Selected Poems*, the piece entitled 'In the Park'. This describes a farcical incident with one old man urging another to 'pray for the Mute' (with poignant and evocative eloquence), while the other mishears this as an injunction to 'pray for the newt' and can't understand why he should need to pray for so happy a creature. The first man insists (louder) on his urging the other to piety. He is 'Mousing for pain' – a wonderfully unexpected metaphor for the undignified obsession of some religious people with suffering that they think they'll be able to alleviate. But 'Which is Christianer?' asks the poet: praying with solemn and perhaps self-regarding emotion in response to pain or simply praising, like 'the deaf other that rejoices/ So much that the cool amphibian/ Shall have his happiness, all things rejoicing with him?' The first speaker is overcome by the simple praise that the second implies and joins him in this; because, he says, 'Praise is the best prayer, the least self's there, that least's release.'

Is that what the 'airy Christ' is singing? A gospel that is not a programme for 'dealing with' pain (or sin, or guilt), but is in fact the only effective kind of healing – a glimpse of what is totally other, totally untouched by the dramas of suffering that human beings find so strangely and worryingly compelling (remember that devastating phrase, 'Mousing for pain')? No, not the whole gospel, perhaps; but certainly the gospel of one 'we had not thought of'.

John Solilo

Truth

In contemplation I ask myself,
when will the truth ever be spoken
by those who recognise it here on earth?
What kind of smell does this truth exude?

As a priest I'm sometimes criticised,
wherever I go here on earth I'm cornered
and questioned about the truth:
filled with rage they surround me.

My brother came and told me:
show others respect and you'll speak the truth,
on the point of death you'll speak the truth,
before God the truth is spoken.

What is this thing called truth?
The truth's a tale that actually happened.
When you tell the truth you relate a story
of the way it was, as it came to pass.

If you don't tell it straight your rest's disturbed
by constant hedging and circling facts.
A blindfolded man teaches this way.
To those lacking faith the truth stinks.

Who always holds to the truth?
Only the son of God, he alone.
Indifferent to being loved on earth
those lacking faith despise the truth.

The truth disgusts, its stench overpowers.
Those lacking faith don't like it at all.
Believers are saved by their faith,
the soul's eye reveals the Almighty.

John Patrick Solilo (Qhanqolo, to give him his clan name in Xhosa) was an Anglican priest and writer who was also renowned as a praise singer (*imbongi*) in the African tradition. In addition to praise poems in this style, he composed satirical and polemical poems on current questions, often sharply challenging the colonial government and lamenting the dissolution of African communal binds and the relentless appropriation of land by white settlers and administrators, Boer and British alike. He uses the techniques of Xhosa poetry with skill and energy and English translations lose the allusiveness of the originals. His recent editors and translators point to how, in Xhosa verse, especially praise poetry, there is no clear notion of a 'line' of poetry: there are sequences of clustered questions, exclamations, images and so on. Although Solilo published his poems in conventional European format, they need to be imagined as scripts for oral performance, with successive bursts of connected ideas and words. And even when he is not composing what is strictly praise poetry, celebrating prominent men and women in his community, his style is shaped by that remembered rhythm.

'Truth' is one such piece, not a personalized eulogy but a meditation, one that reflects very clearly his awareness of the tensions he lives with as a priest committed to peace-making but also committed to truth-telling. Solilo was an outspoken commentator in the English language press of South Africa, never backwards in naming and castigating abuses of colonial power, although some of his material was toned down by himself and his publishers when reproduced in book form. He was, predictably, attacked from all sides at times, surrounded, as he says, by angry critics and aggressive enquirers. How do we learn and how are we able to speak the truth?

Truth is drawn out of us in three kinds of circumstance: it grows out of respect for the humanity of others; it is all that is left for us to say in the face of death; and it is what must be spoken in the sight of God. It is telling the story as it happened; but that is a rather inadequate summary of what the whole poem is saying on the subject. Untruthfulness is a kind of inhumanity: the distortion of truth leaves us at sea, confused and afraid, never at peace. Lack of faith makes us unable to cherish or value the truth; indeed it makes us hate the truth and react to it with disgust.

But Solilo introduces into this the crucial conviction that only Christ can be fully truthful. The implication is that only Christ has complete respect for others, complete transparency to God and complete honesty in the face of death. As for the rest of us, to one degree or another we have to recognize our liability to ignore or reject truth. In Solilo's vivid image, truth will 'stink' in our nostrils, like something dead or diseased. Our untruthfulness is a kind of incapacity to know health or life when we encounter it. And it is this aspect of the poem that will strike home in a cultural context so often described as 'post-truth'. Solilo would say that 'post-truth' is a euphemism for 'anti-truth': indifference to truth is a denial of the distinction between life and death, health and sickness, and so is a kind of *post-human* phenomenon: we have lost our orientation to what gives life and – again by implication – we have forgotten that we shall die. We imagine that there will be no circumstance in which truth is drawn out of us (dragged out of us) whether we like it or not; but even if we have no intrinsic respect left for the humanity of others (the first condition for truthfulness), we cannot finally evade the confrontation with death and with God. And if truth still stinks in our nostrils in the presence of death and God, we are in serious trouble, locked in disgust at and revolt against what is *real*, including our own reality as mortal creatures.

A deceptively simple poem, perhaps; but it foregrounds some plain facts about what sustained public lying does to our humanity, and underlines with force and clarity the connection between pervasive untruthfulness and a contempt for humanity itself that will ultimately make us despise and hate ourselves. It is a connection not too hard to identify in certain kinds of politics today; but Solilo also reminds us that we are all in some degree implicated in faithlessness and untruthfulness. The claim to be innocent is another kind of lie, and we need to have faith enough to recognize this.

A. E. Stallings

First Miracle

Her body like a pomegranate torn
Wide open, somehow bears what must be born,

The irony where a stranger small enough
To bed down in the ox-tongue-polished trough

Erupts into the world and breaks the spell
Of the ancient, numbered hours with his yell.

Now her breasts ache and weep and soak her shirt
Whenever she hears his hunger or his hurt;

She can't change water into wine; instead
She fashions sweet milk out of her own blood.

The Gospel of John tells us that the first miracle or 'sign' that Jesus performed was the turning of water into wine at the wedding feast at Cana, and the poem's title might lead us to expect that this would be the subject. But Stallings presses back behind the story of Cana to the initial miracle of birth itself – the 'ordinary' miracle of human birth, but also the miraculous interruption of the 'numbered hours' by the arrival of something unprecedented, a new human identity, which is in this particular case, an identity that will indeed interrupt the steady sequence of time; and as well as this, the miracle of the nourishment that a mother gives to a baby.

The opening image is not casual: Alicia Stallings's poems regularly work with or allude to Greek mythology, and the pomegranate is a significant metaphor here. In the mythical story, when Persephone, daughter of the fertility goddess Demeter, is abducted by the underworld god Hades, her rescue is conditional on her never having tasted food in the underworld; because she is tricked by Hades into eating some of the seeds of a pomegranate, she is obliged to spend part of the year in Hades' kingdom as his consort. In Stallings's poem, the picture of the pomegranate opening (and spilling its seeds) connects the Nativity immediately with the mythology of death and rebirth. Mary's body 'splitting' as she gives birth speaks of the way in which the child she bears is fated to go down among the dead, yet is also free to restore life and fertility to the earth.

Mary 'bears what must be born': the sound of the line leaves us with an ambiguity about the meanings of 'bears' and 'born', though the text itself is clear. Mary gives birth to what must be born from her, but she also carries the load that must be carried, 'borne' – the burden of attention to, and response to, the hunger and hurt of the child. Both are in this case beyond human capacity to assuage – the hunger that is the infinite divine longing for the world's healing, the hurt that is the total self-emptying of Christ's suffering. Bearing all this is deeply painful; the language here picks up the prophecy of Simeon in Luke's Gospel that Mary will experience a sword piercing her own soul. The solidarity in suffering that in Christian devotion is associated with Mary standing at the foot of the cross is here associated already with her birth-giving and breastfeeding.

And the final couplet points to the transformative miracle already at work here, the transition from the blood of birth-giving to the 'sweet milk' of breastfeeding. What is given in and through the pain of birth somehow makes possible the giving of nourishment. The miracle foreshadows the miracle of Cana, and also (since that miracle is traditionally seen as itself a foreshadowing of the transforming of human nature into divine by the death and resurrection of Jesus) it looks forwards to the sacramental transformation of the blood shed on the cross into the nourishment of believers. The half-rhyme of 'instead' and 'blood' suggests both the continuity and the discontinuity between Mary's pain and the Passion of Jesus.

What the poem also suggests is that the miraculous sign at the wedding feast depends on the unnoticed 'sign' or 'miracle' of human birth, the arrival of a new centre of personal life who must be nursed and fed into full capacity, as well as the transformations or transubstantiations theology speaks of in respect of Jesus, grounded in the proximity and mutual 'exchange' of pain and fruitfulness in the experience of giving birth (a connection already made in John's Gospel – 17.21 – when Jesus compares the grief felt by his disciples when he will be separated from them by death with the pangs of childbirth, intense and almost intolerable, but quickly forgotten when the new life has arrived). It is a reminder of the forgotten feminine perspective on the narrative of salvation through Christ – but also of the forgotten grounding of supernatural change in natural transformation. Stallings invites us to look at the miraculous 'interruption' of the sequence of human history by the events of salvation in the context of the everyday story of human cost and gift – not as something which sweeps all that away or strips it of transfiguring value. The split pomegranate is a sign of all those aspects of our world that cross the boundary between life and death, sterility and fruitfulness, pain and fulfilment, the uncanny territory where worlds intersect – even before the first Christmas.

Avrom Sutzkever

The Lead Plates of the Rom Printers

Like fingers stretched out through the bars in the
night
To catch the free light of the air that is shed –
We sneak in the dark to grab up, as in spite,
The Rom printing plates, with old wisdom inbred.
We dreamers now have to be soldiers and fight
And melt into bullets the soul of the lead.

And now, once again, we broke open the seal
Of a strangely familiar, a timeless dark cave.
And armored in shadows, with candles concealed,
We poured out the letters – in lead lines engraved.
Thus did, in the Temple, our forefathers wield
The golden menorahs, poured out oil that was
saved.

Liquid lead, brightly shining in bullets so fine,
Ancient thoughts – in the letters that melted hot.
A line from Babylonia, from Poland a line,
Boiled, flooded together, in the foundry pot.
Jewish valor, hidden in word and in sign
Must now explode the whole world with a shot!

And he who saw Jewish youths in their prime
Clutching the weapons in ghetto halls –

He saw the last struggle of Yerushalayim,
The heroic fall of those granite walls;
Took in the words, poured in lead, out of time,
And heard in his heart: their ancient voice calls.

Avrom Sutzkever, recognized as probably the foremost Yiddish poet of the last century, is unusual in many respects, not least in what he writes about the experience of Jewish resistance during the years of the Shoah. This is one of the poems originating in the terrible history of the Vilna Ghetto in 1942–43, when the Nazi administration effectively imprisoned the Jewish population of what is now Vilnius in a tiny area of the city, so as to guarantee a more efficient process of extermination. Vilnius had long been a major centre of Jewish scholarship and intellectual life, and the Ghetto proved a seedbed for some extraordinary creativity. But it also nurtured militant activists who pursued their guerrilla campaigning within the city and alongside the partisans in the surrounding region, where young recruits were regularly despatched in secret. Sutzkever – who survived and eventually escaped to Israel – represents both these elements, and this poem brilliantly draws together in a bold, ironic image the history of the traditional Jewish theological and cultural identity of the city and the unprecedented pressures of the new situation. It is about Jewish partisans raiding a Jewish printing press so that the lead plates once used for printing can be melted down for bullets.

The inherited 'dreaming' of a would-be timeless scholarship – from the Babylonian Talmud to the exegesis of the great rabbis of Poland – has to be turned into action: the inherited identity has become a prison, the acceptance of a passivity that is now fatal, and the partisans are – paradoxically – breaking into the press building so as to break out of its legacy. Yet it is that legacy at its deepest levels which quite literally enables the resistance of the militants. They melt down the metal plates in the glow of a menorah-like lamp; the lines of plates themselves are shining, they reflect a kind of glory that must now be revealed in another shape (it is illuminating to read this poem together with Shapiro's 'The Alphabet', p. 283). Sutzkever is harshly direct about this: whatever has been concealed in the historical words must now 'explode'. Real shots are to be fired.

But the poem does not put before us a simple 'ploughshares into swords' narrative. The transformation of words into bullets is a detonation of *the world*, and the militants in their resistance are in fact absorbing the words of the tradition 'by heart'. Active resistance to appalling evil – more specifically to the appalling evil represented by the effort to eradicate Jewish identity itself by the murder of Jewish people – is something that the tradition in some sense mandates, even if this has been forgotten. To be a light to the nations, the Jewish people has to *exist*, and the defence of the Jewish community becomes an act of radical obedience to the God who is written about in those lines on the metal printing plate. God's purpose, it seems, is to 'explode' the human world through the fidelity of the Jews to their calling; here and now, that fidelity has to be expressed in a literal battle against the annihilation of a people who are a sign of the divine presence and the divine freedom to transform the world.

A good deal of rather futile discussion has gone on as to whether Sutzkever is reporting an actual event or not. The point (as the more perceptive critics have stressed) is to do with Sutzkever's own internal struggles over the justification of poetry itself. Auden notoriously said that poetry 'makes nothing happen'. Sutzkever offers a different perspective: words that are genuinely shot through with the flaming illumination of God's purpose can be turned into explosive agency. If they can't, we have to question their apparent sacredness; and this applies to the 'sacredness' of the poet's self-defined justification, just as it does to the holiness of the texts printed at the Rom works.

Not, then, a simple turn from scholarship or poetry to militancy, but a challenge – a self-challenge for Sutzkever – about the risk of being trapped in poetry for poetry's sake, of dividing 'holy' words from the active defence of a community that serves the truth. Sutzkever did not stop writing, but he had taken the risk of action as well. He is in an obvious sense a 'poet of the Holocaust', given his immediate involvement in the horrors of the genocide that unfolded in Eastern Europe, but he is not simply a poet of lament or theological protest. For him, any poem about the death of Jews has to be made of the same stuff as action for the life of Jews – which is action for the life of the world.

Avrom Sutzkever

Who Will Be Left? What Will Be Left?

Who will be left? What will be left? A wind;
A blindness left when there are no more blind;
A streak of foam, a relic of the sea;
A scrap of cloud left snagged in a tree.

Who will be left? What will be left? One syllable
  alone
To start a second Genesis of grass fresh-sown;
A fiddle-rose existing just for its own glory;
Perhaps seven growths of grass will grasp the story.

And more than all the stars from the North Star to
  here,
That star is left that we see falling like a tear.
And in the jug, a drop of wine left too.
God is left. Or is that not enough for you?

Writing in Yiddish in modern Israel, many would say, can never escape a certain elegiac tone. Yiddish is the language of a culture brutally extinguished, existing only in word and memory. Sutzkever's decision to continue writing in Yiddish is testimony to his concern that this history should not be lost; in the light of what we have seen in his poem that we have just read about the printing press, it is important that his Yiddish poetry is still an action for the sake of the Jewish people, not an indulgent or nostalgic exercise. This poem – brilliantly economical and evocative in Yiddish and notoriously hard to translate – is another kind of self-interrogation. What is it that has not been destroyed in the conflagration of the Shoah? Does poetry really have the active role claimed for it?

The imagery is at first (appropriately) elusive and almost abstract – wind, sea foam, cloud – but it is interrupted by an unexpectedly sharp phrase about blindness surviving when the blind person has disappeared. What makes for blindness is not something that fades with the passage of time; and the memory of the past must be also a memory of the persistence of all that confines human life as well as all that enriches it. It is against this background of persistent danger that the hope of the second stanza comes into full focus: blindness remains, but so does the primordial creating word that 'regrasses' (it is tempting to translate, 're-wilds') a ravaged creation. The possibility of renewal is not destroyed: the rose that exists in its own right or for its own sake, like the music of the violin (the characteristic fiddle music of the Eastern European Jewish communities), will grow again. There will always be, in art and nature, that which exists for its own sake, inviting contemplation, not exploitation. As for the mysterious seven grasses or seven blades of grass, they appear to represent the stable intelligibility of the world, despite its brokenness. The image may be of seven successive annual growths of grass (and other vegetation), the 'week of years' mentioned in Leviticus in connection with the regulations for the cultivation of the land and the year of Jubilee: in the sixth year, no crops are to be sown, so that there can be a 'sabbath' from harvesting in the seventh year; and this is possible because the natural growth of the sixth year will be especially abundant. But whatever the exact reference, the main point is clear, that what remains is a hope for the earth itself to generate new life.

The final stanza brings us back to the human context by means of a sharp contrast. There is a star that will endure long beyond the lifetime of the furthest stars in the sky – the stars 'northward from here' (the Yiddish for 'northwards' borrows the word used in Hebrew Scripture – as in Psalm 48.2 – for the distant realm of divine glory and authority). This star is a human tear, the abiding reality of inconsolable lament; but it is at once juxtaposed with the drop of wine that remains in the pitcher, the abiding reality of celebration. And the poem ends with an abrupt question and challenge: 'What will be left? . . . God is left. Or is that not enough for you?'

The abruptness of the last line suggests that the God who remains is identical with, or at least embodied in, all that has been so far listed – the continuing riskiness of our lives, the blindness that always needs divine light, the regenerative freedom of the earth, the deep rootedness of lament and celebration in the human imagination. If we are to claim that God endures through the horrors of human loss, this claim has to be 'earthed' in things like these. The concluding question can be read both as a rhetorical flourish (surely this is enough?) or as a real interrogation (is this really adequate?): it is precisely the poet's dilemma. Is the 'remaining' of God (as spelled out in these images) 'enough' to make it worth memorializing what is lost? In other words, is the poem a real *act* of obedience or witness or service to God's people? The very fact of the poem has to answer the question. Enough to be going on with, enough to make sense of the labour of writing.

Dylan Thomas

The Conversation of Prayer

The conversation of prayers about to be said
By the child going to bed and the man on the stairs
Who climbs to his dying love in her high room,
The one not caring to whom in his sleep he will
  move
And the other full of tears that she will be dead,

Turns in the dark on the sound they know will
  arise
Into the answering skies from the green ground,
From the man on the stairs and the child by his
  bed.
The sound about to be said in the two prayers
For the sleep in a safe land and the love who dies

Will be the same grief flying. Whom shall they
  calm?
Shall the child sleep unharmed or the man be
  crying?
The conversation of prayers about to be said
Turns on the quick and the dead, and the man on
  the stairs
To-night shall find no dying but alive and warm

In the fire of his care his love in the high room.
And the child not caring to whom he climbs his
prayer
Shall drown in a grief as deep as his true grave,
And mark the dark eyed wave, through the eyes of
sleep,
Dragging him up the stairs to one who lies dead.

What exactly Dylan Thomas believed is elusive. He could describe his poems as written 'for the love of Man and in praise of God', and he deploys the imagery of sacramental Christianity in very many poems; in his later years, he would sometimes sit in silence at the back of the parish church in Laugharne during the early morning Eucharist. But his comments on institutional religion are mostly dismissive, and there is little evidence that he thought much about the claims of any doctrine.

All that being said, this poem has an unusually pronounced theological grounding. Thomas knew something of Charles Williams, the idiosyncratic poet, novelist and playwright who so influenced C. S. Lewis and his circle, and who, in different ways, made a deep impression on W. H. Auden and Geoffrey Hill. One of Williams's most distinctive ideas (see p. 341) was that Christianity brought into the world not primarily a new set of principles but a new possibility of human interrelation – what he called 'coinherence'. In the deep interconnectedness of human lives that characterize the Mystical Body of Christ, believers are able to take on the experience of others as if it were their own; you can offer others the chance to offload their fear or physical pain or anxiety and carry it yourself. You may or may not then *experience* it in the same way, but what matters is that you have made yourself 'available' to carry it on behalf of others, and have lifted from those others the weight that they cannot bear. What God does with your availability for this substitution is unpredictable. You may sense in some way the anguish or horror that those others shrink from; or it may find its way elsewhere to another soul capable of bearing it.

It is a bold, difficult and risky doctrine, about which theologians still worry and disagree. But while there may be disagreement about how strictly or literally it is taken, Williams's vision reflects something deeply bound up with the central Christian belief that no one's experience is theirs alone, that the suffering of any one member of the Mystical Body is everyone's suffering and the joy or fulfilment of any one is a gift to all (1 Corinthians 12.26) – and also the injunction of St Paul to 'bear one another's burdens' (Galatians 6.2).

So here, Thomas sets up a case of such 'coinherence'. A child is saying bedtime prayers, an adult man is keeping watch at the deathbed of a partner or lover. The child may not consciously be offering himself to relieve the agony of the adult, but the mere fact of stepping into the 'conversation of prayers' exposes him to the suffering of another whom he may not know. The child is paradoxically strong enough, protected enough, to bear the incomprehensible weight of adult misery, to 'drown in a grief as deep as his true grave', so that the man may find a moment of hope in the presence of death. The poem does not say directly whether the prayer literally saves the lover's life: all we know is that 'To-night' the grief-stricken man finds his love warm and alive. 'His love': the person he loves or the love he feels for them? Never mind. What matters is that he is delivered from the terror of death; while the child is drawn, carried by a 'dark eyed wave', into the pain of witnessing the death of someone passionately loved.

It is a poem typical of Thomas's sheer technical skill: the intricate rhyme pattern – reminiscent of the complex rhyme schemes of classical Welsh poetry – illustrates the poem's central theme, the *crossing-over* of experience from one soul to another in this new and strange world of prayer. The ends of lines regularly rhyme with the middle of those that follow, the first and last lines of each verse rhyme with each other – except for the very last line, which rhymes with the first line of the whole poem. You could trace over the text a complex visual pattern of criss-crossing and circling movements, like one of those mediaeval Irish 'carpet pages' in illustrated manuscripts, a close-woven fabric of knotted strands. To enter the 'conversation' is to risk being caught in this tight fabric, where the exchange 'turns', pivots, so that experiences are passed from one person to another – and in a different sense, the conversation 'turns on' the praying person, rounds on them unexpectedly and painfully.

Prayer is something the workings of which we cannot chart. 'Answers' to prayer are not a matter of some tidy yes or no to a request, but of what unpredictable movement of transformation or healing is opened up when the praying person genuinely yields space to the infinite presence and action confronted in prayer. The sound of prayer is 'the same grief flying': grief taking wing to the one who makes grief bearable, grief fleeing from one heart to another.

R. S. Thomas

Sea-watching

Grey waters, vast
   as an area of prayer
that one enters. Daily
   over a period of years
I have let the eye rest on them.
Was I waiting for something?
                                        Nothing
but that continuous waving
   that is without meaning
occurred.
   Ah, but a rare bird is
rare. It is when one is not looking,
at times one is not there
                                that it comes.
You must wear your eyes out,
as others their knees.
   I became the hermit
of the rocks, habited with the wind
and the mist. There were days,
so beautiful the emptiness
it might have filled,
                        its absence
was as its presence; not to be told
any more, so single my mind
after its long fast,
                    my watching from praying.

It is not easy to select poems from R. S. Thomas's copious work. Like Eliot, he is anthologized freely and quoted widely and sometimes uncritically by writers on the spiritual life; he is almost too familiar. But it is also a difficulty that so many apparently similar poems prove on examination to be significantly distinct, with an unexpected new metaphor or a startling twist to something we think we have heard before. This poem, from a collection of the mid-1970s, deploys two images that recur especially in the later poems – looking out over the sea, and bird-watching. The title brings the two together, as if 'sea-watching' were an activity like bird-watching, a deliberate suspension of movement and thought in the hope of catching sight of something.

As so often in Thomas's poems, the run-on of the lines allows some teasing moments. 'Was I waiting for something?/ Nothing/ but that continuous waving': we are briefly tricked into thinking that 'Nothing' is the answer to the question posed. 'Nothing . . . occurred', we are told, but that does not mean that the speaker has not been waiting for 'something'. Looking at the immense expanse of water is like entering the state of prayer; and that state of prayer is one in which for most of the time nothing happens. Yet there is an expectation of sorts: hence the association with bird-watching. The point of watching like this for a rare bird is precisely the rarity of the bird. Its visible presence cannot ever be taken for granted. It comes when 'one is not there' – which could be either, frustratingly, when one is literally not around to see, or when the busy 'I' is not there, when self-preoccupation has been silenced and the attention rests fully on what is there beyond the self. The 'waving/ that is without meaning' fleetingly acquires a significance. Once again, the language teases us, since 'waving' is a sign of someone trying to attract our attention (and most readers of modern poetry would catch an echo of Stevie

Smith's famous 'Not Waving but Drowning'); it is a moment when someone else initiates a connection. But the speaker's watching/praying is not one in which any such initiative can be relied on. If we expect it, if we take it for granted, we shall either be systematically disappointed or we shall fill the gap with fantasy. 'You must wear your eyes out.' The watching is an unremitting call to attention, yet without any suggestion that the intensity of the watching can produce the longed-for vision. Effort and grace are never cause and effect.

And at times, the emptiness that might have been filled by the presence of the long-awaited visitant becomes itself a kind of visitation: the beauty of the empty seascape is all we need to absorb (or to be absorbed in). Absence and presence coincide, not in some sort of glib evasiveness, attempting to explain away the fact that prayer/watching finds no object for itself. It is that the expanse of waving water reveals itself as the object we have been waiting for: the 'visitant' is not an intruding item coming in from somewhere else, and in that sense the act of watching at its most sustained and intense, with the mind 'fasting' from thoughts and images, imperceptibly transmutes into prayer, into something that (however silently) affirms a relation, a dimension of grace.

Thomas's staring out on the Atlantic from his station in North Wales and Kevin Hart's night-time gaze on the Pacific from the coast of eastern Australia (p. 119) may at first seem similar; but they embody different moments of attention or vision. Hart's poem presents a moment of 'suspension', convergence and fulfilment, a 'here and now' beyond but in the depths of the world of time; Thomas focuses on the unswerving patience and costly practice required for such a moment to be possible not simply as an unexpected gift but also as a habitual temper of mind or heart or sight. No contradiction, ultimately (though they are poets of radically diverse tonality and temperament); in an important sense, poems don't 'contradict' one another. But two perspectives on the way our human/poetic sensibility receives the gift of grace in the presence of what is immeasurable and uncontainable: the knowledge that nothing conditions or controls the reality we are facing, that the passage of time is irrelevant to it, that there is nothing to do or say except to recognize your being gathered up into it; and the knowledge that the gift demands that you day after day set aside the pictures and ideas you are always slipping back towards and sit resolutely with the emptiness until it becomes light.

R. S. Thomas

Neither

Not a person, neither
less than, since we are so,
personal. Impassible
yet darkening your countenance
once for a long moment
as you looked at yourself
on a hill-top in Judea.
Your mastery is to be both
outside and inside, standing off
from the primary explosion,
entering in to its quieter
repetitions in acorn and spermatozoa.
You have given us the ability
to ask the unanswerable question,
to have glimpses of you
as you were, only to stand dumb
at the limits of our articulation.
Is it our music interprets you
best, a heart-beat at the very centre
of your creation? Is it art,
depicting man's figure as the conductor
to your lightning? Had I
the right words, it is the poem
that would announce you to
an amazed audience; no longer

a linguistic wrestling but a signal
projected at you and returning quick
with the unpredictabilities at your centre.

This late poem (1995) is as near as Thomas gets to anything like a programmatic theological statement. The formulation that God cannot be 'less than' personal is one that can be found in the writings of various theologians of the past century or so; here it is starkly presented as bound up with the recognition that God cannot be less than *us*. As always in Thomas's work, we are up against what exceeds our imagining – which is why in some poems he sets out to shock by apparently anthropomorphic language, nakedly mythological pictures, riffs on the divine cruelty or indifference and so on. We have to be shaken out of any domestication of God, even if this is done – as in another celebrated poem, 'Raptor', from the same 1995 collection – by picturing God as a hunting owl, fastening his talons in 'some lesser/ denizen, maybe, like you or me'.

But the language here is more measured, if no less intense. God is supposed to be 'impassible', beyond suffering, yet the mirror in which he looks at himself is the 'long moment' of Jesus' suffering on the cross. The problem around which we cannot get our heads is the fact that God is inside and outside what has been made: God is independent of the Big Bang, yet God is equally within the repeating patterns of the physical world, not least in the processes of sexual generation (compare Larissa Miller on the 'unoriginality' of God's actions, p. 204). We are created so as to ask unanswerable questions; we catch a fleeting sight of the reality but it brings us to the limit of what we can say. Significantly, Thomas says that we glimpse God 'as you *were*': in several poems, he reflects on the undeniable fact that Christianity as a culturally 'available' frame of reference is fading fast in the Western world. We cannot speak of God directly as our forebears could, and yet we can acquire some sense of what it meant for them to speak, even as we struggle to find words to express that today.

Music may be a better option for keeping us in touch, since it provides what is still a compelling metaphor for God's presence in the world, the presence of rhythm within the music, neither something that can be abstracted from the actual sequence of sounds nor something that depends on the sounds themselves. Visual art can portray the human as 'conductor/ to your lightning', and so may also be a vehicle of sorts for conveying the divine (I suspect that these lines are there to give a home to the single striking metaphor of the lightning conductor rather than contributing to the advancing argument of the poem). And poetry, finally, *ought* to be where God can be visible, not in the complexities of 'wrestling' with its subject – think of Eliot's 'intolerable wrestle/ With words and meanings' in 'East Coker' – but in the instantaneous flash of an electronic signal sent and returned like the firing of a neuron in the brain. The word is spoken into the darkness and is reflected back pregnant with the unsuspected possibilities that belong to the life of God. When language is suffused with possibilities in this way, it displays God. This is what poetry aspires to.

But not necessarily what it achieves. The poem's end is, of course, inconclusive. Just as Eliot throughout the *Quartets* repeatedly gestures towards what poetry *might* be – 'The complete consort dancing together', in the image towards the end of 'Little Gidding' – but leaves us to decide whether or not this has in any way been attained, so Thomas tells us what it would be like 'Had I/ the right words'. And the implication is that these words are not the right ones – or perhaps the *recognizing* that these words are not the right ones is our only way of finding 'right' words? To say that we are at the end of what we can say is, after all, a truthful statement here, and its truthfulness can be shown in at least two ways: in the spaciousness of the empty margins created around the struggling words, and in the ambition and strangeness of the images. Something will be said that tells us of God, even if we cannot speak the word that unequivocally *shows* God 'to/ an amazed audience'. The quietly satirical inflection of this phrase – a very Thomas touch – suggests strongly that, while we are not wrong to expect something of poetry where God is concerned, we should be just a little sceptical of our chances of staging the 'complete consort' or the neural fire. But for all that, the gift of the unpredictable may still be there, in the shock and excess of metaphor and in the ways in which we are made aware of the vastness of the 'margin'. Thomas may be ironically realistic about what poetry may realize, but he is – quite properly – never falsely modest.

Sally Thomas

biddan (to pray)

There is the rope's moan on the well-lip.
There is the cold sky, cloud-combed.
There is the sea, the headland's headdress,
Folding, folding, far afield,
Sun born from barn roofs, the tree-bare rise.
There is the lick of Lauds-bell, the wind's weeping.

Biddan: Ic bidde. We bidden.
Bed-making. Bidden, the soul's housewife sweeps
Clean the clod-cold hearth, furnishes fire
To see by, with sighs more wordful than words.

So she might have written.
So she surely said – *Ic bidde. We bidden.*
So I say, because her words lie hidden.

Walsingham in Norfolk is a pilgrimage centre with a history going back to the eleventh century, when the widow of a local landowner built a small chapel in obedience to a vision of the Virgin Mary. The tradition is that this chapel was constructed according to the exact dimensions of the house of the Holy Family in Nazareth. Destroyed at the Reformation, the shrine was restored in the twentieth century; both Roman Catholic and Anglican churches on or near the site attract substantial numbers of pilgrims. Sally Thomas's poem is part of a sequence meditating on the history of Walsingham, each poem headed by a single Anglo-Saxon word, in this case the verb for praying (we still occasionally hear the expression 'bidding prayer' – strictly speaking a tautology, as a 'bidding' in this context is precisely a request made in prayer).

The poem begins by evoking – economically and beautifully – an early mediaeval landscape in winter as Richeldis, the eleventh-century visionary, might have known it – the level clouds of a cold morning, the sun coming up over buildings and bare trees, the sea not so far away, draped around the headland like an elaborately pleated coif, the creak of the well-bucket, the bell announcing the morning office of Lauds, literally 'praises'. The lines are shaped around the kind of alliterations and vowel rhymes or half-rhymes that characterize Anglo-Saxon (and indeed traditional Welsh and Irish) poetry – 'cold . . . cloud-combed', 'folding, far afield', 'see by, with sighs', and so on; and this gives the poem an air of close-woven solidity. The interweaving of the words fits the thick, tactile image of the second stanza.

The Saxon verb is picked up and 'fingered over' in this verse, so that we are made aware of its echo of more familiar words, 'bed', for example, and 'bidden' in the modern sense of 'commanded'. The household duties to be done on this chilly morning are indeed 'bidden', they have to be performed; the bed must be made, just as the water must be drawn from the well. So with our own early morning activity: things must be put in order, water fetched, fires lit so that we can see. And the 'sighs more wordful than words' allude to the well-known language of St Paul in Romans 8.26 about the Holy Spirit assisting us in our prayers 'with sighs too deep for words'. The wordless longing that arises is 'wordful' because it best communicates what needs to be expressed.

The mediaeval housewife does what is 'bidden', what is enjoined on her, and perhaps as she does so she acknowledges that she is involved in *biddan*, in prayer. But we cannot know; all we can do is to speak for her and voice her possible hidden words, claiming the dignity of prayer for our own labour of putting mind and heart in order in the morning. We make our beds, we light the fires we need so that we shall be able to see what the day offers to us; we let the Spirit sigh wordlessly in us, awakening the longing for God that will move us forwards in the day's business.

Like Les Murray's 'loving repetition' or Sally Ito's metaphor of the steady moistening of a hard surface, the language of this poem offers an image of prayer as a kind of undramatic housekeeping, making sure that the door is left open for the Spirit. We do what must be done. We clear the space, and unless we do this faithfully, daily, undramatically, we cannot expect our hearts to be ready for change, or for joy. Perhaps Sally Thomas wants us to remember that a 'bidding' can also be an *invitation*. Making the bed, sweeping the hearth, lighting the fire – these are all signs of expectation, making room for life to go on and grow. And we find the courage and patience for this in the knowledge that we are 'bidden' as guests ourselves.

Derek Walcott

A City's Death by Fire

After that hot gospeller has levelled all but the
  churched sky,
I wrote the tale by tallow of a city's death by fire;
Under a candle's eye, that smoked in tears, I
Wanted to tell, in more than wax, of faiths that
  were snapped like wire.
All day I walked abroad among the rubbled tales,
Shocked at each wall that stood on the street like a
  liar;
Loud was the bird-rocked sky, and all the clouds
  were bales
Torn open by looting, and white, in spite of the fire.
By the smoking sea, where Christ walked, I asked,
  why
Should a man wax tears, when his wooden world
  fails?
In town, leaves were paper, but the hills were a
  flock of faiths;
To a boy who walked all day, each leaf was a green
  breath
Rebuilding a love I thought was dead as nails,
Blessing the death and the baptism by fire.

In 1948, the main city in Derek Walcott's native island of St Lucia was almost completely destroyed by fire. Not surprisingly, it was an event that left a long memory and a deep communal trauma. Walcott, 18 years old at the time of the disaster, recalls it in this earlyish poem, which shows some strong echoes of Dylan Thomas in both style and direction: we encounter a certain amount of alliterative play ('tale by tallow'), nouns turned into adjectives (the sky is 'churched'), the image of a young boy walking in a green landscape. And the underlying themes – purgation by fire and the recollecting of an innocent perception of the natural world – have many parallels in Thomas. But it is far more than a pastiche. Its opening metaphor is immediately distinctive and striking: the fire spreads the good news. It leaves the 'churched sky' exposed, while levelling everything else in sight. The implication is that the skyline is still punctuated by church spires: but this does not mean that conventional or traditional piety has been vindicated. 'Faiths' have snapped – *faiths*, not simply faith: different sorts of trust have been broken, and the 'wire' to which they are compared may be the wire of telegraph communication. Something that connects us has been shattered, and the remains of built structures seem like 'liars'. The way we have joined up, mapped out, and divided the world we live in so as to master it is swept away and shown to be illusory.

It is not hard to see behind these lines the strong hint that such a dissolution of structures and boundaries is also a tacit judgement on the colonial imposition of boundaries and on the colonial aspiration to a literal 'mastery' of persons and landscapes. The speaker's shock is not so much at the devastation as at the *persistence* of the marks of division, the surviving wreckage of the walls. The tempting metaphorical convergence of dripping candle wax, eyes watering in smoke and tears shed is teasingly proposed and then rejected: why should we 'wax tears' for the destruction of an artificial world? The phrase 'wax tears' is a close-packed bit of wordplay and imagery, taking us back to the running down of melting wax from the tallow light, while also gesturing towards the verbal sense of 'waxing' as 'growing': why should we think that lamenting for this destruction is any sort of growth? Why are tears to be thought of as the natural 'growth' coming from the organism of our minds and feelings? And this leads into the mention of leaves and the different ways in which they are seen or experienced. In the town they are 'paper' – crumpled waste in the landscape (and perhaps also occasions for writing in an artificial mode); in the hills outside, they can be rediscovered as 'green breath', active signs of spirit, of another sort of growth or waxing.

The sky – now 'bird-rocked' rather than 'churched' – is alive with sound, and the ragged clouds, like looted bales, overflow with white material, the white, perhaps, of the baptismal ritual that has been enacted in the fire, the destructive and disruptive arrival of a different sort of hope. And the seawater may be steaming with the fire's heat, but it is where Christ has walked, and that memory prompts the defiant question about why we need to grieve for the fire. The final words pick up the familiar cliché of 'baptism by fire' and give it a freshly literal application: this is indeed a death and resurrection, a restoration of the lost greenness of loving vision that is felt by the child.

There have been some critics who have read the poem as offering too easy a consolation for collective trauma. But consolation is not at all what it seems to be doing. It certainly forbids lament, and its bold opening tells us to expect good news; but the faith reaffirmed is not a melancholic injunction to trust a mysterious providence but a sharper, even a more aggressive, claim that something creative has happened which strips away various kinds of falsehood. The church towers may still be standing but the church walls are not, or not as they once did. Dylan Thomas's poem 'A Refusal to Mourn the

Death, by Fire, of a Child in London', which is unavoidably called to mind by Walcott's piece, takes us to a very different place, a more individual exploration of the fear of dying and the resources with which we face it. Walcott's 'baptism of fire' from the 'hot gospeller' pushes more fiercely towards a recognition of liberation from controlling maps and walls, from paper resolutions and representations of human reality, from a world that is shaped by concerns for mastery. Sea, hills, clouds, the abiding natural environment of the island, all promise a re-greening of imagination and so of life together.

Vernon Watkins

A Christening Remembered

for Rhiannon

Water of life no prophet could divine,
Whose eyes now know a month more light than
  shade:
The font in your awakening is waylaid,
Where fell that christening moment from the vine.
If I look deeply there, I see time fade
And light grow perfect, dark; and darkness shine.
Again I see the curve her body made,
Bearing you like a pitcher doomed to wine.

That ancient miracle makes moist your lip
With Cana's feast; and babblings none could spell
Recall great buckets that a chain let slip
Down the dark, echoing walls of some deep well
Where a stone, plunging, woke you from your
  sleep:
Your angel spoke the moment that it fell.

Vernon Watkins' poetry was, in its day, unfashionably formal; his tight-woven verses could all too easily be unfavourably compared to the expansive and extravagant diction of his close friend Dylan Thomas. But the dense, sophisticated metaphors and sheer verbal control – in a variety of complex forms – have repeatedly drawn readers back, and made it hard to write off his achievement, in spite of the archaisms and the occasional drop into a self-conscious 'poetic' manner. He might best be read alongside the seventeenth-century 'metaphysicals', with their formal ingenuity and intricate chains of images.

This brief piece about his daughter's baptism illustrates the characteristic intricacy and depth of the writing. It is a poem in which water serves as the central symbolic focus. The child to be baptized is addressed as herself a manifestation of the 'water of life', the unpredictable and unique lightning-flash of novelty that a birth embodies. The newborn baby wakens to unfamiliar light after the womb's darkness, an anticipation of the grace of the sacrament: the font is 'waylaid', ambushed, we could say, by the fact of the natural light dawning on and in the newborn's eyes. Looking at those eyes, we see – in a typical Watkins paradox – light so intense that it becomes darkness, darkness that is at the same time radiant with the reflection of the new world. The reference that follows to the curve of the pregnant mother's body pursues the metaphor. That body has been a container for the water of life, swollen with its burden and 'curved' like a pitcher; and this image in turn calls up the pitchers of water at the wedding feast of Cana, where water is turned into wine. The startling phrase 'doomed to wine' insists that the transformations of growing into maturity are both promise and menace: the wine of adult sensibility, sensuality and intelligence is inseparable from the loss of water's transparency, the clarity and directness of the newborn vision.

So the infant's 'babblings' in this moment of sacramental transition are like a foreshadowing of drunkenness, the wine of the future (the experience of growing up) anticipated in the incomprehensible chaos of infant speech. And the imagery swerves abruptly to evoke the noise of buckets dropping down into a well – the rattling chain, the knocking against stone walls, the splash. The new life has been woken as suddenly and audibly as a stone dropping into the well, and the language of that new life, the unintelligible sound of the waking self, echoes against the well shaft as if the apparatus of the buckets had been 'let slip', literally unchained. The life of speaking and thinking that lies ahead is something which is *released*, and it is the speech of an angel. Should we think here of St Paul's 'tongues of men and of angels' at the beginning of his meditation on love in 1 Corinthians 13? But the final line also carries an ambiguity: what is the 'it' that falls? The stone? Or the angel? 'Angels are bright still, though the brightest fell': the line from *Macbeth* echoes inescapably in the background. The baptized child is given the tongues of angels, but there is always the danger that our human speech becomes that of the fallen angel.

It is a poem that points us into the unfathomable darkness of human identity – darkness in the sense of mystery, darkness in the sense of tragic risk. But the overall mood of the poem is one of wonder at this impenetrable darkness rather than one of fear or lament. In another (longer and slightly later) poem, 'For a Christening', Watkins uses a very 'metaphysical' image for the sacrament:

> We are come to see that prism
> Take fire, where Christ's own tear
> In your baptism
> Consecrates, first each drop, then all the sphere.

The 'water' of the new life is to be made holy, and this is done by the single drop of water that is Christ's sorrow touching the child's body; through that simple contact, the whole 'sphere' – the whole of a life, the whole of a world – is changed. 'Sink; then wake' is his injunction to the infant and to the reader in this later poem. We are always already defeated by the darkness of risk and pain; we are always already rescued by Christ's sharing of it. Human identity is indeed an unfathomable depth, a long well shaft. But when the stone is dropped into it that wakes us into life, it is also the stone of Christ's life on which we may always be rebuilt and remade.

Vernon Watkins

Adam

When Adam stood beneath the Knowledge Tree
Naked, and felt the full strength of the sun
Shine on his body, he had mastery
Of every visual form, not yet begun.

When Adam found a leaf, and God called out:
'Who told thee thou wast naked?' he began
To build that heaven from which God cast him out
With all the effort of a conscious man.

He hates the praise his false admirers give,
Who have not suffered. Always his eyes stared,
While these robustly found a way to live,
Into a heaven for which they never cared.

An unusual take on the fall of Adam: the forbidden fruit of the Tree of Knowledge in the garden of Eden brings an awareness of both mind and body in (literally) a new light: Adam feels for the first time both the heat and the light of the sun, and he is aware of his physicality in a new way. And as he begins to exercise his newfound ingenuity by plaiting the leaves to cover his nakedness, he implicitly begins to construct for himself the home from which he is banned. He cannot simply accept the raw vulnerability of the nakedness it has been granted him to see.

There have been those who have said that human art is an attempt to re-enter Paradise – possibly not the most obvious way to understand *Antigone* or Cormac McCarthy or Damian Hirst, but the point is that the creative artist has often been seen as someone seeking to address the broken relationship between the human mind and its environment, whether by images of reconciliation or by images that leave no doubt about the extent of the brokenness. Watkins' Adam deploys 'all the effort of a conscious man' not to re-enter Paradise but to build an alternative Paradise.

Modernity tends to celebrate the secular courage and honesty of those who recognize that Paradise is unattainable and seek to maximize human achievement and originality. But Adam cannot bear to be celebrated in this way; those who respond 'robustly' to the secular vision do not understand the suffering that lies behind his intense effort. He really experiences *loss*: he, more than any other imaginable being, knows that Paradise is not an illusion, and his eyes are still fixed on its remembered geography. Those souls who have 'never cared' for what he has lost understand nothing of what he is doing.

So this compact and enigmatic poem recognizes the truth in the idea of art as seeking to reopen a paradisal vision, but refuses to see that enterprise as any kind of substitute for the actual garden. For art to be fully itself, something involving all our resources of feeling and imagination, it has to be driven by the consciousness of something irreparable, a loss or wound that cannot be mended. Adam's inventiveness, the concentration of his consciousness in clothing his naked humanity, depends on a desire that is intensified by the expulsion from Eden. In other words, human creativity is only seriously itself when it recognizes the tragic. We are not where we should be or who we should be as humans; and this is why we struggle with such energy to go on reimagining what it is to be human, over and over again.

Art can only reconnect us with Paradise when it recognizes that Paradise has been *lost*. If it constructs its own version of Paradise without that acknowledgement of loss, it falls painfully short of what it sets out to do. Watkins is tacitly insisting on a necessarily 'religious' dimension to creative art, in the sense that art flourishes when it confesses its limitations. Finding a way to live ('robustly') in a self-made Eden, a secular utopia, has nothing to do with the urgency and cost and perennial unfinishedness of art. Behind the relatively simple surface of Watkins' poem lies his commitment to a kind of Platonic philosophy of creative vision, in which the memory of lost harmony plays a key role; and it is a specifically Jewish–Christian Platonism in that he sees the fading of the primordial vision not just as 'a sleep and a forgetting', in Wordsworth's phrase, but as a traumatic (and self-inflicted) injury. Full human consciousness – 'all the effort of a conscious man' – is always, in one way or another, a consciousness of this wound.

Aled Jones Williams

Faith

Clumping along
the back streets of my
imagination
(nid-nad, nid-nad, nid-nad)
and sometimes
through a grubby window
catching the sound
of your voice in mine, like
an accent in the words
betraying that we come from the same place
but is this any more
than bickering inside my head –
me and my self, Aled and this man here . . .
nid-nad, nid-nad, nid-nad.

Neither a confession of doubt or denial exactly, nor an affirmation of belief, this is a poem from a writer of exceptional depth and complexity – a skilled and much-acclaimed dramatist and novelist, who uses a stark simplicity of manner and a plain, almost offhand, colloquial tone (using local North Welsh dialect forms and pronunciations) to frame unexpected metaphors probing the border of faith and the absence of faith. It is tempting to compare him a bit too quickly to R. S. Thomas. In fact, Williams left the ordained ministry, unlike Thomas, and his poetic voice is even more stripped and reticent. Thomas is manifestly a major influence, gratefully acknowledged by Williams; but Williams has a barbed comment in one of his poems about the 'English accent' of Thomas's God and his 'lyrical indifference'. Williams's mostly very brief poems look at what comes 'after' faith and raise the ironic possibility that what is found on the far side of religious belief is doubt about doubt itself – certainly doubt about the kind of scepticism that assumes we know enough to refuse the possibility of 'god'; he has written about his poetry as trying to make space around the words, so that the words – so to speak – 'absent' themselves and lead us into what cannot be said directly or descriptively. This continuing doubting of doubt is what the writing of the poetry enacts. Tellingly, one page of the collection is entitled 'Duw', 'God'; it has no other words on it. A more recent collection has a whole series of pages headed 'duw' (the lower case is deliberate), followed by a brief set of phrases or images. The title poem of his 2010 collection, *Y Cylchoedd Perffaith* (*The Perfect Circles*) imagines writing poems as throwing pebbles into the lake of 'speechlessness' or 'muteness' (*mudandod* in Welsh), so that the circles spread out and resolve into a 'quiet' (*distawrwydd*) that is not the same as speechlessness, a 'long waiting' on the water's surface. This looking towards a waiting that is free from self-orientated expectations is of course one of the themes that does connect him with R. S. Thomas, but there is a keener suspicion of getting involved in a sort of literary resolution of the problem of 'god'.

In this poem, the speaker is trudging through a murky and drab mental/imaginative environment, 'back streets', houses with 'dirty windows'; the 'nid-nad' sound of heavy feet represents two Welsh words of negation. But the sound still comes through of what might be a voice that is not just the human voice. In the central metaphor of the poem, this overheard voice has the same accent as the human speaker, a sign of common origins. Does this mean that the human voice comes from the divine or the divine from the human? That is what nothing outside is going to tell us definitively. There is an inner dialogue of some kind; is it only me talking to myself? The steady beat of negation goes on as a sort of ground-bass. But catching words spoken through a window (a window we can't see through because of the dirt obscuring it) might suggest that we're hearing something we haven't simply constructed for ourselves, something that might surprise us.

In the collection, this poem is immediately followed by another with the same title, 'faith'. It is little more than a single poignant metaphor, presenting us with faith as the 'widow' of speech – the voice that is left when language has died on us.

Language's latest
widow,
going through the pockets
of its words.

Language may be dead, but you can rifle its pockets, the folds that may hide something you hadn't suspected, to see what remnants may be there, which may even be useable. As in the longer poem, the point is not simply the bankruptcy of faith and its conventional language. We do not know just what words may still be alive, what words may still come through a dirty window to speak to us from outside the self.

Charles Williams

Taliessin on the Death of Virgil

Virgil fell from the edge of the world,
hurled by the thrust of Augustus' back; the shape
he loved grew huge and black, loomed and pushed.
The air rushed up; he fell
into despair, into air's other.
The hexameter's fullness now could find no ground;
his mind, dizzily replete with the meaningless
  sweet sound,
could found no Rome there on the joys of a noise.
He fell through his moment's infinity
(no man escapes), all the shapes of his labour,
his infinite images, dropping pell-mell; above,
loomed the gruesome great buttocks of Augustus
  his love,
his neighbour, infinitely large, infinitely small.
In the midst of his fall others came, none to save.
While he was dropping they put him in a grave.
Perpetual falling, perpetual burying,
this was the truth of his Charon's ferrying –
everlastingly plucked from and sucked from and
  plucked to
  and sucked to a grave.

Unborn pieties lived.
Out of the infinity of time to that moment's infinity

they lived, they rushed, they dived below him, they
rose
to close with his fall; all, while man is, that could
live, and would, by his hexameters, found
there the ground of their power, and their power's
use.
Others he saved; himself he could not save.
In that hour they came; more and faster, they sped
to their dead master; they sought him to save
from the spectral grave and the endless falling,
who had heard, for their own instruction, the
sound of his calling.
There was intervention, suspension, the net of their
loves,
all their throng's songs:
Virgil, master and friend,
holy poet, priest, president of priests,
prince long since of all our energies' end,
deign to accept adoration, and what salvation
may reign here by us, deign of goodwill to endure,
in this net of obedient loves, doves of your cote and
wings,
Virgil, friend, lover, and lord.

Virgil was fathered of his friends.
He lived in their ends.
He was set on the marble of exchange.

Williams's large and diverse literary legacy includes novels, plays, criticism, theology and a body of uneven and often obscure poetry, the most significant examples being the pieces that make up his two 'Taliessin' volumes (*Taliessin through Logres*, 1938, and *The Region of the Summer Stars*, 1944).

Using the imagined perspective of the sixth-century Welsh poet Taliesin (the more accurate spelling, though Tennyson had popularized the version used by Williams), he creates an intricate symbolic and mythological world, centring on the court of King Arthur and drawing in a wide range of legendary material to do with the Holy Grail, as well as deploying an idealized Christian 'Byzantium', the Eastern Roman Empire, which was at its widest extent in the sixth century.

The poems are impossible to categorize or summarize; they include soliloquies by figures in the Arthurian legend, a meditation by the Pope, narrative episodes involving characters like Merlin and Lancelot, and Taliessin's own musings on the interconnection of individual persons within the mystical unity of the Christian Church and the implications of this for human society. Many set out Williams's thinking about 'substitution' and 'co-inherence' – the idea, central to his theology, that we are radically responsible for one another's well-being and even salvation, and that it is even possible literally to take on the suffering or fear of others and endure it on their behalf so they are spared the pain. It is a bold extrapolation from themes in the New Testament about 'bearing one another's burdens' (for example, Galatians 6.2). Williams encouraged those whom he felt to be spiritually close to him to undertake this as a voluntary mutual service – though the exchange or substitution need not always be a conscious matter; Dylan Thomas's 'The Conversation of Prayer' (p. 312) gives a powerful picture of an involuntary case of this.

It is this bundle of ideas that is at the heart of the present poem. Some of the Taliessin pieces are elaborately formal in construction; this one is at first reading untidy and uneven, but closer study will show – for example – that the rhyming lines in the first section are not as arbitrarily placed as they initially seem to be (they follow, respectively, five, three, and one unrhymed lines, and the final cluster of rhyming lines falls into an AABBA pattern). Similarly, internal rhyme and alliteration are carefully placed through the whole section. There are jarring moments (is the line about Augustus' 'great buttocks' a deliberate grotesquerie?), as often in Williams's work. But as the pace settles and the slightly meandering and repetitive tone of the first section gives way to a more focused development of the theme.

Virgil – not wholly unlike the Taliessin figure of the sequence – has written his poetry to build and serve a social order, the new global empire of Augustus; but, like every worker in any medium, he has to let go of the works of his hands in the presence of death, and to acknowledge the emptiness of individual achievement. The music of his hexameters no longer has the power to build anything. But more than this, as death approaches, it is as if the elaborate political structure Virgil has served, personified in the Emperor Augustus, reveals its true nature, becoming dark and monstrous, pushing the poet away and into the abyss – a stark image of the disillusion of the poet seduced into propaganda. Virgil dies, aware not only of the transience but also of the falsehood of what he has made or said.

Now comes the theological twist: Virgil's poetry has made things possible for future writers, created a world of imaginative vitality and depth. Famously, his Fourth Eclogue was read by Christians as a prophecy of the birth of Jesus, and he was regularly regarded as a sort of honorary Christian prophet: it is this that makes him a fitting guide through Hell and Purgatory for Dante in the *Divine Comedy* (no coincidence that Williams wrote quite a bit on Dante). So those who have learned their craft because of Virgil and who, still more, have learned something of the truth of God's workings through Virgil gather around him as he falls into the darkness. He has given more than he knows; and so he has *lived in the life of others*, he has done more for them than he could for himself (notice the direct parallel with Christ on the cross: 'Others he saved; himself he could not save'). And so those who have been brought closer to God and God's love because of Virgil are there to intervene and intercede for him: he is 'fathered of his friends', born afresh because of what he has unwittingly done, so that his fate becomes an example of 'exchange', the hidden connections that save those who cannot save themselves. We are given the gift of eternal life not by our merits but by virtue of what – through the all-pervading grace of Christ – we have been allowed to make possible for others, which is well beyond our knowledge or capacity. This, for Williams, is what it is to live in the Body of Christ, who is the one in and through whom all exchange is made real and effective, the Christ who stands in the place of each and every human person to carry all failure and hurt, and who heals each and every person by giving everyone a share in his own life-giving freedom; so that we too are able to carry the hurt of others and stand in for them when they fail.

Waldo Williams

What Is Man?

What is living? The broad hall found
between narrow walls.
What is acknowledging? Finding the one root
under the branches' tangle.

What is believing? Watching at home
till the time arrives for welcome.
What is forgiving? Pushing your way through
  thorns
to stand alongside your old enemy.

What is singing? The ancient gifted breath
drawn in creating.
What is labour but making songs
from the wood and the wheat?

What is it to govern kingdoms? A skill
still crawling on all fours.
And arming kingdoms? A knife placed
in a baby's fist.

What is it to be a people? A gift
lodged in the heart's deep folds.
What is love of country? Keeping house
among a cloud of witnesses.

What is the world to the wealthy and strong? A
wheel,
turning and turning.
What is the world to earth's little ones? A cradle,
rocking and rocking.

Waldo Williams was a Quaker, a peace activist and a primary school teacher and inspector, a man whose calm and steadily compassionate vision made him profoundly loved in his native West Wales. That vision permeates his small but very significant body of poetry, generally agreed to belong with the lastingly important poetic work of the twentieth century in the Welsh language. Like Gwenallt (p. 155), he wrote both in strict classical metre and in a freer and more exploratory form. Here is a poem that is essentially a series of aphoristic metaphors for thinking about human nature.

Our life is a matter of discovering freedom, expansiveness, within the narrow limits of mortality; and this freedom is enabled by 'recognizing' or 'acknowledging' – *adnabod* in Welsh, a word that Waldo uses many times to evoke the current of mutual respect that runs between human beings and grounds the entire moral world. We are limited in our physical and mental or spiritual possibilities and must learn our limits; but our capacity for recognizing one another in love and veneration is what enables us to find the 'broad hall' of hospitality and communion, and the patience of faith – staying at home, waiting confidently for insight and connection to arrive.

This confidence in human connectedness (celebrated especially in Waldo's most famous poem, 'In Two Fields') makes forgiveness possible, the costly business of working through pain and resentment to arrive at renewed solidarity. We must learn to sing together – to make sense in art and play, which are the work of *awen*, another important word for Waldo drawn from traditional Welsh vocabulary. It is not the 'Muse', the pseudo-classical spirit invoked in other poetic traditions, but something more like 'spirit' (hence the 'gifted breath/ drawn in creating' this translation); and it is the presence of this spirit that works through human labour, that makes the production of food and tools a matter of art not just necessity.

Our collective consciousness is not always a matter of communion and recognition, though. We are still at an infantile level in our politics; and our militaristic fantasies are the equivalent of putting 'A knife . . ./ in a baby's fist'. And the shared identity of a nation is not a triumphant exclusionary possession but something buried invisibly in our affections – so that patriotism is (in a phrase that has become almost proverbial in Wales) *Cadw ty mewn cwmwl tystion*, 'Keeping house/ among a cloud of witnesses', a translation that, sadly, loses the alliteration in the original, which gives it something of its aphoristic quality. We are to 'keep house', to carry on our prosaic human business with the material that we have inherited, conscious of the eyes on us, past, present and future; we are in some way responsible to those witnesses for our fidelity to their humanity as it was and will be lived out in this place, in this language – but in the context of this poem and many others by Waldo, it is clearly a fidelity to a way of *being human* not to a set of national peculiarities and privileges.

Waldo's life and writing exemplify the strong link in much twentieth-century Welsh nationalism between the uncompromising affirmation of local identity and the recognition of a global vocation to making and keeping peace – the spirit that inspired the Welsh Women's Peace Appeal of 1923, calling for international women's advocacy for reconciliation; that welcomed the African American Paul Robeson to the Welsh valleys in the 1920s and 1930s, and supported him in the 1950s when he was under threat in the USA for his political convictions. The final stanza of this poem contrasts the world of the prosperous, the ceaseless cycle of 'getting and spending', in Wordsworth's familiar phrase, and the world of the biblical 'poor in spirit', the 'little ones' Jesus speaks of in the Gospels, for whom the world is always a cradle of new life. The whole poem is a striking fabric of images for the balance of limit and creativity in human life. Belonging to a tradition with deep local roots makes us heirs to not a possession that has to be violently defended but a security which allows us to seek mutual recognition between people, not opposition and rivalry, to fight our way through the thorns because we are confident of finding a human face on the far side of the struggle with the thorns of our pride and fear.

Christian Wiman

Coming into the Kingdom

Coming into the kingdom
I was like a man grown old in banishment,
a creature of hearsay and habit, prayerless, porous,
  a survivor of myself.
Coming into the kingdom
I was like a man stealing into freedom when the
  tyrant dies,
if freedom is freedom where there are no eyes to
  obstruct it,
if the cold desert and the hard crossing were still
  regions of me.
I remember unremembered mountains,
  unspeakable weeds,
a million scents and sights I did not recognize
though they flowed through me like a land I
  inhabited long before belonging or belief.
Coming into the kingdom
I was like a man who imagines a city in flames and
  a city at peace
and sets out not knowing whether his
  homecoming
will be cause for sorrow or rejoicing,
or if indeed there will be one soul that knows him,
or if he is even the same assemblage of cells this
  side of exile,

or if exile is no longer what he once entered but
  what he is.
I tried to cry out in the old way
of thanksgiving, ritual lamentation, rockshriek of joy.
There was no answer. Had there ever been?
Remembering it now I do not remember
the arduous journey that must have rendered me a
  beast,
nor the broad gates opening at the last,
nor the children gathering around me in wonder,
nor the slow reclamation of a life I had been so
  long denied,
the million instants of exile told in tears.
Coming into the kingdom
I came into the damp and dirtlight of late
  November in north Chicago,
where the water-lunged bus chuffs and lumbers up
  Montrose,
and Butch's back gate's broken latch is impervious
  to curses,
and wires crisscross the alley like a random rune,
and an airplane splits and sutures the blue as it
  roars for elsewhere.

How to write about 'conversion'? The word is already laden with stale meanings that shrink rather than enlarge our understanding. Wiman's is a lapidary, intense voice, whose poetry pays an unusual degree of attention to patterns of sound, to the musical coherence of a line; he writes as someone who has a story to tell not only of discovering faith but also of living with untreatable long-term disease; whatever is going to be said about faith in this perspective is not likely to be a simple tale of darkness-to-light, error-to-truth.

'Coming into the kingdom' takes up the central biblical language about the transformation that faith entails. It is less like acquiring a new set of ideas than arriving in a new landscape, and this is the background to this poem. The speaker is 'a survivor of myself', someone who has with difficulty pulled himself out of the habits of estrangement and distance. Job says at the end of the book that bears his name, he has known God only 'by the hearing of the ear' (Job 42.5). But to move away from this 'hearsay' into something else is not necessarily to move into greater peace or clarity at once (Eliot's magi might have told us as much; do Wiman's 'cold desert and . . . hard crossing' allude directly to them?). Some controlling and alien power has died, and freedom has arrived, not as a blaze of achievement but as the slow recognition of a changed world; is it truly freedom when we do not even see it as an object of thinking ('no eyes to obstruct it')? When the legacy of the ages of banishment from home is still engrained in the body and imagination?

And will anyone recognize the new entrant into the kingdom? Having arrived in the new landscape, will the speaker be welcomed, understood, accompanied? The uncertainty remains as to whether his whole identity is bound up with the state of exile from which he is being reclaimed, whether the person he now is or must learn to be in the kingdom is going to be a totally new physical being, a new 'assemblage of cells'. But it's worth noticing how the lines here ('or if indeed there will be one soul that knows him,/ or if he is even the same assemblage of cells this side of exile') play with a continuous stream of echoing sounds – 'soul', 'cell', 'exile' – as if to make audible the continuities under the story of rupture. The form of the verse itself begins to answer the question (in the only way it can be answered that is not a cosy simplification).

But entry into the kingdom does not guarantee that you will at once find fluency in the native language. The speaker attempts to reproduce the accepted idioms of religious behaviour, but finds no response. But the question, 'Had there ever been [a response]?' is ambiguous. It may be, 'Had there ever been a response to *anyone's* cries of gratitude or lament?' Had this received language ever been effective? But it is equally a question for the speaker: 'Had there ever been a response *for him*?' Somehow the journey towards faith has stupefied the memory, so that the moment of transition – 'the broad gates opening', the wondering children gazing at the exotic stranger, the released tears that bear witness to the incalculable daily particularity of banishment from home – is no longer accessible. What the speaker comes into is the urban 'dirtlight' that might be waiting on the far side of a tunnel on the road; he is still surrounded by the random, the broken. But above is the plane tearing and then stitching the sky as it flies. It 'roars for elsewhere': it roars as it speeds onwards – but also, surely, roars in longing for that other world which has been in some way opened up.

To find your way into faith is to become another sort of person. You can't imagine in advance what that will mean or feel like; even as the transition is made, and perhaps for a long time after, you can't imagine what it amounts to. And at the same time, you can't think or feel your way back to how it was before: the old random landscape is irreversibly a site of longing and of grace. Once again, the sounds weave together – 'curses' and 'crisscross', 'rune, 'blue', 'roars' – to tell us that the world is at once completely different and faithfully, irreducibly the same in the light of this grace.

Franz Wright

Wake

I saw my friend the other day
we were all attending his wake
and he was the only one there
who looked like he was well
Somehow he'd gotten well
He looked like he was doing fine There
Everyone else in the room looked just awful

Strange how little say I had in all I said

That's what his relaxed and now youthful face
  seemed
just about to say
anyway those were the words
that abruptly appeared in my head

And: I have heard God's silence like the sun
and longed to
change

And one way or another I was going to
And if I could not manage to do it, it would be
  done
to me

You can't choose
where you come from

But looking down into the white face I knew
one day I would have to
choose

Heaven

Only Your friends can
render, here, visible
the kingdom
that bright glory

Look my friend is there

The title could be a noun or a verb, pointing us to the event of the pre-funeral gathering around the coffin or delivering an imperative, 'Wake up!' Wright, very much a poet who explores trauma, failure and struggle, sees his friend's dead body as the only presence in the room that is not somehow damaged and diminished. The living are ill, the dead man is healed.

People sometimes describe the recently dead as looking as though they had unexpectedly stumbled on some big secret. Wright sums up the secret in the wry observation, 'Strange how little say I had in all I said': looking back on life, the dead man sees a pattern of unfreedom, things said/done that were not really ever chosen or decided. Death releases and relaxes because it finally puts an end to the illusion that we are in charge.

We know we have to change – or at least we know this if we have 'heard God's silence like the sun' (a phrase that Wright uses several times in this particular collection of poems from

2006), if we have in any way found ourselves faced with the light of what has no beginning and no end. But we continually put off that change. A bit like Eliot's magi back in their kingdoms, we know something has happened but need 'another death' if we are truly to live in the presence of grace. Holy people ('Your friends') are the ones who show us in their lives what most can only show in their death.

Yes, our lives are haunted by passivity, reacting to what we did not choose or make ('You can't choose/ where you come from'), but this will not finally do as an alibi; and the confidence that the choice will one day be made for you, done to you, is no excuse either. The 'But' that follows pulls us back to the acknowledgement that heaven must be chosen – and so *death* must be chosen. We have to choose to be well; and this means choosing to let go of our deceptive stories about our independence and the simultaneous lazy acceptance of being at the mercy of events, instincts, cravings and so on. If actual physical death is to be something other than a prospect we approach with the unhappy apprehensiveness that we shall find all we've ever done to be empty, there are choices to be made now, and the strange 'wellness' that is visible in the face of the departed just might be visible in a living face too.

The idea that the life of faith is a 'daily dying' is familiar, though it is usually heard as a merely negative turning from the delights of the material world. But if death releases from the sickness of a passivity that we dress up as action and drama and control, we can begin to choose that release here and now. We can begin to be well, to be 'there' – and once again, Wright gives us a word the meaning of which is fluid. At the start of the poem, the dead friend 'looked like he was doing fine There': the capital letter suggests that 'There' is somewhere other than the place where the unhealthy living souls are trapped. But at the very end, the final word is 'there', in lower case and without any concluding punctuation (though Wright seldom punctuates his poems): 'my friend is *there*' – he is simply present to what is. Such presence is not only for the dead, it is also for the living who have taken note of the release to be seen in the faces of the dead and have begun to make the choices that will release them. They have begun to choose heaven, and so to let the light in. They have responded to the command to 'Wake!'

James Wright

Saint Judas

When I went out to kill myself, I caught
A pack of hoodlums beating up a man.
Running to spare his suffering, I forgot
My name, my number, how my day began,
How soldiers milled around the garden stone
And sang amusing songs; how all that day
Their javelins measured crowds; how I alone
Bargained the proper coins, and slipped away.

Banished from heaven, I found this victim beaten,
Stripped, kneed, and left to cry. Dropping my rope
Aside, I ran, ignored the uniforms:
Then I remembered bread my flesh had eaten,
The kiss that ate my flesh. Flayed without hope,
I held the man for nothing in my arms.

This arresting sonnet with its stark opening phrase invites us to look at human contradictoriness in its most extreme manifestation. Judas is – in most accounts – a uniquely guilty human being; he has acknowledged that guilt in the bleak conviction that there is no forgiveness or reparation possible. He has accepted that his life is over.

And then, on the far side of this embrace of death, he is moved to a completely spontaneous act of compassion. He *forgets his guilt.* The immediacy of the suffering of another detaches him from his own story or memory and he simply responds. It is an act beyond calculation. He has 'slipped away' from the tumult of Good Friday, having 'Bargained the proper coins': he has worked out what his debt is, seasoned economist that he is, and the payment that has to be made is his life. It is a sharply compressed image, picking up the story of Judas' bargaining with the enemies of Jesus over his fee for betraying his master: the 'proper coins', the just payment, will be death.

But faced with the man being beaten up in the street, all this fades away for a moment, both the tormenting memory and the despairing resolve to die ('Dropping my rope'). And what is then remarkable is that, as the memory returns, the resolve of compassion is unchanged. He remembers the bread shared with Jesus at the Last Supper, and the kiss of betrayal 'that ate my flesh', that wounded or consumed the calculating, betraying self. There is nothing to hope for; Judas has eaten and been eaten in his act of betrayal, he has destroyed and been destroyed. The final line is a sort of 'freeze-frame' image of love without hope of reward, love for which death is irrelevant.

So the poem intimates that Judas, cradling the suffering victim in the street, becomes a kind of image of Christlike love, love that continues unaffected over and beyond the certainty of death, the reality of failure: 'Saint Judas'. Two insights come together. The person we assume to be beyond grace or love can surprise us dramatically: a Judas can show a self-forgetful love that shocks and judges us. And the love of neighbour is not a calculating matter, looking to reward. You could almost say that *only* a Judas, convinced of being 'Banished from heaven', can show this kind of love, totally divorced from any thought of its result or effect, since his future is already determined.

Judas *runs* towards the suffering man; is this meant to recall Peter and the Beloved Disciple in John 20 running to the empty tomb of Jesus? It is as though Judas' capacity for love is itself a kind of 'empty tomb', a manifestation of the indestructible reality of what Jesus' life and death signify or make possible, a firstfruits of 'resurrected' life. The poem glances sideways at 'the garden stone', the stone that seals the tomb of Jesus, guarded by soldiers. Judas has turned away from this, the site of the new discovery of life and mercy, but a kind of resurrection comes upon him unawares in the impulse of compassion. The image that closes the poem is a pietà: Judas cradling the suffering body cannot but call up for us the image of Mary holding her dead son – an image of death and tragedy, but also inescapably an image of some sort of newness, a life being 'mothered' afresh into existence. Holiness like that of Judas' unselfconscious act is always a sign of resurrection and rebirth, all the more compelling here because it is a sign lifted up in the middle of the certainty of death and damnation in Judas' mind.

Betrayal is about surrendering to the world of debt, payment, merit and demerit, mechanical effect; guilt belongs in this world, too, especially the guilt with which we punish and destroy ourselves. Love is 'for nothing'. The bread shared and the flesh kissed consume not the fragile seed of love but the fantasy of irreparable guilt, mechanical punishment.

Does Judas pick up his rope again? Birth or death?

Adam Zagajewski

Mysticism for Beginners

The day was mild, the light was generous.
The German on the café terrace
held a small book on his lap.
I caught sight of the title:
Mysticism for Beginners.
Suddenly I understood that the swallows
patrolling the streets of Montepulciano
with their shrill whistles,
and the hushed talk of timid travelers
from Eastern, so-called Central Europe,
and the white herons standing – yesterday? the day
  before? –
like nuns in fields of rice,
and the dusk, slow and systematic,
erasing the outlines of medieval houses,
and olive trees on little hills,
abandoned to the wind and heat,
and the head of the *Unknown Princess*
that I saw and admired in the Louvre,
and stained-glass windows like butterfly wings
sprinkled with pollen,
and the little nightingale practicing
its speech beside the highway,
and any journey, any kind of trip,
are only mysticism for beginners,

the elementary course, prelude
to a test that's been
postponed.

The mild (well, actually not that mild) silliness of a book title like *Mysticism for Beginners* prompts the question as to what that unhelpful word 'mysticism' really refers to. Zagajewski responds to the unspoken question with, first, a wonderfully varied catalogue of perceptions: the light under which these are seen is indeed 'generous', as the opening line tells us. Birds; tourists murmuring hesitantly; birds again, standing still as if they were dedicated contemplatives; darkness falling on houses and hills; art; more birds, also speaking experimentally ('practicing . . . beside the highway'); any experience of travelling – all this fleshes out the absurd title or, rather, recasts it radically. The sights and sounds of the Italian landscape (and the French museum) encountered by the shy Eastern European tourist (or 'Central' European, a nicely ironic or self-deprecating qualification; can a Pole really claim to be 'central' to Europe in the face of the massive Franco-Italian stake in the cultural Olympics?) all blend into one another as night falls on a countryside returned to 'wind and heat'. The journey will continue, with the nightingale's experimental noises accompanying it.

'Mysticism for Beginners' is what is going on in all this – a journey involving the experience of being a stranger without the right words to speak, of listening to the universal 'speech' of the birds, of watching the view being steadily wiped away by the dark, of noticing the brightness of dusty and light-flecked church windows (the butterfly image suggests the impression of the light quivering through the glass). What is 'beginning' here for the speaker is a hesitancy about speech combined with a clarity of seeing and an impulse to keep moving while giving each moment its full weight of attention. If we must talk about the 'mystical', it has something to do with the kind of seeing or hearing (or overhearing, as with birdsong perhaps) that silences us, but also refuses to stay still, as a thing for us to try to 'own'. It is certainly not something that we can learn from a self-help book, as if it were a skill or subject among others (*Plumbing for Beginners, Astronomy for Beginners* . . .).

And all this is indeed only a beginning, an 'elementary course'. This is where the poem finally takes us – beyond the fairly familiar insight that the receptive attentive perception of the world around us is the ground of the mystical, or that the willingness to keep moving into a process of growing the end of which we don't see is somewhere close to the heart of the life of spirit. We are not to confuse beginnings with maturity. Somewhere ahead is a 'test', postponed for now: the learning has started, but there is something we are not ready for yet.

Zagajewski implies that mysticism begins with a separation opening in us between perception and the urge to possess. We begin to experience without clutching, without freezing our relation with what we encounter or trying to pin it to a collector's board. Those moments of experience cannot – almost by definition – come with effort; they cannot be piled up as successful evidence of our learning. Keep moving, and the test, postponed for now, will arrive (though without notice): the test of a radical letting go of the self that really will 'erase outlines', the outlines of my pictures of God and myself. The experiences represented by the various glimpses listed all point beyond themselves ultimately; yet they are to be celebrated in this moment that the poem catches – a moment of release and immediacy, and the freedom to love and then pass on. And the problematic book title becomes just another of those things perceived and enjoyed as a doorway to a journey still unfolding and never fully mapped out.

Jan Zwicky

Grace Is Unmoved. It Is the Light that Melts, excerpt from 'Philosophers' Stone'

Grace is unmoved. It is the light that melts,
the spring where words and world
fill up with meaning. We will see things
stark and dead if we see only things
themselves and not the pattern that informs them.
What must be understood, not collectivity, not
substance, is the depth of an embrace.
Resist the great temptation. What rests within
without floats freely. By any words
the truth is unsupportable. To see
is to be unafraid to cast away the ladder
we have cherished.

Jan Zwicky is unusual (in recent times, anyway) in being a teacher of philosophy as well as a poet – though she is anything but a conventional philosopher, and is sharply critical of the style of academic philosophy as it is generally practised. Her collection of *Wittgenstein Elegies* comes from long absorption in the writing of probably the twentieth century's most elusive and original philosophical mind. Ludwig Wittgenstein moved from a philosophy in which the task was conceived as definitively clarifying what could be said plainly in the form of propositions (as opposed to 'that which we cannot speak of', the ambient reality which cannot be the subject of clear propositions because it is not a matter of fact among other matters of fact) to a far more subtle and tantalizing understanding of language. For the mature Wittgenstein, language is always something that we as humans are *doing*. We identify meanings not by looking for items that correspond to the different bits of a proposition or statement but by attending with all our capacity to the ways in which words are used and heard, their embeddedness in other kinds of shared practice. We look and listen for a 'grammar' that helps us to see how speakers expect to be heard and answered, how they understand what will count as a contribution to the conversation and so on.

So Zwicky draws out the implication: engaging with any object as an item sufficient in and to itself ends up by showing us only a world of dead stuff. Zwicky has written powerfully about the ecological crisis, and the theme is tacitly present in the deeper background of this poem. What language shows, even embodies, is a reality that is properly seen neither as a 'collectivity', the sum total of things rolled up together in a single system, nor as a list of 'substances', individual things that simply happen to be lying around in proximity to one another. To *understand* the world is to sense a deep embrace, a mutuality or interpenetration that does not simply negate the reality of individual subjects or individual moments, but forbids us from thinking of those moments as enclosed or absolute. When we speak, we 'suggest' shape and form, the intelligible pattern that lives in the interaction of things, that makes a face out of particular features, a concept out of assorted sense data; but this is never a 'scaffolding' of description that enumerates a complete set of component parts. Truth does not need the support of words in this way. The wording ('the truth is unsupportable') simultaneously says that truth is beyond what we usually call proof and that it is more firmly established than we can imagine, needing no shoring up; and it hints, too, at the thought that truth may be *unbearable*, that we do not have the capacity to support or endure it ourselves in its nakedness – hence our anxiety to surround it with the structures we construct.

She is telling us to sit light to the names that we give things, not to obsess about how our words can contain what is there before us. Naming is necessary, but it is a ladder to climb, not a fixed carapace surrounding the world we see. Or, to put it a bit differently, our words are part of a varied set of practices in which we interact with the world we inhabit; ways of adjusting to what the environment presents to us, a little like steps in a dance, perhaps. Not to be ignored or refused, but not to be abstracted and absolutized.

It is no accident that the poem begins by setting all this in the context of 'grace', a nakedly theological word. Grace is what supplies meaning to our language because it is the eternally moving and unmoved flow of connection between the various centres of agency in the world; it is something not unlike the image of divine Wisdom in Hebrew Scripture, and much subsequent Christian thought. If you were to ask, 'Is this a "religious" poem?', the answer would have to be yes, to the extent that Zwicky – like her philosophical hero – sees the right use of language as an intensely moral and spiritual enterprise. Shedding our ambitions for totalizing explanations, for surrounding reality with our scaffolding, is a necessary part of shedding that deep distortion of our humanity which sets us over and against (literally 'against', in opposition to) the material world we're part of: the distortion that creates the environmental wreckage we see all around us. Early Christian writers insisted that the true understanding of how we fitted into this material world and its interwoven harmony was one of the steps towards the (wordless) contemplation of God.

Using language mindfully thus becomes indeed a mark of grace; and poetry exhibits grace when it loosens the tight constraints of any search for final meanings and total explanations and recovers that primordial sense of language as one of the things we must learn in order to be where we are in a world that is both ours and not ours.

A good place to stop.

Copyright acknowledgements

The publisher and author acknowledge with thanks permission to reproduce extracts from the following:

Gillian Allnutt, 'Verger, Winter Afternoon, Galilee Chapel': reproduced by kind permission of the Poetry Foundation.

Yehuda Amichai, 'Jews in the Land of Israel': from *The Poetry of Yehuda Amichai*. Copyright © 2015 by Yehuda Amichai. Reprinted by permission of Hana Amichai. Source: *The Poetry of Yehuda Amichai* (Farrar, Straus and Giroux, 2015).

Yehuda Amichai, 'The Real Hero': in *The Selected Poetry of Yehuda Amichai*, trans. Chana Bloch and Stephen Mitchell (Berkeley: University of California Press, 1996), p. 156. Permission to reproduce sought from Farrar, Straus and Giroux.

Mia Anderson, 'Prayer Is Scrubbing': taken from the collection, *Light Takes*, by Mia Anderson, published by Cormorant Books Inc., Toronto. Copyright 2014 © Mia Anderson. Used with the permission of the publisher.

W. H. Auden, 'Friday's Child': copyright © 1958 by W. H. Auden, renewed 1986 by The Estate of W. H. Auden; from *Collected Poems* by W. H. Auden, edited by Edward Mendelson. Used by permission of Random House, an imprint and division of Penguin Random House LLC. All rights reserved. Permission to reproduce also sought from Curtis Brown.

W. H. Auden, 'Luther': copyright 1940 and © renewed 1968 by W. H. Auden; from *Collected Poems* by W. H. Auden, edited by Edward Mendelson. Used by permission of Random House, an imprint and division of Penguin Random House LLC. All rights reserved. Permission to reproduce also sought from Curtis Brown.

Jay Bernard, 'Tympanum': reproduced by permission of Jay Bernard; permission to reproduce also sought from Suresh Ariaratnum (Sprung Sultan) and Penguin Random House.

John Betjeman, 'Norfolk': permission to reproduce sought from PLSClear.

Chaim Bialik, 'Alone': permission to reproduce sought from the National Library of Israel.

Ruth Bidgood, 'The Pause': permission to reproduce sought from the Estate of Ruth Bidgood.

Yves Bonnefoy, '*Noli me tangere*': reproduced by permission of Rowman and Lexington.

Euros Bowen, 'Lazarus': ET in Rowan Williams, *Collected Poems*, reproduced by permission of Carcanet Press.

George Mackay Brown, 'Epiphany Poem': reproduced by permission of PLSClear.

John Burt, 'Sonnets for Mary of Nazareth III': permission to reproduce sought from Princeton University Press and the Copyright Clearance Center.

Charles Causley, 'I Am the Great Sun': permission to reproduce sought from Pan Macmillan.

Charles Causley, 'Eden Rock': permission to reproduce sought from Pan Macmillan.

Paul Celan, 'Count Up the Almonds': permission to reproduce sought from Penguin.

Paul Celan, 'Your Beyondness': permission to reproduce sought from Penguin Random House.

Jack Clemo, 'Cactus in Clayscape': reproduced by permission of Enitharmon Press and the Estate of Jack Clemo.

Copyright acknowledgements

Adam Czerniawski, 'Self-judgement': permission to reproduce sought from Salt Publishing.

Hilary Davies, 'Penance': reproduced by permission of Enitharmon Press and Hilary Davies.

Imtiaz Dharker, 'Prayer': in *Postcards from God* (Bloodaxe Books, 1997). Reproduced with permission of Bloodaxe Books. <www.bloodaxebooks.com>

Imtiaz Dharker, 'Living Space': in *Postcards from God* (Bloodaxe Books, 1997). Reproduced with permission of Bloodaxe Books. <www.bloodaxebooks.com>

Isabel Dixon, 'One of the First Times After': permission to reproduce sought from Cambridge University Press and Salt Publishing.

T. S. Eliot, 'Journey of the Magi': in *Collected Poems 1909–1962*, reproduced by permission of Faber and Faber Ltd; permission to reproduce also sought from HarperCollins.

Rhina Espaillat, 'Martha Considers the Lilies': permission to reproduce sought from Truman State University.

U. A. Fanthorpe, 'Half-past Two': reproduced by permission of Enitharmon Press and the Estate of U. A. Fanthorpe.

Caleb Femi, 'At a House Party, "Ultralight Beam" Came on and It Started a Church Service': permission to reproduce sought from Penguin Random House.

Kate Foley, 'Tikkun Olam: Mending the World': reproduced by kind permission of Shoestring Press.

Louise Glück, 'Vespers': in *The Wild Iris*, reproduced by permission of Carcanet Press; permission to reproduce also sought from HarperCollins.

Jo Harjo, 'Don't Bother the Earth Spirit': permission to reproduce sought from the University of Arizona Press.

Kevin Hart, 'Facing the Pacific at Night': permission to reproduce sought from Notre Dame University.

Geoffrey Hill, 'The Orchards of Syon XLIII': permission to reproduce sought from PLSClear.

Geoffrey Hill, 'The Orchards of Syon XLV': permission to reproduce sought from PLSClear.

John Hodgen, 'Visitation': permission to reproduce sought from the University of Pittsburgh Press.

Fanny Howe, 'The Angels': reproduced by permission of the Poetry Foundation.

Fanny Howe, 'The Descent': permission to reproduce sought from the University of California Press.

Sally Ito, 'At the Beginning of Lent: Ash Wednesday': © 2011, reprinted with permission from *Alert to Glory*, Turnstone Press (Winnipeg, MB).

Mark Jarman, 'Unholy Sonnets 7': reproduced by kind permission of Mark Jarman.

Mark Jarman, 'Unholy Sonnets 17': reproduced by kind permission of Mark Jarman.

Elizabeth Jennings, 'A Childhood Horror': permission to reproduce sought from David Higham Associates.

D. Gwenallt Jones, 'Sin': ET in Rowan Williams, *Collected Poems*, reproduced by permission of Carcanet Press.

Brigit Pegeen Kelly, 'The Music Lesson': from *Song*. Copyright © 1995 by Brigit Pegeen Kelly. Reprinted with the permission of The Permissions Company, LLC on behalf of BOA Editions Ltd., <boaeditions.org>.

Sarah Klassen, 'Advent': reproduced by kind permission of the St Thomas Poetry Series and Sarah Klassen.

Avraham Yitzhak Kook, 'Sukkot: The Light in the Sukkah': permission to reproduce sought from Rav Kook List and Elizabeth Topper.

Avraham Yitzhak Kook, 'Sukkot: The Sukkah of Peace': permission to reproduce sought from Rav Kook List and Elizabeth Topper.

Copyright acknowledgements

Denise Levertov, 'Jacob's Ladder': in *New Selected Poems* (Bloodaxe Books, 2003). Reproduced with permission of Bloodaxe Books. <www.bloodaxebooks.com>

Denise Levertov, 'A Place of Kindness': in *New Selected Poems* (Bloodaxe Books, 2003). Reproduced with permission of Bloodaxe Books. <www.bloodaxebooks.com>

Gwyneth Lewis, 'How to Read Angels': in *Chaotic Angels: Poems in English* (Bloodaxe Books, 2005). Reproduced with permission of Bloodaxe Books. <www.bloodaxebooks.com>

Saunders Lewis, 'Prayer at the End': reproduced by kind permission of the Estate of Saunders Lewis.

Maitreyabandhu (Ian Johnson), 'The Postulant': in *Yarn* (Bloodaxe Books, 2015). Reproduced with permission of Bloodaxe Books. <www.bloodaxebooks.com>

Thomas Merton, 'The Fall': from *The Collected Poems of Thomas Merton*, copyright ©1963 by The Abbey of Gethsemani. Reprinted by permission of New Directions Publishing Corp.

Larissa Miller, 'It was on the Very Last Day of Creation': reproduced by kind permission of Arc Publications on behalf of Larissa Miller.

Larissa Miller, 'I'm on about My Own Stuff Again, and Again': reproduced by kind permission of Arc Publications on behalf of Larissa Miller.

Les Murray, 'Poetry and Religion': permission to reproduce sought from Black Inc Books and the Estate of Les Murray.

Les Murray, 'The Chimes of Neverwhere': permission to reproduce sought from Black Inc Books and the Estate of Les Murray.

Paul Murray, 'The Rock': reproduced by permission of Dedalus Press.

Dorothy Nimmo, 'The Pottery Lesson': reproduced by permission of Poetry Business.

Naomi Shihab Nye, 'Fundamentalism': from *Fuel*. Copyright © 1998 by Naomi Shihab Nye. Reprinted with the permission of The Permissions Company, LLC on behalf of BOA Editions Ltd., <www.boaeditions.org>.

Naomi Shihab Nye, 'The Words Under the Words': permission to reproduce sought from Marketplace Books.

Alice Oswald, 'Seabird's Blessing': in *Woods, Etc.*, reproduced by permission of Faber and Faber Ltd; permission to reproduce also sought from United Agents.

Ruth Padel, 'Learning to Make an Oud in Nazareth': permission to reproduce sought from Penguin.

Sylvia Plath, 'Mystic': in *Collected Poems*, reproduced by permission of Faber and Faber Ltd; permission to reproduce also sought from HarperCollins.

Michael Symmons Roberts, 'On Easter Saturday': permission to reproduce sought from Penguin.

Michael Symmons Roberts, 'A New Song': permission to reproduce sought from Penguin.

Tadeusz Różewicz, 'Unrecorded Epistle': permission to reproduce sought from Anvil Publishing.

Tadeusz Różewicz, 'Thorn': permission to reproduce sought from Anvil Publishing.

Gjertrud Schnackenburg, 'A Gilded Lapse of Time 12': permission to reproduce sought from Macmillan.

David Scott, 'The Friends' Meeting Room': in *Beyond the Drift: New & selected poems* (Bloodaxe Books, 2015). Reproduced with permission of Bloodaxe Books. <www.bloodaxebooks.com>

David Scott, 'Canon Fenton, Theologian': in *Beyond the Drift: New & selected poems* (Bloodaxe Books, 2015). Reproduced with permission of Bloodaxe Books. <www.bloodaxebooks.com>

Olga Sedakova, 'The Angel of Rheims': permission to reproduce sought from Olga Sedakova.

Olga Sedakova, 'Chinese Journey 18': permission to reproduce sought from Olga Sedakova.

Martha Serpas, 'Poem Found': permission to reproduce sought from Norton.

Vikram Seth, 'This': permission to reproduce sought from PLSClear.

Copyright acknowledgements

Karl Shapiro, 'The Alphabet': permission to reproduce sought from Harold Ober Associates and Wieser & Elwell, Inc.

C. H. Sisson, 'Steps to the Temple': in *A C. H. Sisson Reader*, reproduced by permission of Carcanet Press.

Dana Littlepage Smith, 'Thoughts Without Order Concerning the Love of God': permission to reproduce sought from Cinnamon Press.

Stevie Smith, 'The Airy Christ': taken from *Two in One: Selected Poems and The Frog Prince and Other Poems*, by Stevie Smith, published and copyright 1971 by Darton Longman and Todd Ltd, London, and used by permission of the publishers.

John Solilo, 'Truth': in *Umoya Wembongi: Collected poems (1922–1935)* ed. and trans. by Jeff Opland and Peter Mtuze (University of KwaZulu-Natal Press, 2016).

A. E. Stallings, 'First Miracle': permission to reproduce sought from Macmillan.

Avrom Sutzkever, 'The Lead Plates of the Rom Printers': permission to reproduce sought from the University of California Press.

Avrom Sutzkever, 'Who Will Be Left? What Will Be Left?': reproduced by permission of the University of California Press.

Dylan Thomas, 'The Conversation of Prayer': reproduced by permission of Penguin Random House.

R. S. Thomas, 'Sea-watching': permission to reproduce sought from Pan Macmillan.

R. S. Thomas, 'Neither': in *Collected Later Poems 1988–2000* (Bloodaxe Books, 2004). Reproduced with permission of Bloodaxe Books. <www.bloodaxebooks.com>

Sally Thomas, '*biddan* (to pray)': From *Motherland: Poems* © Sally Thomas, 2020. Used by permission of Able Muse Press.

Derek Walcott, 'A City's Death by Fire': in *Collected Poems 1948–1984*, reproduced by permission of Faber and Faber Ltd; permission to reproduce also sought from Farrar, Straus and Giroux.

Aled Jones Williams, 'Faith': permission to reproduce sought from Gwasg y Bwythyn.

Charles Williams, 'Taliessin on the Death of Virgil': permission to reproduce sought from Oxford University Press.

Waldo Williams, 'What Is Man?' ET in Rowan Williams, *Collected Poems*, reproduced by permission of Carcanet Press.

Christian Wiman, 'Coming into the Kingdom': permission to reproduce sought from Macmillan.

Franz Wright, 'Wake': from *God's Silence* by Franz Wright, copyright © 2006 by Franz Wright. Used by permission of Alfred A. Knopf, an imprint of the Knopf Doubleday Publishing Group, a division of Penguin Random House LLC. All rights reserved.

James Wright, 'Saint Judas': reproduced by permission of Wesleyan University Press.

Adam Zagajewski, 'Mysticism for Beginners': permission to reproduce sought from Macmillan.

Jan Zwicky, 'Grace Is Unmoved. It Is the Light that Melts': excerpt from 'Philosophers' Stone' from *Wittgenstein Elegies* by Jan Zwicky, 2nd rev. edn, Brick Books, 2015, reprinted by permission of the author.

Every effort has been made to seek permission to use copyright material reproduced in this book. The publisher apologizes for those cases where permission might not have been sought and, if notified, will formally seek permission at the earliest opportunity.

Bibliography

Allnutt, Gillian, 'Verger, Winter Afternoon, Galilee Chapel', *Poetry*, October 2005.

Amichai, Yehuda, *The Poetry of Yehuda Amichai*, trans. Chana Bloch, New York: Farrar, Straus and Giroux, 2015 ('Jews in the Land of Israel', 'The Real Hero').

Anderson, Mia, *Light Takes*, Toronto: Cormorant Books, 2014 ('Prayer Is Scrubbing').

Auden, W. H. *Collected Poems*, London: Faber & Faber, 1976 ('Friday's Child', 'Luther').

Bernard, Jay, *Surge*, London: Chatto & Windus, 2019 ('Tympanum').

Betjeman, John, *Collected Poems*, London: John Murray, 2006 ('Norfolk').

Bialik, Chaim Nachman, *Shirim*, Tel Aviv: Dvir, 1966 ('L'vaddo'; ET: 'Alone' by Rowan Williams).

Bidgood, Ruth, *Time Being*, Bridgend: Seren Books, 2009 ('The Pause').

Bonnefoy, Yves, *Début et fin de la neige*, Paris: Mercure de France, 1998 ('*Noli me tangere*'; ET by Rowan Williams).

Bowen, Euros, *Achlysuron*, Llandysul: Gwasg Gomer, 1970 ('Lazarus'; ET: 'Lazarus', in Rowan Williams, *Collected Poems*, Manchester: Carcanet, 2021).

Mackay Brown, George, *The Collected Poems of George Mackay Brown*, ed. Archie Bevan and Brian Murray, London: John Murray, 2006 ('Epiphany Poem').

Burt, John, *The Way Down*, Princeton: Princeton University Press, 1988 ('Sonnets for Mary of Nazareth III').

Causley, Charles, *Collected Poems 1951–2000*, London: Picador, 2000 ('I Am the Great Sun', 'Eden Rock').

Celan, Paul, *Selected Poems*, London: Penguin, 1996 ('Count Up the Almonds', 'Your Beyondness'; German text; ET by Rowan Williams).

Clemo, Jack, *Selected Poems*, ed. Luke Thompson, London: Enitharmon, 2015 ('Cactus in Clayscape').

Czerniawski, Adam, *The Invention of Poetry: Selected poems*, Cambridge: Salt Publishing, 2005 ('Self-judgement').

Davies, Hilary, *Imperium*, London: Enitharmon, 2005 ('Penance').

Dharker, Imtiaz, *Postcards from God*, Newcastle upon Tyne: Bloodaxe, 1997 ('Living Space').

Dharker, Imtiaz, *Purdah and Other Poems*, New Delhi: Oxford University Press, 1989 ('Prayer').

Dixon, Isabel, *A Fold in the Map*, Cambridge: Salt Publishing, 2007 ('One of the First Times After').

Egbunu, Emmanuel, *Birth Pangs and Other Poems*, Zaria, Nigeria: Tamaza Publishing Company, 2009 ('Farewell').

Eliot, T. S., *Collected Poems 1909–1962*, London: Faber & Faber, 1963 ('Journey of the Magi').

Espaillat, Rhina, *Playing at Stillness*, Kirksville, MO: Truman State University Press, 2005 ('Martha Considers the Lilies').

Espaillat, Rhina, *Where Horizons Go*, Kirksville, MO: New Odyssey Press, 1998 ('Falling').

Fanthorpe, U. A., *New and Collected Poems 1978–2009*, London: Enitharmon, 2010 ('Half-past Two').

Femi, Caleb, *Poor*, London: Penguin, 2020 ('At a House Party, "Ultralight Beam" Came on & It Started a Church Service').

Foley, Kate, *One Window North*, Nottingham: Shoestring Press, 2012 ('Tikkun Olam: Mending the World').

Glück, Louise, *The Wild Iris*, New York: Ecco Press, 1992 ('Vespers').

Harjo, Joy, *Secrets from the Centre of the World*, Tucson, AZ: University of Arizona Press, 1989 ('Don't Bother the Earth Spirit').

Kevin Hart, *New and Selected Poems*, Sydney: HarperCollins, 1995 ('Facing the Pacific at Night').

Hill, Geoffrey, *Broken Hierarchies: Poems 1952–2012*, Oxford: Oxford University Press, 2013 ('The Orchards of Syon XLIII', 'The Orchards of Syon XLV').

Hodgen, John, *Grace*, Pittsburg, PA: University of Pittsburgh Press, 2006 ('Visitation').

Howe, Fanny, 'The Angels', *Poetry*, 1973.

Howe, Fanny, *Gone*, Oakland, CA: University of California Press, 2003 ('The Descent').

Ito, Sally, *Alert to Glory*, Winnipeg: Turnstone Press, 2011 ('At the Beginning of Lent: Ash Wednesday').

Jarman, Mark, *Questions for Ecclesiastes*, Ashland, OR: Story Line Press, 1998 ('Unholy Sonnets 7', 'Unholy Sonnets 17').

Jennings, Elizabeth, *Times and Seasons*, Manchester: Carcanet, 1992 ('A Childhood Horror').

Gwenallt Jones, D., *Cerddi Gwenallt: y casgliad cyflawn*, ed. Christine James, Llandysul: Gwasg Gomer, 2001 ('Pechod'; ET: 'Sin', in Rowan Williams, *Collected Poems*, Manchester: Carcanet, 2021).

Pegeen Kelly, Brigit, *Poems: Song and the orchard*, Manchester: Carcanet, 2008 ('The Music Lesson').

Klassen, Sarah, 'A Prairie Credo', in Margo Swiss, ed., *Poetry as Liturgy: An anthology by Canadian poets*, Toronto: St Thomas Poetry Series, 2007 ('Advent').

Yitzhak Kook, Avraham, ET: *Parasha Poems*, <parashapoems.wordpress.com/tag/rav-kook> ('Sukkot: The Light in the Sukkah', 'Sukkot: The Sukkah of Peace')

Levertov, Denise, *Selected Poems*, Newcastle upon Tyne: Bloodaxe, 1986 ('The Jacob's Ladder' and 'A Place of Kindness').

Lewis, Gwyneth, *Chaotic Angels: Poems in English*, Newcastle upon Tyne: Bloodaxe, 2005 ('How to Read Angels').

Lewis, Saunders, *Selected Poems*, trans. Joseph P. Clancy, Cardiff: University of Wales Press, 1993 ('Prayer at the End').

Maitreyabandhu (Ian Johnson), *Yarn*, Hexham: Bloodaxe, 2015 ('The Postulant').

Mariani, Paul, *Ordinary Time: Poems*, Eugene, OR: Slant/Wipf and Stock, 2019 ('Holy Saturday').

Merton, Thomas, *In the Dark Before the Dawn: New selected poems* ed. Lynn Szabo, New York: New Directions, 2005 ('The Fall').

Miller, Larissa, *Guests of Eternity*, trans. Richard McKane, Todmorden: Arc Publications, 2008 ('It was on the Very Last Day of Creation', 'I'm on about My Own Stuff Again, and Again').

Murray, Les, *Collected Poems*, Collingwood, Australia: Black Inc Books, 2018 ('Poetry and Religion', 'The Chimes of Neverwhere').

Murray, Paul, *These Black Stars*, Dublin: Dedalus Press, 2003 ('The Rock').

Nimmo, Dorothy, *The Wigbox: New and selected poems*, Huddersfield: Smith/Doorstop, 2000 ('The Pottery Lesson').

Shihab Nye, Naomi, *Fuel*, Rochester, NY: BOA Editions, 1998 ('Fundamentalism').

Shihab Nye, Naomi, *Words Under the Words: Selected poems*, Portland, OR: Far Corner Books, 1995 ('The Words Under the Words').

Oswald, Alice, *Woods, Etc.*, London: Faber & Faber, 2005 ('Seabird's Blessing').

Padel, Ruth, *Learning to Make an Oud in Nazareth*, London: Chatto & Windus, 2014 ('Learning to Make an Oud in Nazareth').

Plath, Sylvia, *Collected Poems*, London: Faber & Faber, 1981 ('Mystic').

Symmons Roberts, Michael, *Drysalter*, London: Jonathan Cape 2013 ('On Easter Saturday', 'A New Song').

Różewicz, Tadeusz, *They Came to See a Poet: Selected poems*, trans. Adam Czerniawski, Vancouver: Anvil Press, 2004 ('Unrecorded Epistle', 'Thorn').

Schnackenburg, Gjertrud, *A Gilded Lapse of Time*, London: Harvill, 1992 ('A Gilded Lapse of Time 12').

Scott, David, *Beyond the Drift*, Hexham: Bloodaxe, 2014 ('The Friends' Meeting Room', 'Canon Fenton, Theologian').

Sedakova, Olga, *Collected Works*, vol. 1, *Stikhi*, Moscow, 2001 (Russian text of 'The Angel of Rheims', 'Chinese Journey 18'; ET by Rowan Williams).

Serpas, Martha, 'Poem Found', in Harold Bloom, ed., *American Religious Poems*, New York: Library of America, 2006.

Seth, Vikram, *The Rivered Earth*, London: Hamish Hamilton, 2001 ('This').

Shapiro, Karl, *Poems of a Jew*, New York: Random House, 1958 ('The Alphabet').

Sisson, C. H., *A C. H. Sisson Reader*, ed. Charlie Louth and Patrick McGuiness, Manchester: Carcanet, 2014 ('Steps to the Temple').

Littlepage Smith, Dana, *The Skin of Mercy*, London: Cinnamon Press, 2012 ('Thoughts Without Order Concerning the Love of God').

Smith, Stevie, *Two in One: Selected Poems and The Frog Prince and Other Poems*, London: Longman, 1971 ('The Airy Christ').

Solilo, John, *Umoya Wembongi: Collected poems (1922–1935)*, Pietermaritzburg, South Africa: University of KwaZulu-Natal Press, 2016 ('Truth').

Stallings, A. E., *Like*, New York: Farrar, Straus and Giroux, 2018 ('First Miracle').

Sutzkever, Avrom, *Selected Poetry and Prose*, trans. Barbara and Benjamin Harshav, Oakland, CA: University of California Press, 1991 ("The Lead Plates of the Rom Printers', 'Who Will Be Left? What Will Be Left?'; ET by Rowan Williams).

Thomas, Dylan, *Collected Poems 1934–1952*, London: J. M. Dent, 1952 ('The Conversation of Prayer').

Thomas, R. S., *Laboratories of the Spirit*, London: Macmillan, 1975 (Sea-Watching').

Thomas, R. S., *No Truce with the Furies,* Newcastle upon Tyne: Bloodaxe, 1995 ('Neither').

Thomas, Sally, *Motherland: Poems*, San Jose, CA: Able Muse Press, 2020 ('*biddan* (to pray)').

Walcott, Derek, *Collected Poems 1948–1984,* London: Faber & Faber, 1986 ('A City's Death by Fire').

Watkins, Vernon, *The Collected Poems of Vernon Watkins*, Boston: Golgonooza, 2000 ('A Christening Remembered', 'Adam').

Jones Williams, Aled, *Y Cylchoedd Perffaith*, Caernarvon: Bwthyn Press, 2010 ('*ffydd*'; ET: 'Faith' by Rowan Williams)

Williams, Charles, *Taliessin through Logres and the Region of the Summer Stars*, Grand Rapids: Eerdmans, 1974 ('Taliessin on the Death of Virgil').

Williams, Waldo, *Dail Pren*, Llandysul: Gwasg Gomer, 1956 ('Pa Beth yw Dyn?'; ET: 'What Is Man', in Rowan Williams, *Collected Poems*, Manchester: Carcanet, 2021).

Wiman, Christian, *Once in the West: Poems*, New York: Farrar Straus and Giroux, 2014 ('Coming into the Kingdom').

Wright, Franz, *God's Silence*, New York: Knopf, 2006 ('Wake').

Wright, James, *Above the River: Collected poems*, Middletown, CT: Wesleyan University Press, 1972 ('Saint Judas').

Zagajewski, Adam, *Without End: New and selected poems*, New York: Farrar, Straus and Giroux, 2002 ('Mysticism for Beginners').

Zwicky, Jan, *Wittgenstein Elegies*, Edmonton: Brick Books, 1986 ('Grace Is Unmoved. It Is the Light that Melts' excerpt from 'Philosophers' Stone').